Drywall Installation and Finishing

Karen Goad

Sterling Publishing Co., Inc. New York

NOTICE TO THE READER

Publisher does not warrant or guarantee any of the products described herein or perform any independent analysis in connection with any of the product information contained herein. Publisher does not assume, and expressly disclaims, any obligation to obtain and include information other than that provided to it by the manufacturer.

The reader is expressly warned to consider and adopt all safety precautions that might be indicated by the activities described herein and to avoid all potential hazards. By following the instructions contained herein, the reader willingly assumes all risks in connection with such instructions.

The publisher makes no representations or warranties of any kind, including but not limited to, the warranties of fitness for particular purpose or merchantability, nor are any such representations implied with respect to the material set forth herein, and the publisher takes no responsibility with respect to such material. The publisher shall not be liable for any special, consequential or exemplary damages resulting, in whole or in part, from the readers' use of, or reliance upon, this material.

Delmar staff
New Product Acquisitions: Mark Huth
Assistant Editor: Nancy Belser
Project Editor: Mary P. Robinson
Production Coordinator: Mary Ellen Black
Art/Design Coordinator: Brian G. Yacur

Library of Congress Cataloging-in-Publication Data

Goad, Karen.
Drywall : installing & finishing / Karen Goad.
p. cm.
Includes index.
ISBN 0-8069-0304-X
1. Dry wall. I. Title.
TH2239.G62 1993b
690′.12—dc20 92–38241
CIP

10 9 8 7 6 5 4 3

Published 1993 by Sterling Publishing Company, Inc.
387 Park Avenue South, New York, N.Y. 10016
Text edition originally published and

3 Columbia Circle, Albany, N.Y. 12212
Distributed in Canada by Sterling Publishing
c/o Canadian Manda Group, P.O.Box 920, Station U
Toronto, Ontario, Canada M8Z 5P9
Manufactured in the United States of America

Sterling ISBN 0-8069-0304-X

Contents

Preface

For centuries trade skills have been passed from generation to generation or learned through apprenticeship, with the experienced craftsperson teaching the student. The student could learn only what the teacher had to pass along, and if the senior person had learned an improper method, the student learned the same mistakes. Today the apprentice or student has the benefit of textbooks, such as *Drywall Installation and Finishing.* This text presents proven techniques that have been reviewed by many drywall experts. Learning to install and finish drywall is still best done with the help of an expert, but this text will reinforce what the expert teaches. It is also a reliable source of accurate, up-to-date information.

Drywall Installation and Finishing covers the three major areas of drywall work. The early chapters discuss drywall hanging—installation of the basic material on walls and ceilings in a variety of conditions. Planning, measuring, cutting, and fastening are covered thoroughly. The book then explains drywall finishing to prepare for the final wall or ceiling covering. The chapter on texturing, in which the author explains how to create special textures, is unique to this book. These techniques are not covered in any other published form.

Karen Goad, author of *Drywall Installation and Finishing,* is a veteran of twenty-three years' experience. She has worked as a drywall mechanic and as a drywall contractor. In addition, she has taught others to install and finish drywall products.

The manuscript for this book was reviewed by the following experts, whose advice helped ensure that it would be a complete and accurate source of information and an effective educational tool.

Stanley Badzinski
Milwaukee Area Technical College

L. Gaylon Huff
Portland Community College

Nathan Kleefisch
South Suburban College

Lester I. Stackpole
Eastern Maine Technical College

Part 1
Hanging

Chapter 1
Drywall Installation Tools and Materials

Introduction to Drywall

The framework of your home has been completed, the major plumbing and electrical work is done, and it's time to hang your walls. Or maybe you've decided to refurbish your house, and you want to replace those old walls. Either way, you must hang your drywall and then prepare the walls for texture, paint, or wallpaper.

This book will introduce you to the basics of hanging drywall.

WHAT IS DRYWALL?

Drywall, Sheetrock, and *Wallboard* are all terms for the paper-wrapped gypsum board that forms the wall and ceiling surfaces of most buildings. The generic term is *drywall.* Sheetrock and Wallboard are trade names.

Drywall is made in various lengths and thicknesses, but the board is always four feet wide. Drywall can be as thin as ¼ inch or as thick as ¾ inch, and it can be from eight to twenty feet long. In residential construction, though, we usually use ½-inch boards, four feet wide and twelve feet long.

There are three types of drywall that you will need to be familiar with as a drywall hanger: regular drywall, fire-rated drywall, and water-resistant (or greenboard) drywall.

Regular Drywall

Drywall is made out of a gypsum composition covered with a type of paper that is used to bind the mixture together and provide a smooth surface.

The sides of the drywall are beveled with what are known as factory edges, so that a recess is formed when two pieces of board are hung side by side. See the illustration in Figure 1-1. The recess is there so that the finisher easily can tape and float the area with joint compound, producing a smooth joint that will blend in with the rest of the wall. The ends of the board, known as butt joints, aren't beveled. This causes problems for the finisher, as we shall see later.

One of the most important rules to remember in hanging drywall is that you must hang a factory edge to a factory edge and a butt joint to a butt joint.

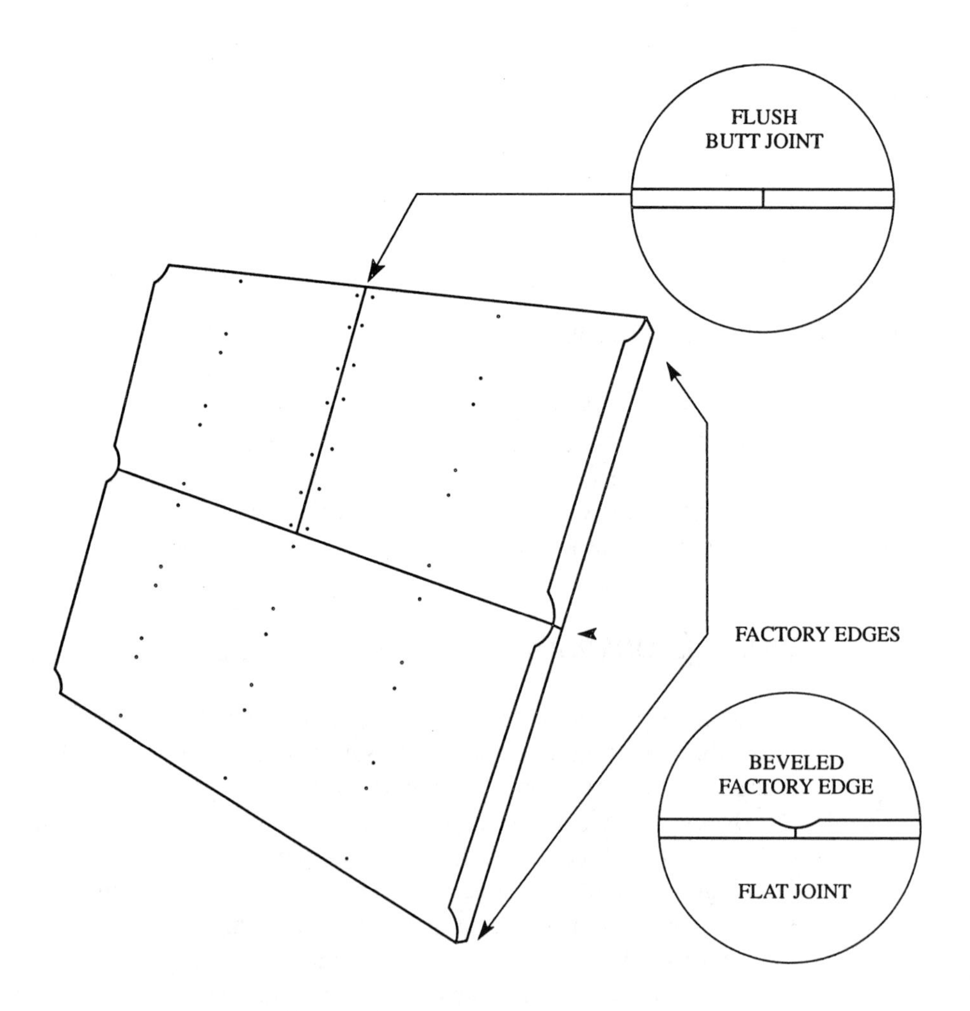

FIGURE 1-1 Factory edges and butt joints

Fire-rated Drywall

Gypsum does not burn, but it will crumble and fall away if its paper covering is burned. If this happens, the framework of the house will be exposed. Fire-rated drywall is fire resistant (not fireproof); therefore, it holds together longer in a fire than does regular drywall. This allows a greater chance that the fire will be discovered and extinguished before it can burn through into another area. Fire-rated drywall is used on all fire walls. A fire wall is any wall separating two units, such as the house from the garage, or one apartment from another. City fire codes vary, so you should check local building codes before you hang any drywall. Fire-rated drywall is also known as type X and has a one-hour fire rating.

Water-resistant Drywall

Water-resistant drywall is commonly used around high-moisture areas such as bathtubs and showers. Its green color distinguishes it from other kinds of drywall, which are usually off-white. Water-resistant drywall also comes with a type X core, which is fire rated.

There are numerous types of drywall, but you will use these three most often. Other types of drywall are used for exterior ceilings and sheathing for building exteriors (usually under brick or masonry). Lead-paneled drywall is used for X-ray rooms. Foil-backed drywall is used for interiors along concrete areas or high-moisture areas.

Hanging Tools and Attachment Methods

WHAT WILL YOU NEED?

To hang drywall, you need the right tools and materials. First, you must figure out how much drywall you need. Since every house is different, it's impossible to say exactly how many sheets you will need, but this formula will give you a good estimate: Determine the number of square feet of floor space in the house. Multiply that number by 3.8, and divide that answer by 48. This will tell you how many twelve-foot-long sheets of drywall you will need for your house. (If you are using eight-foot drywall, divide by 32 instead of 48.)

There are three important forms of attachment. Usually the type of job site will determine the best method.

Nail Attachment

There are many types of nails for hanging drywall. The two main types are the annular ring nail, which perhaps holds better, and the cement coated drywall nail

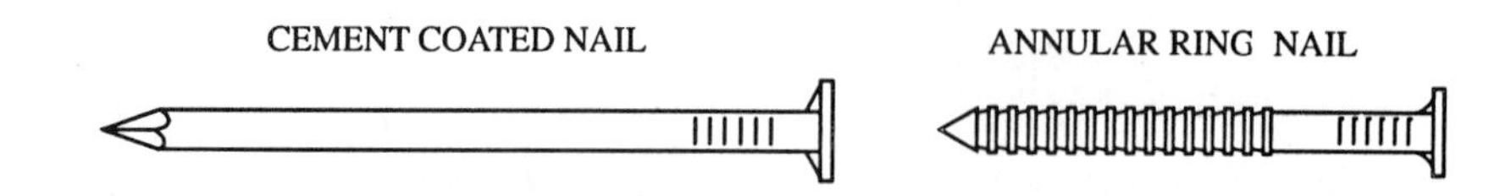

FIGURE 1–2 There are two basic drywall nails: the annular ring nail and the cement coated nail.

(Figure 1–2). The length of the nail you use depends on what you are hanging and how far the material is from the stud. The nail penetration into wood should be at least ⅞ inch.

If you are hanging ½-inch drywall over lath and plaster, make sure the nail goes through the drywall and the lath and plaster and still penetrates the stud ⅞ inch.

Nail spacing varies depending on a number of factors, including location and thickness of the drywall, stud spacing, framing material, and the use of adhesives. Refer to Table 1–1.

TABLE 1–1 Fastener spacing (*Courtesy U.S. Gypsum Co.*)

Wood Framing:	
Single layer	Nails — Ceilings 7″; Sidewalls 8″ Screws — Ceilings 12″; Sidewalls 16″ Screws with RC-1 Channels — Ceiling and Walls 12″
Base layer of double layer— both mechanic attached	Nails — Ceilings 24″; Sidewalls 24″ Screws — Ceilings 24″; Sidewalls 24″ Staples — Ceilings 16″; Sidewalls 16″
Face layer of double layer— both mechanic attached	Nails — Ceilings 7″; Sidewalls 8″ Screws — Ceilings 12″; Sidewalls 16″
Base layer of double layer— face layer adhesive attached	Nails — Ceilings 7″; Sidewalls 8″ Screws — Ceilings 12″; Sidewalls 16″ Staples — Ceilings 7″; Sidewalls 7″
Face layer of double layer— face layer adhesive attached	Nails — Ceilings 16″ O.C. at ends and edges—1 field fastener per frame member at mid-width of board. Sidewalls fasten top and bottom as required.
Steel Framing:	
Single layer	Screws — Ceilings 12″; Sidewalls 16″
Base layer of double layer— both mechanic attached	Screws — Ceilings 16″; Sidewalls 24″
Face layer of double layer— both mechanic attached	Screws — Ceilings 12″; Sidewalls 16″
Base layer of double layer— face layer adhesive	Screws — Ceilings 12″; Sidewalls 16″
Face layer of double layer— face layer adhesive	Screws — Ceiling 16″ O.C. at ends and edges—1 field fastener per frame member at mid-width of board. Sidewalls fasten top and bottom as required.

Screw Attachment

If screw attachment is required, there is a variety of screws to choose from. Your choice will depend on the type of materials you are using. The screws in Figure 1–3 are used most widely. Screws should penetrate metal framing at least ⅜ inch and wood framing at least ⅝ inch. If you are in doubt about how long a screw you need, it is always better to use a longer screw than a shorter one. Remember that building codes vary, so you might wish to check locally.

For screw fastener spacing, refer to Table 1–1.

1¼″ (31.8 mm) Type W Bugle Head
Attaches ½″ or ⅝″ single-layer gypsum panels, or RC-1 Channels to wood framing

Bugle Head
Attaches gypsum board to 20- to 25-ga. steel framing

1½″ (38.1 mm) Bugle Head-Laminating
Temporary attachment of gypsum to gypsum

Frame Spacing—Drywall Construction
Direct Application

board thickness	location	application method(1)	max. frame spacing o.c.	
SINGLE-LAYER APPLICATION			**in**	**mm**
⅜″ (9.5 mm)	ceilings(2)(3)	perpendicular(3)	16	406
	sidewalls	parallel or perpendicular	16	406
½″ (12.7 mm)	ceilings	parallel(3)	16	406
		perpendicular	24(4)	610
	sidewalls	parallel or perpendicular	24	610
⅝″ (15.9 mm)	ceilings	parallel(3)	16	406
		perpendicular	24	610
	sidewalls	parallel or perpendicular	24	610
DOUBLE-LAYER APPLICATION				
⅜″ & ½″ (9.5 mm & 12.7 mm)	ceilings(5)	perpendicular	16	406
	sidewalls	perpendicular or parallel	24(6)	610
⅝″ (15.9 mm)	ceilings	perpendicular or parallel	24(6)	610
	sidewalls	perpendicular	24(6)	610

(1)Long edge position relative to framing. (2)Not recommended below unheated spaces. (3)Not recommended if water-based texturing material is to be applied. (4)Max. spacing 16″ if water-based texturing material to be applied. (5)Adhesive must be used to laminate ⅜″ board for double-layer ceiling construction. (6)Max. spacing 16″ o.c. if fire rating required.

FIGURE 1–3 Gypsum panel application and frame spacing *(Courtesy U.S. Gypsum Co.)*

Adhesives

The use of adhesives reduces the need for screw or nail fasteners. Put strips of adhesive on the studs you are about to cover with drywall. Adhesives are quite effective in high-moisture areas, especially for ceilings. When using adhesives, remember not to put it on the studs ahead of your immediate working area. When adhesives are exposed to air, they set very quickly, losing their sticking properties.

When using adhesives on ceilings, you will have to secure the perimeter of the drywall with screws or nails. You also will need one fastener in the field on each stud. Follow the same procedure when using adhesives on the walls, omitting the use of fasteners in the field. Refer to Table 1–1.

You will need to order the drywall, screws, nails, and adhesive. For corner beads, square or round, you will need a stick for each outside corner. Be sure to allow for windows and door openings. See Chapter 3 for more information about the types of corner bead.

Most drywall supply stores will deliver the materials to your house. If you are not going to hang the drywall soon, it must be laid flat on the floor to distribute the weight evenly. When you start hanging, it will be a lot easier if the board is leaned up against a wall in the living room. This places the drywall in a bigger (and usually more central) work area than the other rooms.

NECESSARY TOOLS

You will need the following tools to hang drywall. See Figures 1–4 through 1–7.

Bench

The drywall bench is similar to a carpenter's sawhorse except that the top of the bench is about six inches wide so the hanger can stand on top of it. The illustration in Figure 1–5 shows how to make a bench. Note that all of the dimensions are given, with the exception of the height. The bench should be high enough so that when you stand on it, your head will touch the ceiling joist, minus the drywall thickness. Therefore, the bench, hanger's height, and drywall thickness equal the ceiling height.

T-Square

The T-square is used as a straightedge for cutting drywall. You can also use a T-square to find the correct angles to cut when you hang walls in a stairwell or a cathedral-type room.

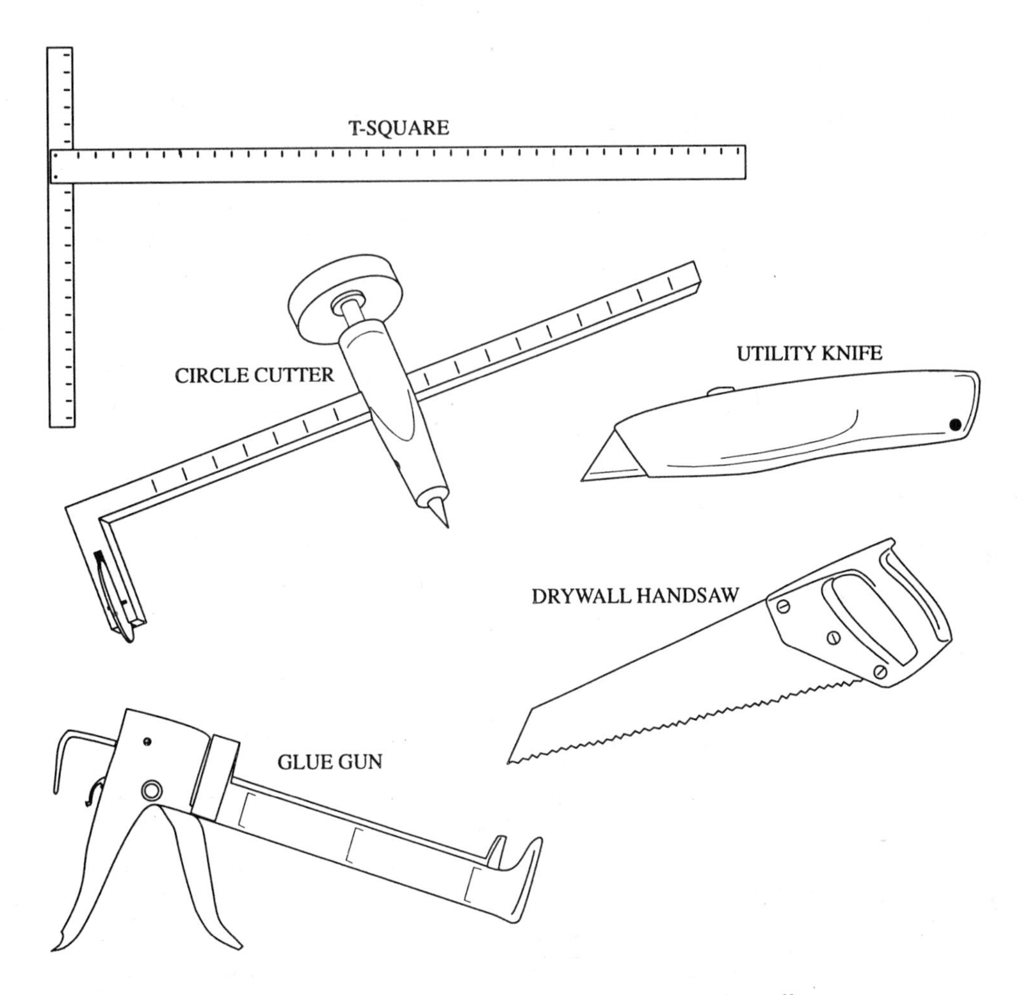

FIGURE 1–4 Tools needed for hanging drywall

Toe Jack

The ceilings in a house are usually an inch or two higher than eight feet. The first board on the wall is hung horizontally with its top edge against the ceiling. The lower board does not reach up to the bottom edge of the top board. The toe jack is placed under the edge of the lower board. When you step down on the toe jack, it will lift the lever board up tight to the top one for easy nailing. (Figure 1–6).

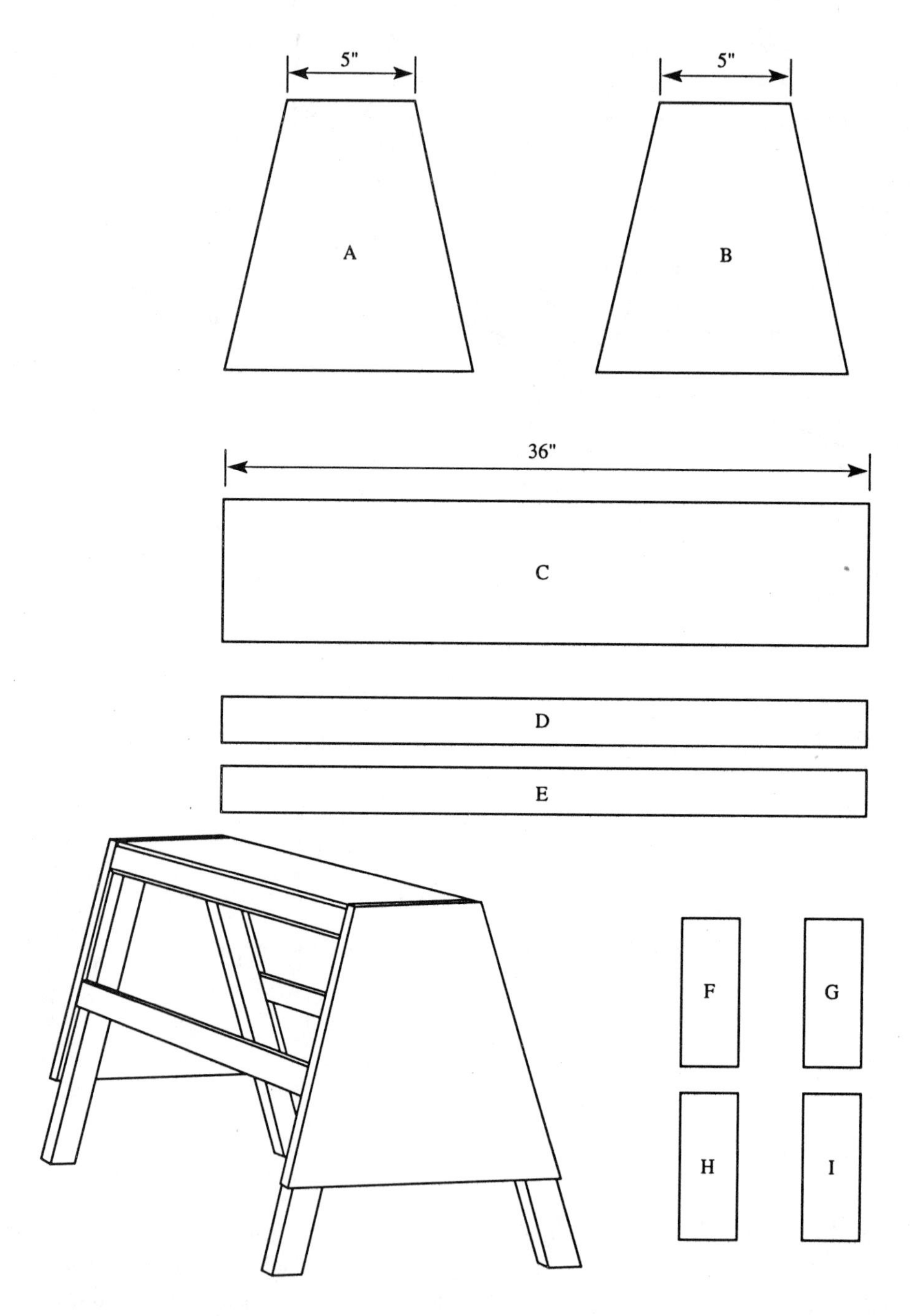

FIGURE 1–5 How to build a drywall bench. Leg length is determined by hanger's height.

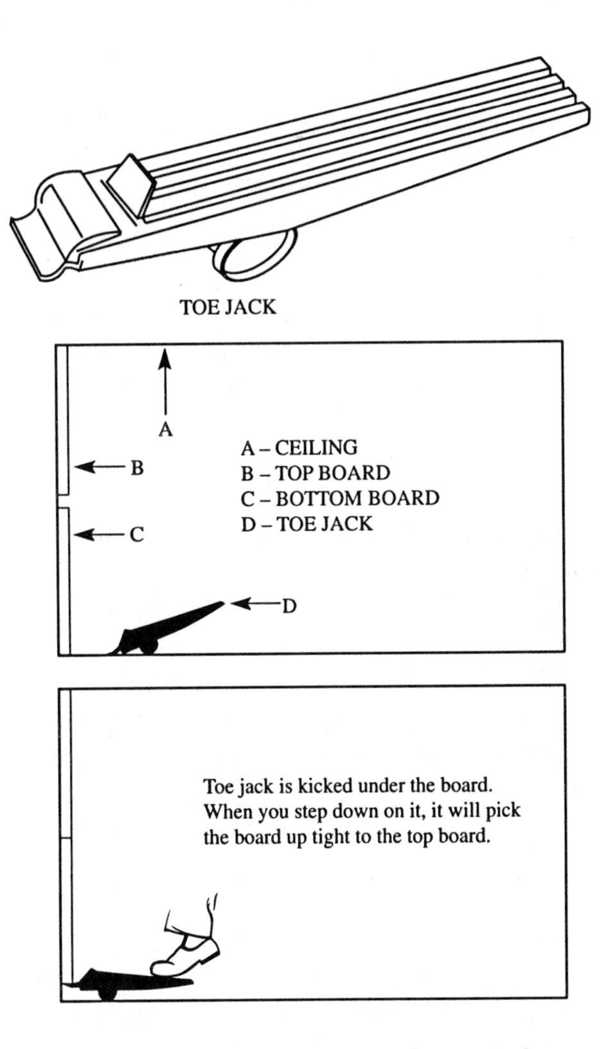

FIGURE 1–6 How to use the toe jack

Hatchet

A hanger's hatchet has a round head with grooves cut in it. The grooves keep the hatchet from sliding off the nail you are nailing. The head is rounded so that when you drive a nail into the drywall, the board around the nail will be dimpled. The dimple is later filled with joint compound to cover the nail.

Knife

For cutting drywall, you will need a carpet or utility knife with a replaceable blade.

Circle Cutter

The circle cutter resembles a drafting compass, but, instead of using a pencil, the circle cutter uses a small round cutting wheel. The circle cutter is used to score around the area to be cut before you knock it out.

Saws

There are two types of saws to use when hanging drywall: a drywall handsaw and a drywall keyhole saw.

Tape Measure

Use a tape measure at least sixteen feet long and ¾ inch wide. You will be hanging drywall that is twelve feet long, but if you buy a tape that is only twelve feet long, it will eventually break on you. The reason for this is that pulling the tape all the way out to the end weakens the tape. Shop around and buy one that's tough.

Pouches

To hang drywall you will need two pouches: one to hold your hand tools and one to hold your nails. If you are right handed, the nail pouch should be on your left side and the tool pouch on the right.

Rasps

This is one of the small hand-held types that has a replaceable blade. The rasp is used to smooth the edge of the drywall after it has been cut.

Pencils

The best pencil to use is a number 2 pencil, the kind commonly used in schools.

TOOLS TO IMPROVE PRODUCTIVITY AND UTILIZE UNTRAINED HELP

Clincher

The clincher is not allowed in all states, so check your building code. This easy-to-use tool helps put on a corner bead (90°). Hitting the top with a mallet forces the two metal teeth to crimp into the edge of the metal. When used correctly, the clincher is quite fast and effective.

Drywall Ripper

It is extremely time consuming to make strips of drywall to wrap around windows and doorways. The ripper is a convenient tool that saves time.

Router, Ream Machine, Drywall Cutout

This handy tool has made it possible for a hanger to learn the trade in half the time. Receptacle boxes have always been difficult to cut out accurately. The router simplifies this task. You place an X in the area of the receptacle box or switch box cutout. After the board is in place, use the router to enter the drill bit into the area with the X. Proceed in one direction until you hit the side of the receptacle box. Place the bit to the outside of the receptacle and let the bit follow around the outside of the receptacle. The bit won't cut into the plastic, metal, or wood. It cuts only the drywall.

Round recess lights are difficult to cut correctly. The router tool is a time saver and money-maker. You can get information about this tool by calling 1-901-665-8600 or check with your local drywall suppliers.

Drywall Lift

Also called dead man lift or drywall jack, the drywall lift is just what the name implies. This lift makes it possible for one person to hang drywall. It saves not only the pocketbook because you won't have to pay for extra help, but it also saves the back. The drywall lift jacks up the drywall and holds it against the ceiling.

Screw Gun Attachment Called the Rocker

The screw gun is something you need if you are going to use screws. This gun has been around for a long time; however, a new attachment has come out that

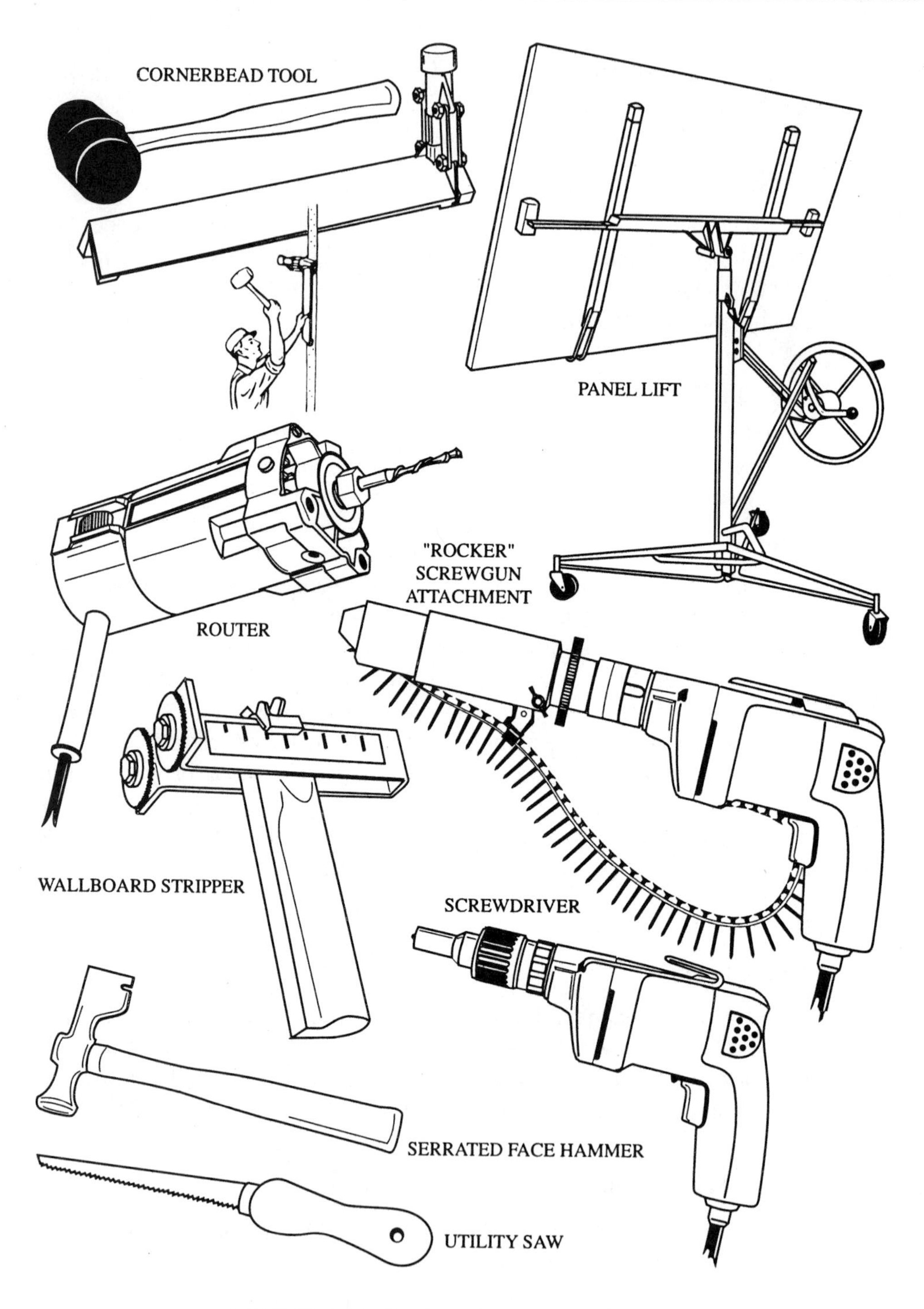

FIGURE 1–7 Tools to improve productivity

makes the screw gun easy to use. The screw gun alone takes skill to work the screws in your hand so they are in place one after another. Also, it's hard to make the screws go in straight. The rocker does all this for you. You can find out more about this new tool by calling 1-800-477-TURN or FAX 510-687-6261. Or write THE ROCKER, 205 Mason Circle, Concord, CA 94520.

Obviously, there are countless materials and tools. I mention only the few that are necessary for a beginner. Visit your local drywall supply store. You will find many interesting tools, but most people end up using only a few with which they are comfortable.

The hanging techniques described in this book are for use without electric tools. You need to know how to cut and hang drywall without depending on electricity. When you know how to hang without electric tools, then adding these tools can only make your job easier. If you are working a job site without electricity (which happens frequently), you can still go on working.

Questions

1. What is drywall made of?
  a. Asbestos and paper board
  b. Paper-wrapped gypsum board
  c. Paper and joint compound
  d. Four-by-eight board

2. What is the main function of drywall?
  a. It ties in the framing of a house
  b. It is used to patch weak places in the wall
  c. It is good insulation
  d. It forms the walls and ceilings of most homes

3. What thickness of drywall is most commonly used in residences?
  a. ¼ inch
  b. ⅝ inch
  c. 1 inch
  d. ½ inch

4. What is a fire wall?
  a. A wall used for fire drills
  b. A wall separating two apartments
  c. A wall separating a bathroom from another room
  d. A wall separating a garage from a living area of a residence

5. Where is water-resistant drywall used?
  a. Around swimming pools
  b. In ceilings of bathrooms
  c. In showers
  d. In tub and shower areas

6. What is a butt joint?
  a. The place where fire-rated and water-resistant boards join
  b. The back side of drywall
  c. The place where two cut edges of drywall come together
  d. The place where two factory edges come together

7. Which type of fastener holds best?
  a. Nail
  b. Screw
  c. Nail and adhesive
  d. Screw and adhesive

8. How high should a hanger's bench be?
  a. The combination of the hanger's height and the bench legs should equal the ceiling height.
  b. The bench should be high enough to reach the ceiling.
  c. The combination of bench height and hanger's height should equal the ceiling height.
  d. The combination of bench height, hanger's height and drywall thickness should equal the ceiling height.

9. What is the toe jack used for?
  a. To open buckets of joint compound
  b. To carry drywall
  c. To hold ceiling boards up until nailed
  d. To lift the lower board up to contact the bottom of the top board for easy nailing

10. What is a T-square used for?
  a. As a level
  b. To make square holes
  c. As a straightedge for cutting drywall
  d. To cut square angles

11. What is a drywall ripper used for?
a. To make factory edges
b. To make butt joints
c. To cut strips of drywall
d. To shred drywall scrap

12. What is a drywall lift used for?
a. To carry drywall from one location to another
b. To lift the hangers so they can reach high areas
c. To jack up the drywall and hold it against the ceiling
d. To lift up the bottom board on the wall to the top board so it can be nailed

13. What is the least amount by which a nail should penetrate wood framing?
a. ⅝ inch
b. ⅜ inch
c. ⅞ inch
d. 1 inch

14. What is the least amount by which a screw should penetrate wood framing?
a. ⅝ inch
b. ⅜ inch
c. ⅞ inch
d. 1 inch

15. When using the router, how would you cut for a receptacle box?
a. Just sight it when the board is in place.
b. Mark top and bottom of box from the floor.
c. Mark left and right side of box from side wall.
d. From middle of box when board is in place, cut to one edge and proceed all around.

16. When using adhesive on walls, how many nails should you use in the field?
a. None
b. One at each end and one in the field
c. Two in the field
d. The same number as you use without adhesive

17. When using adhesive on ceilings, how many nails should you use in the field per joist?
a. Two sets instead of three sets
b. One set of nails in the field
c. One on each edge and one in the field
d. None is required in the field

Chapter 2
Drywall Installation

Hanging the Ceiling

The first thing to hang is the ceiling. Keep in mind that there is no such thing as a perfectly square house, so your drywall won't fit exactly square to the framework. Cut it to fit as well as possible. When hanging the walls later it will fill up ½ inch of ceiling space. Any big spaces will need strips of drywall cut and nailed into place.

MARKING THE CEILING JOISTS

Before hanging the ceiling, mark the ceiling joists throughout the house. When you hold a sheet of drywall against the ceiling, you are unable to see the joists to which you will nail it. The joists rest on a horizontal board called the *top plate.* If you draw a line on the top plate directly beneath the center of the joist, you will be able to see where to nail. This must be done throughout the house, including the closets. Figure 2–1 shows ceiling joists and where to mark them.

CUTTING THE DRYWALL

After marking the ceiling joists, place your benches in one of the back rooms. If you start hanging in one of the back rooms and work your way forward, there

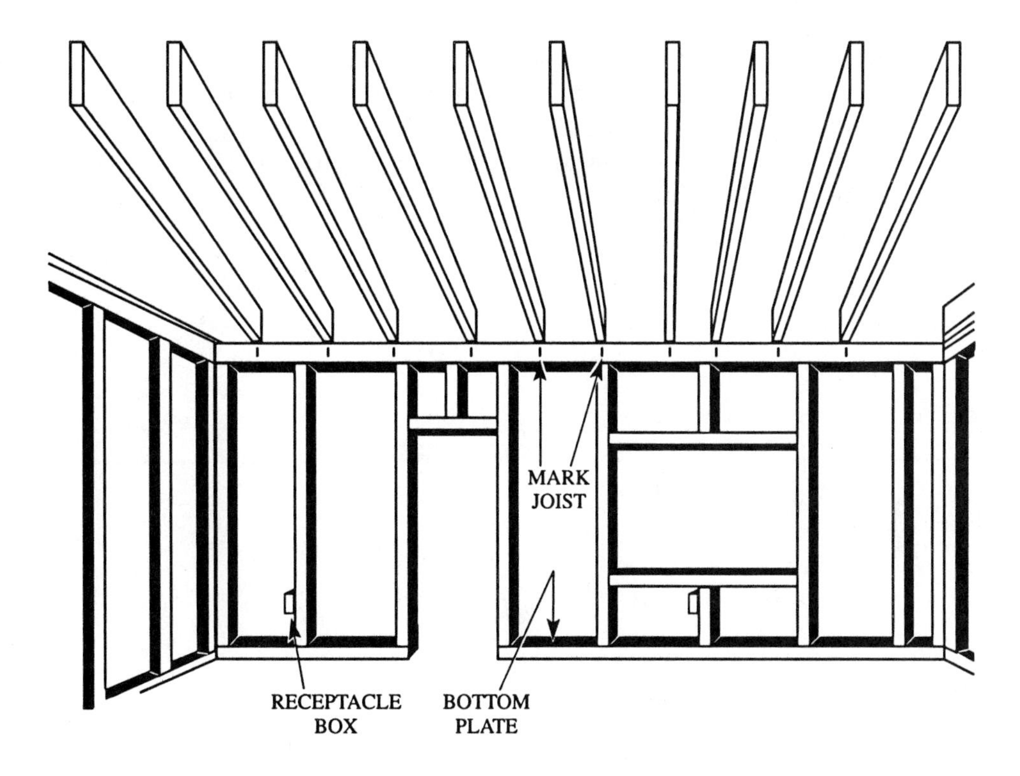

FIGURE 2–1

will not be as much drywall in the way when you get to the front. The drywall will be hung in the opposite direction that the joists run. Place the bench along the outside wall about two feet away from the end. If you do this, you will be under the center of the board when you are standing on the bench.

When you step up onto your bench, have your helper take the end of the tape measure and hold it against the top plate of the wall. You take the other end of the tape and stretch it to the last joist that a twelve-foot sheet of drywall will span. Read the measurement at the exact center of that joist. Step down and go to the stack of drywall. Hook the end of your tape on the end of a sheet of drywall and pull the tape across the board, placing a mark at the correct length. Take a T-square and put it on the drywall with the edge touching this mark. Hold the T-square tight to the board by putting your toe on the bottom and your knee in the middle of the T-square. Hold the top of the T-square with one hand and score down the side of the T-square with your utility knife. Remove the T-square and bend the board back at the score line. Go around to the back side of the board and score along the groove made when it was bent back. Bend it again and it will break off. Set the excess aside to use later. Figure 2–2 shows how to cut the board.

Rasp the end of the board so that it will be smooth. If you have any openings to cut out of the drywall, measure and cut them now. Do not draw the lines for a cutout until the board is cut to the right length.

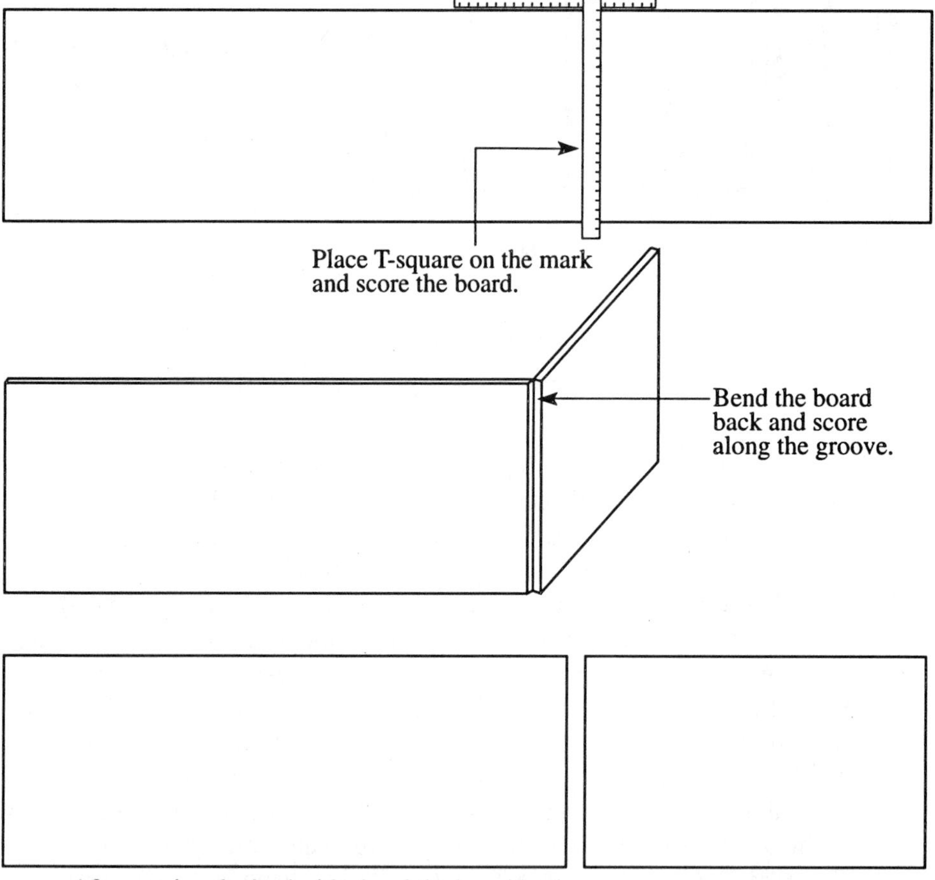

FIGURE 2–2 Cutting the drywall

Cutting Out Openings in the Drywall

To cut out a round hole in the drywall, you must measure from the outside wall to the middle of the hole. Then you must measure from the bottom of the upper board to the middle of the hole. Connect the two points on the drywall and use a circle cutter to score around it. Always allow an extra ¼ inch. For example, if the diameter of a receptacle is four inches, the opening should be 4¼ inches.

To cut a rectangular opening in the drywall, you must measure all four sides. After the lines are drawn on the board, use a keyhole saw to cut out the opening. If you put the point of the saw against the board and push against it, the saw will push through the board and you can start sawing from there.

DRAWING THE CENTER LINE

After the drywall is cut and the openings are cut out, draw a line along the center of the board. You will use this line as a guide for nail placement.

One way to draw this line is to place a T-square on the drywall. Hold a pencil against the T-square at the 24-inch mark. While holding the pencil tight to the square, slowly slide the T-square across the board. A better way to draw this line is to use a tape measure as a guide. With one hand, hold the pencil at the end of the tape, placing the pencil on the 24-inch mark on the drywall. Hold the tape in the other hand, resting that hand on top of the board. Stretch the tape taut and slide your hands across the board, keeping your hands parallel to each other. This method takes practice, but it is worth learning. It is much faster than using the T-square. Figure 2–3 shows where to draw the line and where to place each set of nails.

HOW TO HANG DRYWALL ON A CEILING

When hanging drywall on a ceiling, you will use a special method of nailing. The proper way is to hold the hatchet in front of your chest with the head pointing up. Grip the handle so that your thumb is on the side pointing toward the head of the hatchet. To drive the nail, keep your arm straight and use a wrist action to drive in the nail. This will be awkward at first, but you will improve with practice.

Screw attachment is not as difficult to learn. However, the worker usually will nail around the perimeter of the drywall, finishing the job with screws. Of course, screw attachment holds better.

When you are shorthanded, the tee brace can be a great help in hanging ceilings. The tee brace is simply a two-by-four board of ceiling height, with a two-by-four about two feet long nailed to one end to form a tee. If a worker places the tee under one

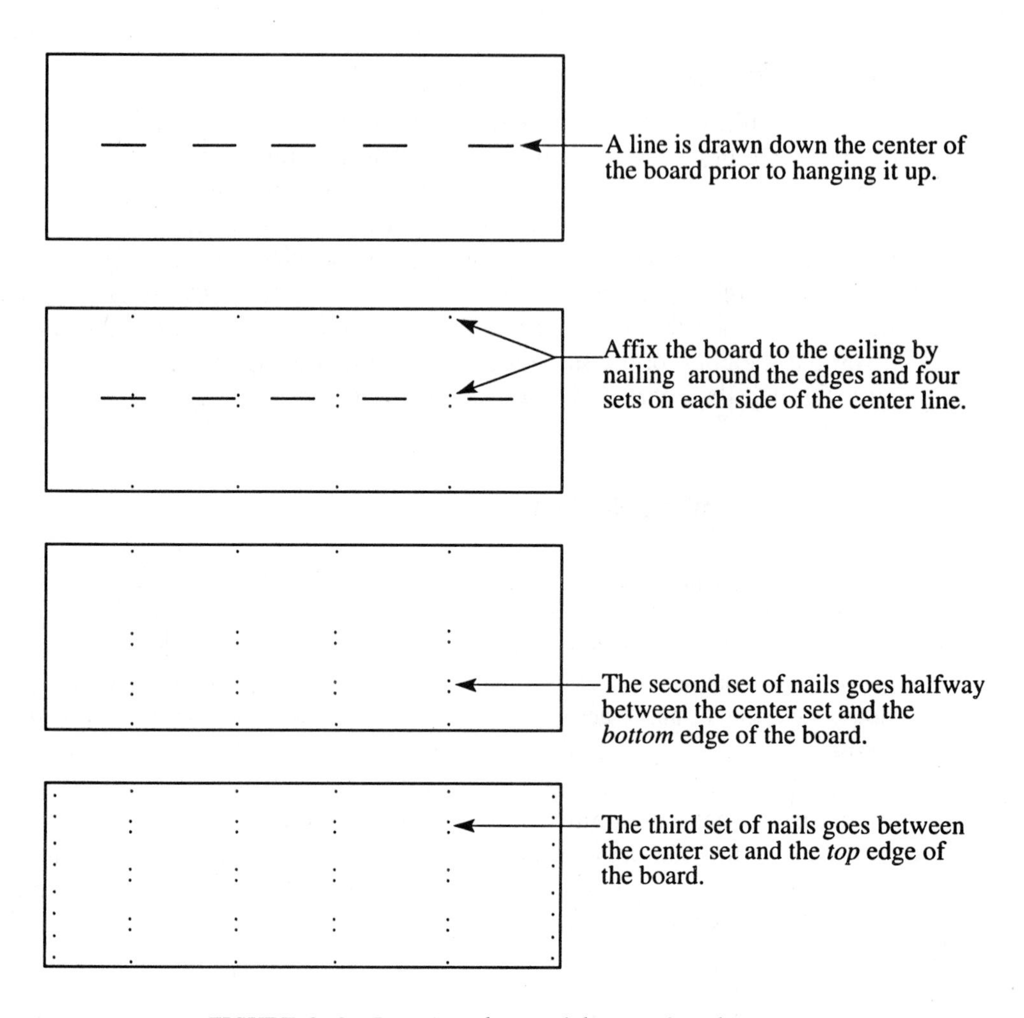

FIGURE 2–3 Drawing the guideline and nailing sets

end of the drywall and braces it against the ceiling, the tee holds one end in place while the worker hangs the drywall.

Hanging the Board

Now you're ready to hang the drywall. If the room you are hanging is longer than twelve feet, you won't have any trouble taking the board into the room. Have your helper pick up one end of the board, and you pick up the other end. If you use your right hand, your helper should also use the right hand. Otherwise, you'll be walking against each other, and this is very awkward. As you carry the board into the room, lift it up to the level of your head, as your helper does the same. Without breaking stride, step up on the benches.

When you are on the benches, place the board tight to the outside wall and tight to the side wall. You should brace the board on the outside wall. Hold the board tight to the ceiling with your head as your helper does the same. Then reach out and drive a nail through the drywall into one of the joists, then into a second joist. After you have nailed the board to the joist, twist around and nail it to two more joists on the opposite side of the board. When you have two joists nailed on each side, you can stop holding the board with your head. Now you can nail the rest of the board. Each time you drive a nail, you must push up on the board to make it tight to the joist. If you fail to do this, the board will not be nailed properly.

The nails on the ends of the board should be seven inches on center, which means you should have seven nails there. Sets of nails are used for the rest of the board. A set of nails is two nails driven one to two inches apart. Each joist must have three sets of nails in the area between the nails on the edges. These nails are placed at intervals of twelve inches. The fastest way to place the sets in proper positions is to nail the first set at the line you drew on the board. The second set can be placed approximately halfway between that set and the edge of the board. The third set will be placed between the center and the other side of the board. The illustration in Figure 2–3 shows the correct method of nailing sets.

After the first board is hung, you are ready to hang the other boards. To hang the second board, measure from the end of the first board to the side wall. This board does not have to fit tight to the wall, so you should allow ¼ inch. If there is a small crack, the board hung on the wall will cover it. This board will be nailed the same way that the first board was nailed. You will also use the same method to cut this board as you did for the first one. When you hang this board, make sure that it butts up tight to the end of the other board.

The next row of drywall is hung so that the butt joint is on the opposite end of the room. The best way to do this is to hang the first row from right to left and the next row from left to right. Figures 2–4 through 2–7 show how to hang each board on the ceiling. All ceilings are hung using the same system.

Hanging in a Small Room

If the room you are hanging is less than twelve feet long, it will be difficult to get the board into the room. When you walk into the room with the board, the first person should hold the end of the board up to the top of the wall next to the ceiling, while the other person bends down with the other end. While the first person holds the board up to the ceiling, the other one walks around to a bench. After both are next to the benches, the second person can then raise the board up. Both can then lift the board up to the ceiling.

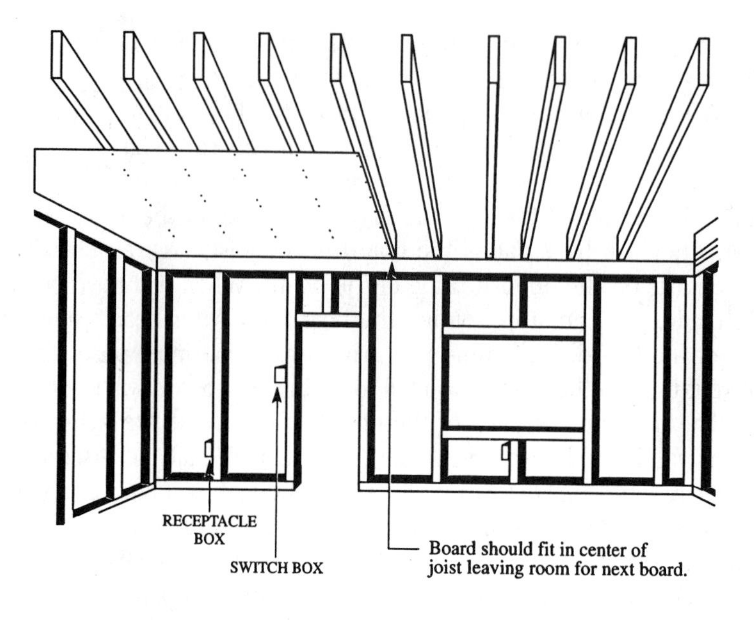

FIGURE 2–4

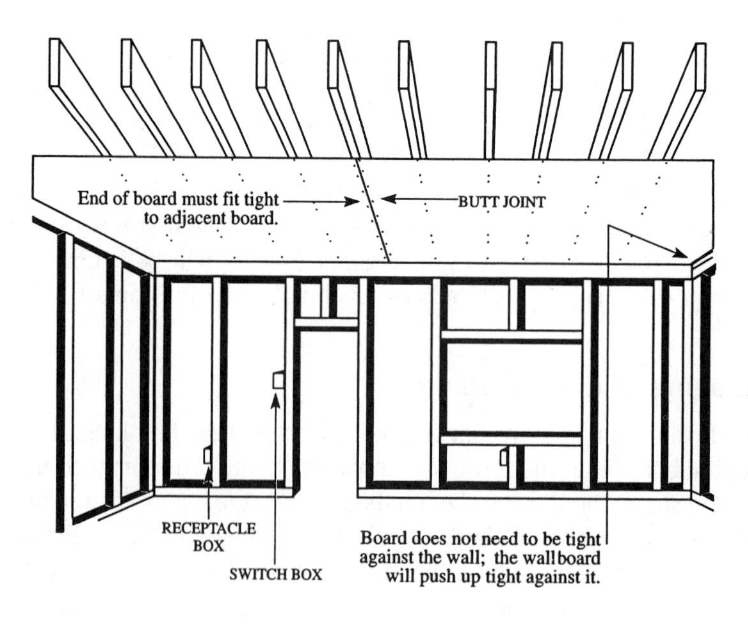

FIGURE 2–5

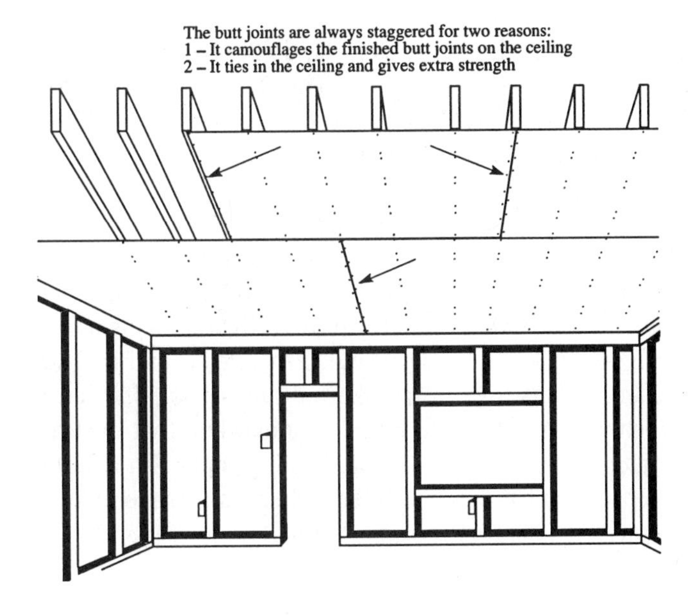

FIGURE 2–6

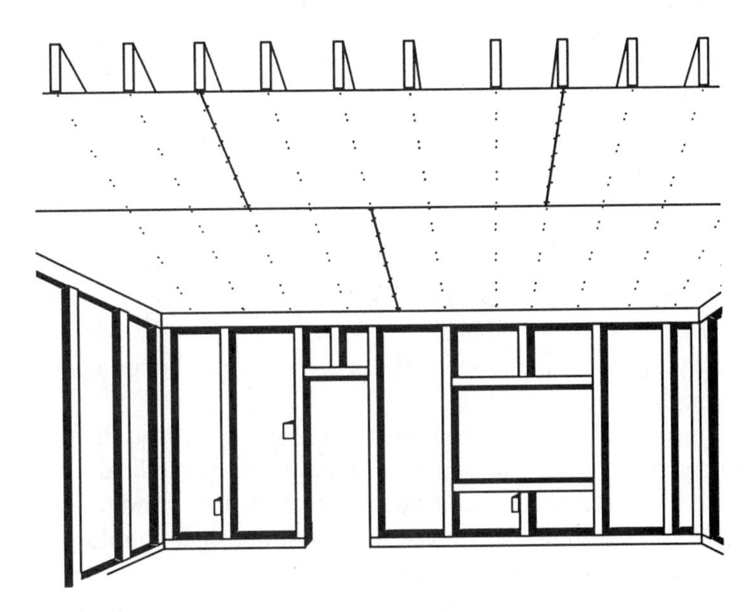

FIGURE 2–7 After nailing off the ceiling, go back and check for loose spots, torn paper, and nails that may have missed the studs.

When hanging drywall in a closet, don't use just little scraps. This is one of the worst mistakes a hanger can make. The closets should be done with the same care as the rest of the house. Too many small pieces of drywall can make the finished job look unsightly. For a more attractive appearance, use the largest excess pieces you can find for small areas like closets.

It's important to check all the nails and pull out any that missed the stud. When you pull a nail out, it will leave a small piece of paper sticking out. This piece of paper should be tapped in with a hammer so that the finisher can cover it with joint compound. Any bent nails with the paper torn around them must be replaced because they won't hold, and the board could crumble around it. Always use a screwdriver, not a hammer, to drive in or take out any screws that have missed studs.

When you hang the first board, you may find that the wall is crooked. The way to alleviate this is to hang the board so it is square in relation to the center of the joist. You can put a piece in later if there is a space at the outside wall.

Hanging the Walls

After you have finished hanging all of the ceilings, you are ready to hang the walls. This section shows you how to hang a wall without any openings in it. The other types of walls will be discussed in the next section.

HANGING THE TOP ROW

Start hanging the walls in one of the back rooms just as you did for the ceilings. Hang the outside wall first, then the side walls, and the wall with the door opening last. This is done so that each board can fit tight to the previous one. When you hang a wall, always hang across the entire wall with the top boards before you start hanging the bottom boards.

The drywall on the ceiling needs three sets of nails in the field. The walls need only two sets. You can use guidelines drawn across the board in the same way you did on the ceiling, except these boards need two lines drawn on sixteen-inch centers. After you have hung a few houses, you will find that you don't need the lines for guides anymore—experience is the best teacher.

Check the nails each time you finish nailing off a board. Pull out any nail that missed the stud, and replace any nail that tore or broke the paper. Make sure that all nails are dimpled (sunk into the drywall). Later, this indentation can be covered with joint compound and no one will ever know a nail or screw was used.

If you are using screw attachment, use a screwdriver to place the screw deeper. Pull out any screw that missed the stud, and tap in any loose paper.

Check and trim all outlet holes before nailing off the board.

After the ceiling is hung, you will notice that the top plate runs the length of the wall, just under the ceiling layer of drywall. The top plate is helpful because you can start nails on the top of the board before hanging it.

To measure the length of the board, have your helper hold the end of the tape to the side wall as high as possible. You stretch the tape out to the last stud that a twelve-foot sheet of drywall will span. Read the measurement at the exact center of that stud. Go to the stack of drywall and cut the board to fit, as you did for the ceiling board. Start a row of nails that will fit to the top of this board against the ceiling.

When you and your helper carry the board into the room, the first to enter the room should walk directly to the corner. Then both of you should pick the board up to the ceiling. After you have the board up, hold it tight to the ceiling, reach up and drive in a couple of nails that you started on the top of the board. Once you have two or three nails driven in, you can let go of the board, but you must push the board up tight to the ceiling each time you drive a nail in until the top is completely nailed off.

Sometimes the ceiling may be bowed in places, and the top board may not fit tight to the ceiling. When this happens, make sure that the ends of the board are level. If there is a space at the top of the board, you can put a piece of drywall there. When you need to cut a piece of drywall for a space, you should try to cut it from a piece of board that still has the factory edge. It will hold together better.

When you nail off the board, the nails on each end should be eight inches on center, which means you should have eight nails there. The field is nailed with two sets of nails on sixteen-inch centers from the edge of the board. The best way to nail on the wall is to stand in front of the stud. Hold a nail against the wall in the approximate area of the stud. Glancing up and down a few times will enable you to see where to nail. To determine if the nail missed the stud, look at the head of the nail. If the head is sunk into the board more on its right side, then that means it is to the left of the stud and vice versa.

A good way to utilize time is to have your helper finish nailing off the board while you cut the next one. When you measure for the next board, remember that you can cut it a quarter inch short to make the board fit into the corner more easily. Also, a quarter inch leaves a little room for settling of the house.

HANGING THE BOTTOM ROW

After the top row is hung, you are ready to hang the bottom row. On the ceiling, in order to stagger the butt joint, you hung the second row in the opposite direction of the first row. You should not do this on the wall because you must keep each board tight to the previous board. Hang from the wall that has already been hung, taking care not to break the joint on the same stud as in the first row. Butt joints should be at least three studs apart.

When you are nailing the bottom board to the wall, do not put the bottom nail any higher than three inches from the floor. The best way is to nail to the bottom plate on approximately twelve-inch centers. If you bend one of the nails, don't worry about pulling it out because it will be covered by the baseboard. But be sure to sink each nail well.

The bottom of each wall usually will have one or two electrical outlets. You can measure and precut the hole for each outlet. This method works because you can get an accurate height measurement from the top. However, the side measurement often will be inaccurate if the wall is off the stud or if the stud is twisted. There is another way that is faster and easier, and the hole will be more on center than it would be by precutting.

Cut the board to the correct length. Then measure from the bottom of the top board (not from the floor up) to the top and bottom of the outlet, drawing a line at these points across the board. Carry the board into the room and put it in place. Using the hatchet, grasp the top of the board and hold it out from the wall just enough to see clearly behind it. Look down at the electrical outlet, then glance from the front side of the board to the back. This should enable you to see where to mark the front. Use the blade of the hatchet to mark the location for each side of the electrical outlet. After making the marks, pull the board out from the wall and saw out the hole. The first few times you do this, you will probably miscut, but don't be discouraged. It takes practice. For more guidance, refer to Router Tool, Figure 1–7.

When you are ready to hang the board, place the toe jack on the floor in the center of the board. Kick it under the board and then step down on it, raising the board up tight to the bottom of the first board so you can nail the board off. Before you finish nailing off the board, check the outlet holes and trim them if necessary. The side walls will be hung the same way, but be sure to keep each board tight to the adjacent boards. Some builders do not use baseboards. When this happens, the bottom row is set on the floor and nailed into place without picking it up to the other board. A board ⅜ inch thick is usually ripped and used in the crack between the boards (Figures 2–8 through 2–12).

USING ADHESIVES

If you want to use glue on the wall, apply it only to the studs or to a board that you will be hanging within a few minutes. After the glue is in the open air for fifteen minutes, it will start to lose its adhesive properties. When you apply the glue, run

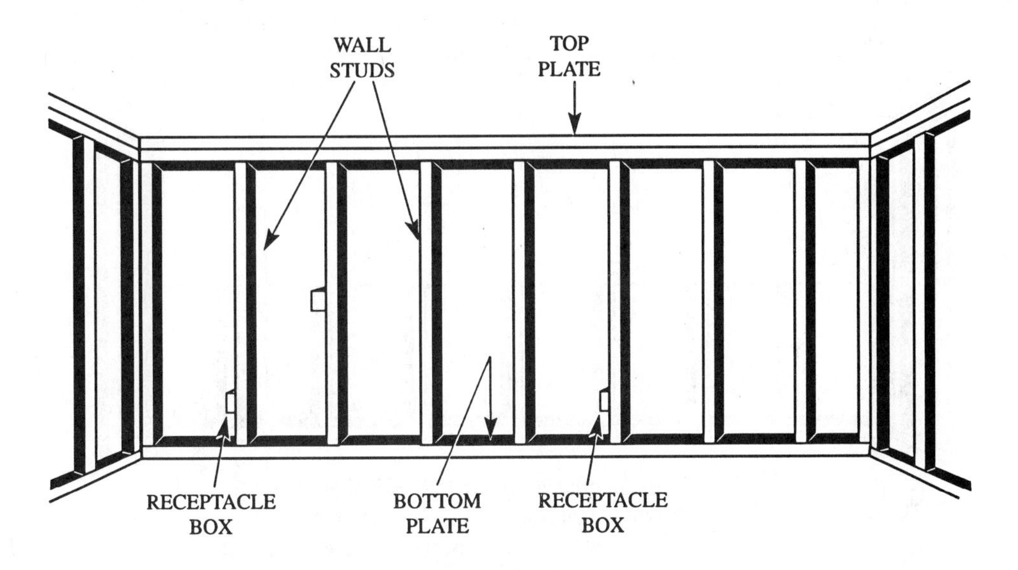

FIGURE 2–8

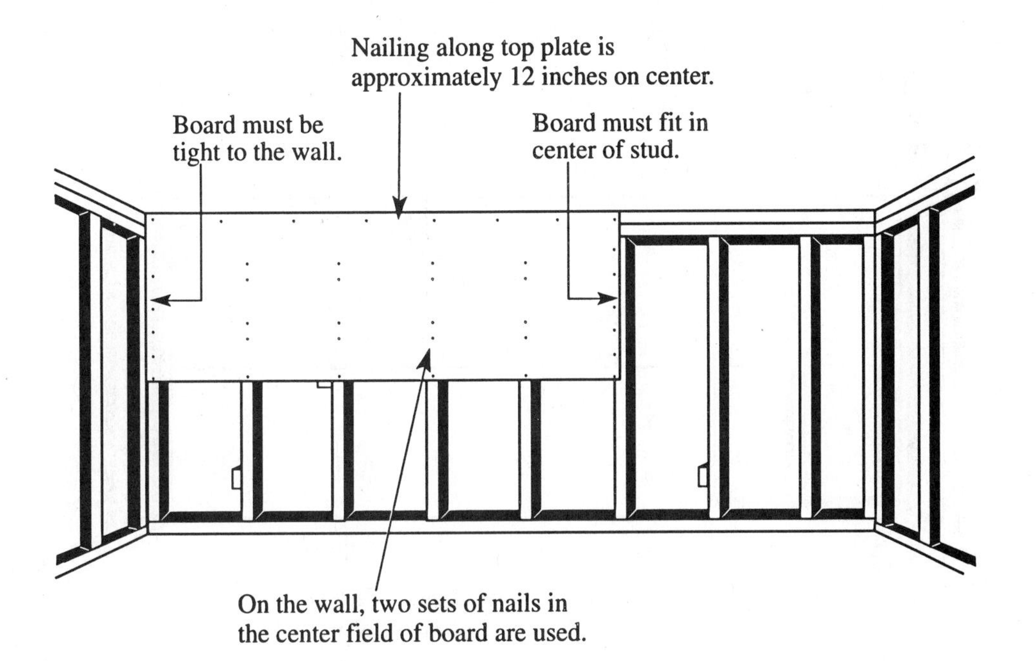

FIGURE 2–9

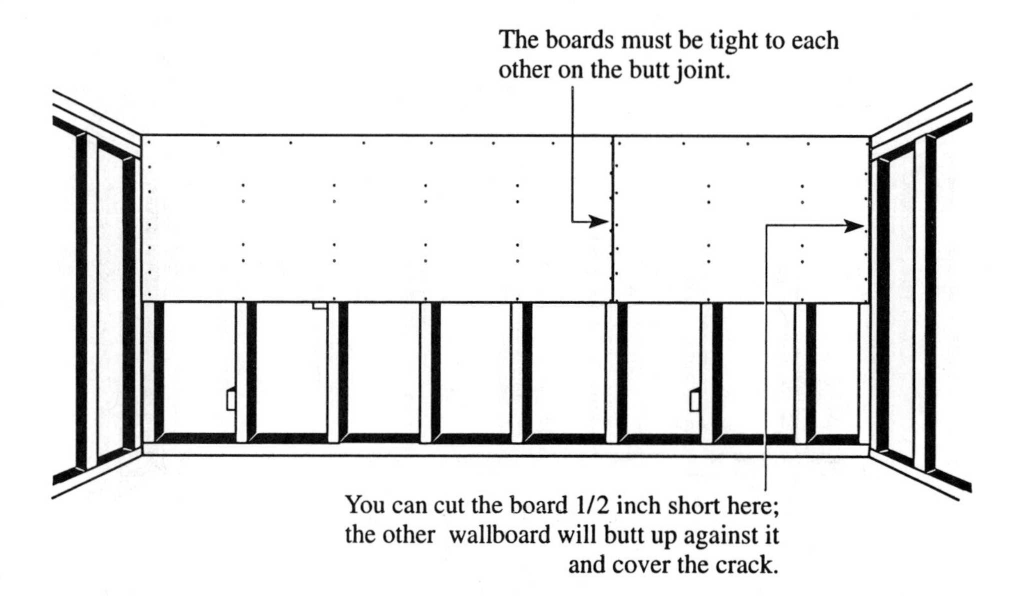

FIGURE 2–10

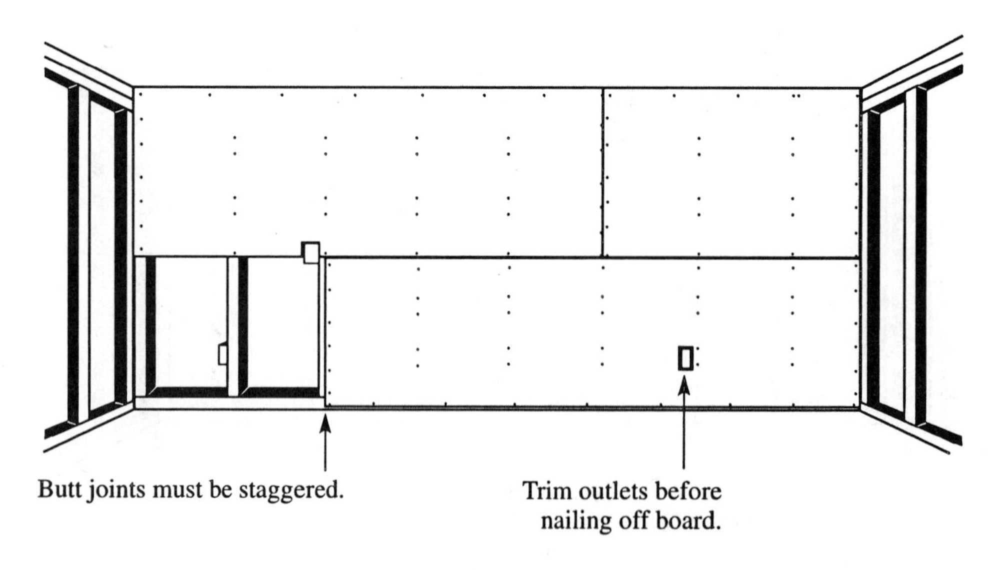

FIGURE 2–11

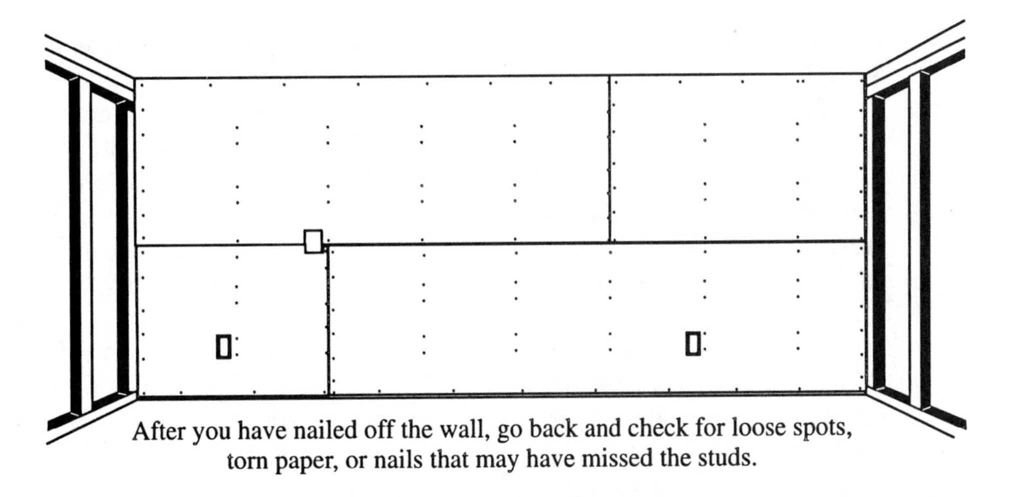

After you have nailed off the wall, go back and check for loose spots, torn paper, or nails that may have missed the studs.

FIGURE 2–12

the gun up the wall with the nozzle pointing forward. Hold it at an angle to the stud. Place the glue in the general area that the nail sets would be. Do not put glue in an area larger than this. The ends and sides of the walls still will have to be nailed, so there is no need to put glue in this area. After the board is nailed on the ends, go back and put one set of nails on each stud to hold the board tight to the wall until the glue sets.

Hanging Walls with Openings

You have seen how to hang a wall without any openings, but a wall with an opening, such as a window or a door, will be hung in a different manner.

There are two ways to hang a wall with an opening. One way is called *picture framing,* and the other way is called *headers.*

PICTURE FRAMING

Picture framing is a method in which you hang the board all the way across the wall and then saw out the opening for the window or door. This is by far the better and easier system. If the board does not reach all the way across the room, you must make the joint over or under the window. The joint over or under a window is a butt joint, but it is much easier to finish than a regular butt joint.

When you picture frame across a door, nail off around the door and then saw up the side of the door frame. Then step behind the board and score across the top of it, along the top of the door. Step back to the front of the board and pick it up as if it were hinged at the top. Score along the groove at the top and then break off the board. When you saw up the sides of the door, it's much easier if you put pressure on the saw against the side of the door. This ensures that the saw will cut a straight line.

When you hang board across a window, you will not be able to get your hand behind the board to score along the top of the window. So you must score the board before you hang it. Measure from the ceiling to the top edge of the window. Score across the back of the board at this line. Do not score all the way across the board or it will break, but extend the score line the width of the window. After the board around the window is nailed, you can saw up the sides of it, pick it up, and break it the same way as you did the door.

HEADERS

The other way to hang a wall with an opening is to use headers. The corner of a door or window is a weak point in the structural framing. If you hang drywall and hang only to the edge of the door or window, this joint will crack because there is movement at the weak point. However, if you hang the drywall past the edge of the door at least six to eight inches, the joint usually will not crack because the weak spot is tied in with the entire wall. You can hang farther over the door or window if you want to, but six to eight inches over is the recommended minimum. The electric router tool is helpful for the picture framing method. It allows you to cut around doors and windows with ease.

The illustrations in Figures 2–13 through 2–18 show how to hang with headers.

Hanging Kitchen Walls

Kitchen walls that are under soffits are hung in a different manner than the other walls. Bathrooms and utility rooms often have soffits in them and are treated in the same manner.

Most kitchens have a soffit running across the top of the wall for the cabinets to hang under. The kitchen window is usually located in the wall, too. There are

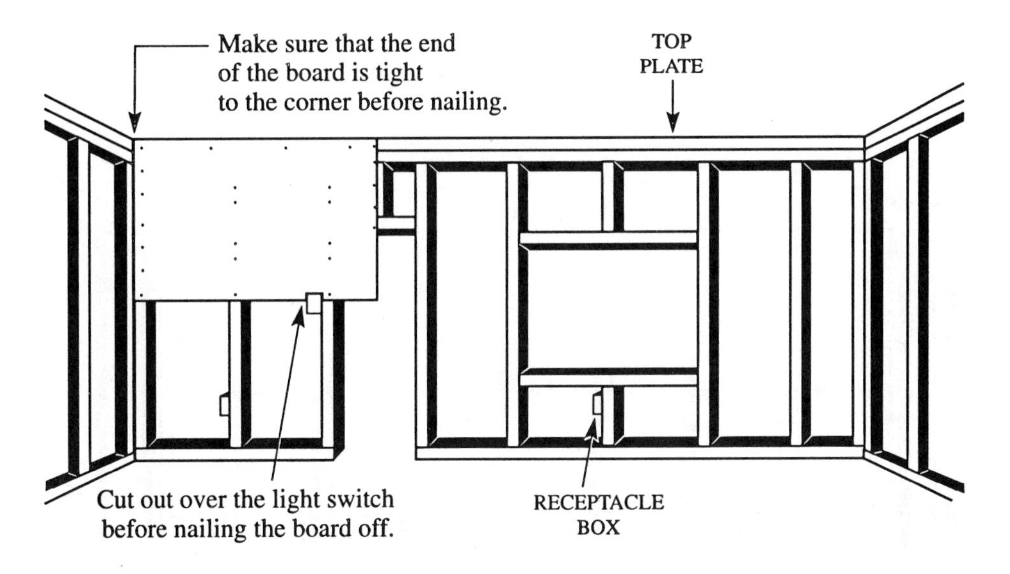

FIGURE 2–13

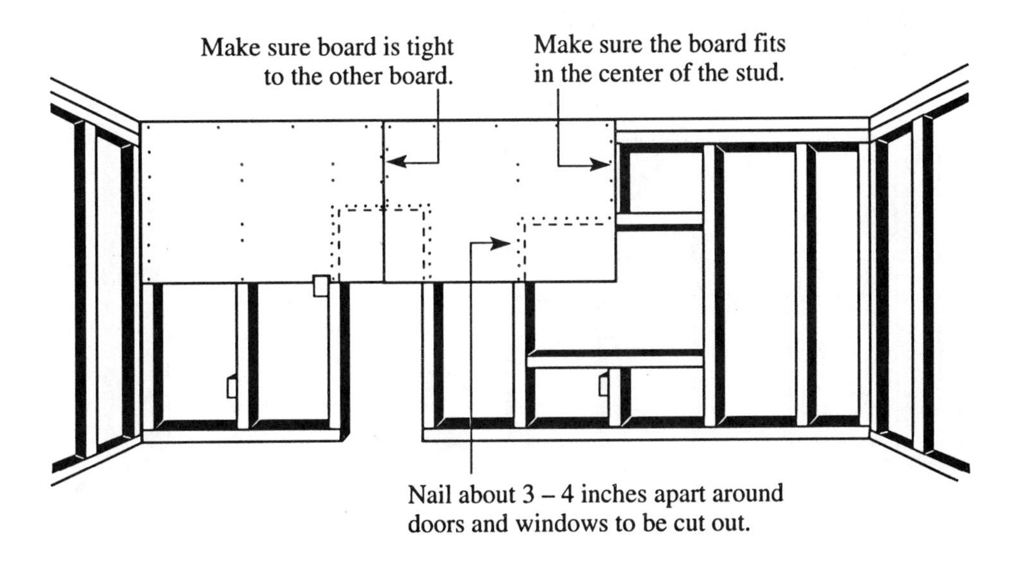

FIGURE 2–14

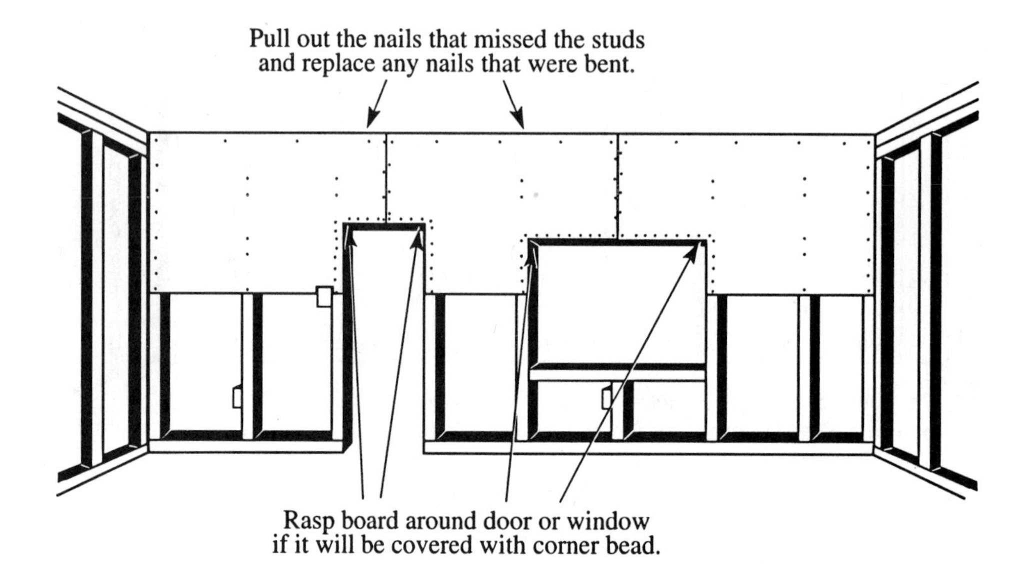

FIGURE 2–15

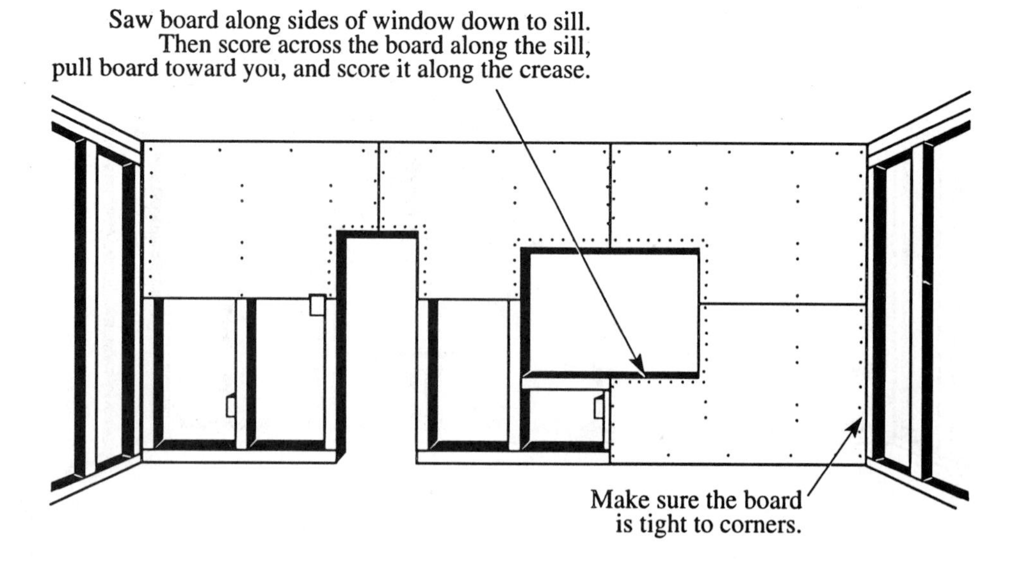

FIGURE 2–16

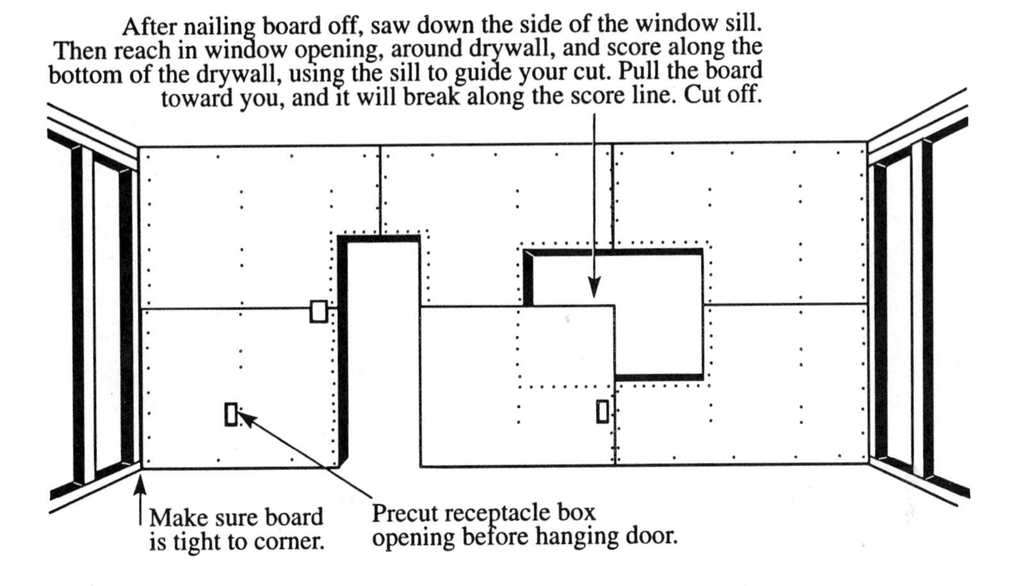

FIGURE 2–17

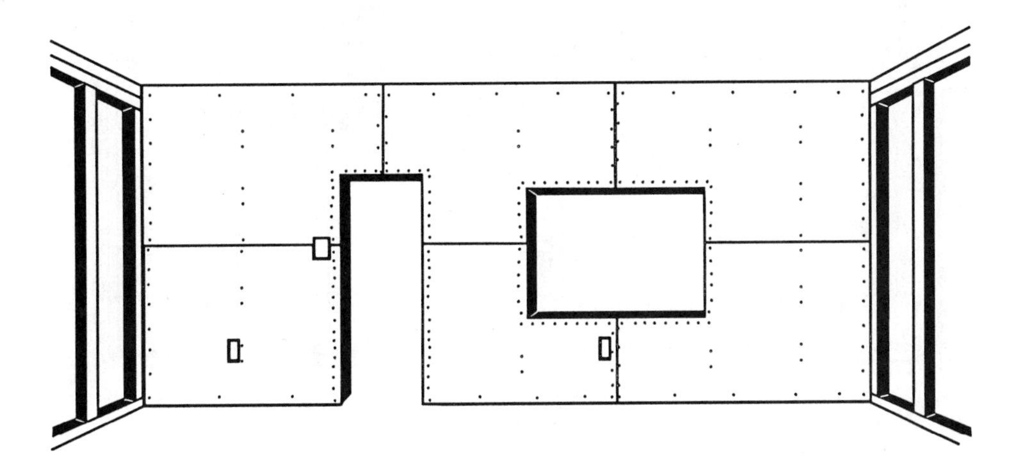

FIGURE 2–18 After nailing off the wall, go back and check for loose spots, torn paper, and nails that may have missed the studs.

more electrical outlets along this wall than anywhere else in the house. These outlets are usually four feet down from the ceiling. To hang under the soffit, you will have to rip the sheet of drywall to fit. After you hang this first piece, the electrical outlets will be right in the way of the finisher when he or she is taping and floating (covering with joint compound) the joint. To aid the finisher, hang a full-width sheet first and then hang a ripped sheet under it.

The illustrations in Figures 2–19 through 2–24 show how to hang a typical kitchen wall with a soffit. The edges of the soffit will be covered with corner bead, so be sure to hang the board to the edge of the frame. When you hang the soffit, use the end pieces left over from cutting the drywall. Remember to put a factory edge to a factory edge, and a butt joint to a butt joint.

Sometimes the two plumbing pipes sticking out of the wall are connected. If you cut a hole to go around both those pipes, there won't be any drywall behind them. To avoid this problem, make a trap door in the drywall by sawing out holes for the two pipes as if they were not connected. After the holes are cut, use a keyhole saw to cut a straight line from the bottom edge of one hole over to the bottom edge of the other. Then go to the back of the board and score from the top edge of one hole to the top edge of the other. Then go to the front of the board, and pick up the drywall as if the top is hinged. You can then put the drywall in place over the pipes and let the trap door close. (Refer to Figure 2–25.)

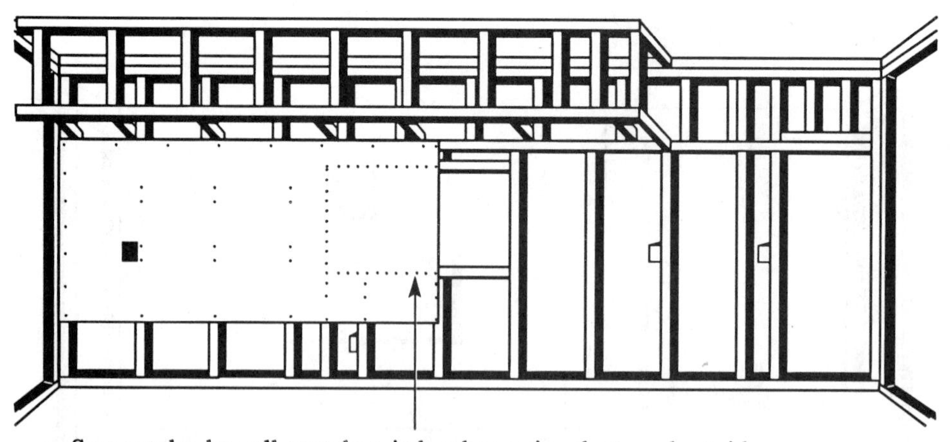

Saw out the drywall over the window by sawing the two short sides with a keyhole saw, reach in, score down the side with a utility knife, bend the drywall, then cut it off.

FIGURE 2–19

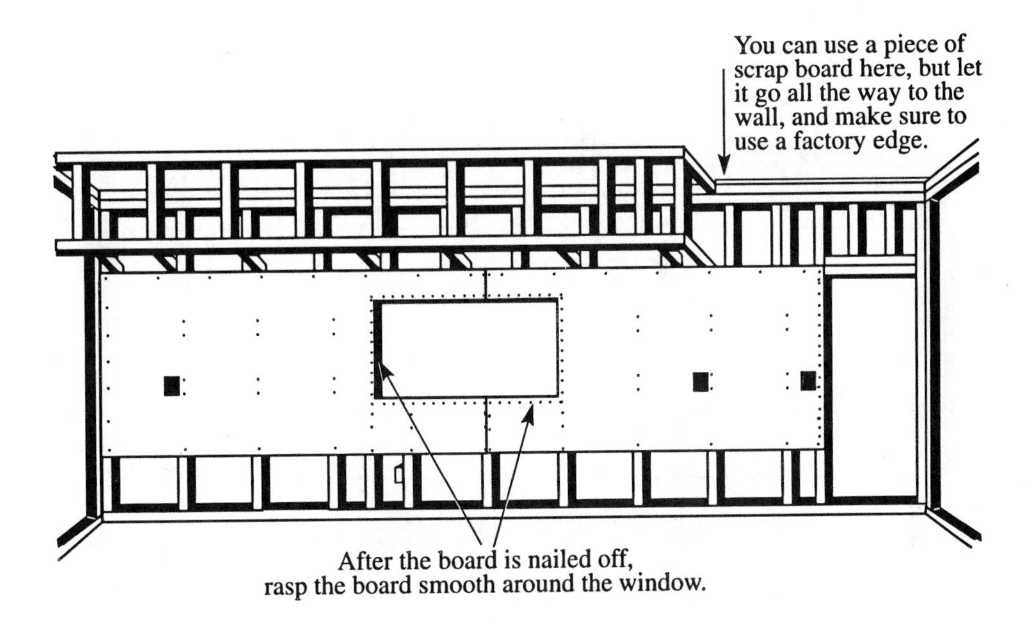

FIGURE 2–20

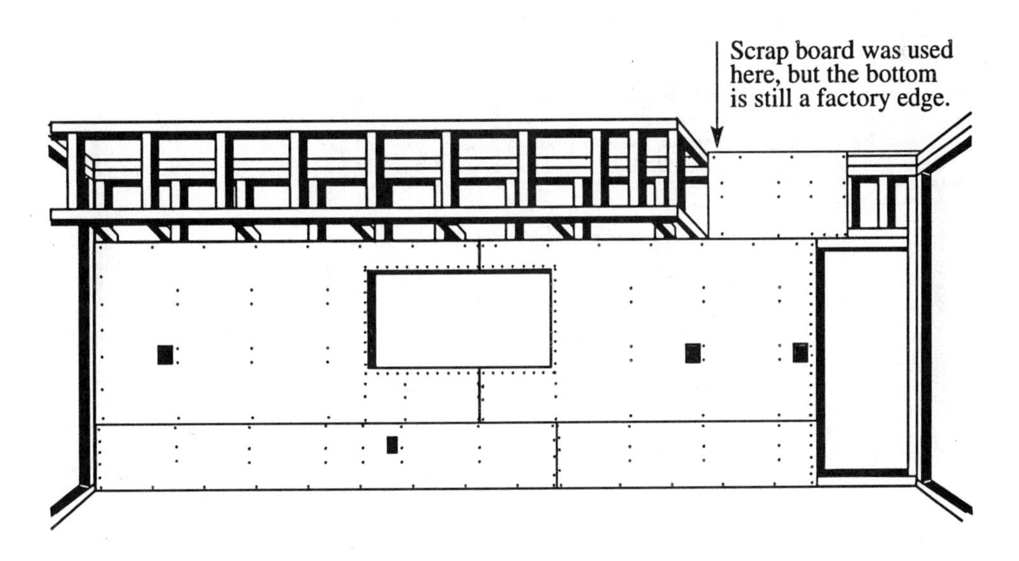

FIGURE 2–21

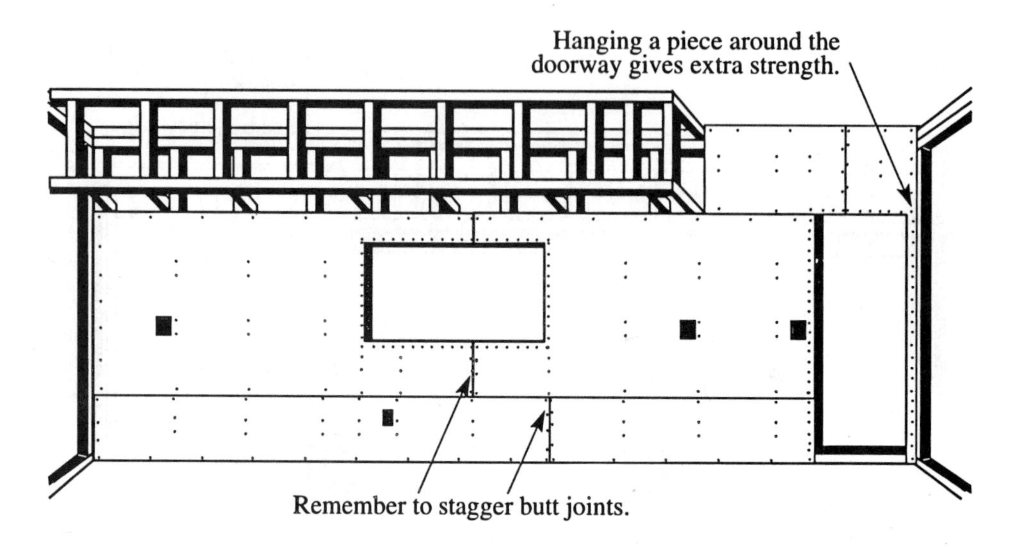

FIGURE 2–22

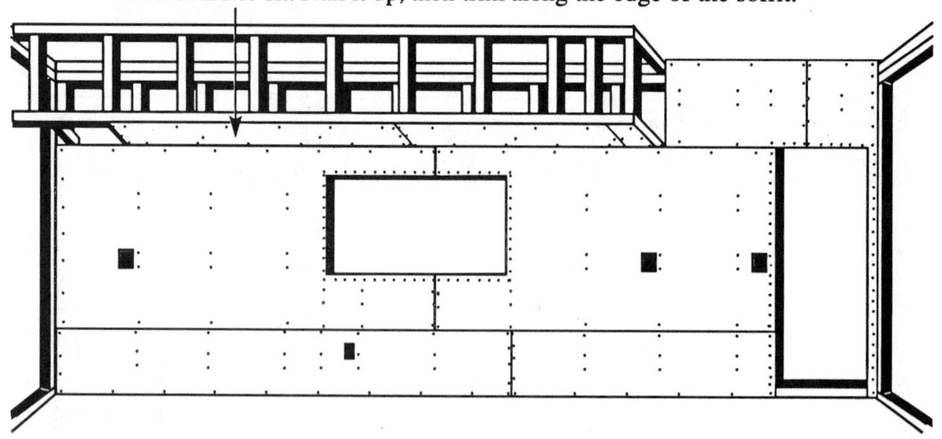

FIGURE 2–23 Use scrap end pieces to hang the soffit. Place butt joint to butt joint and factory edge to factory edge.

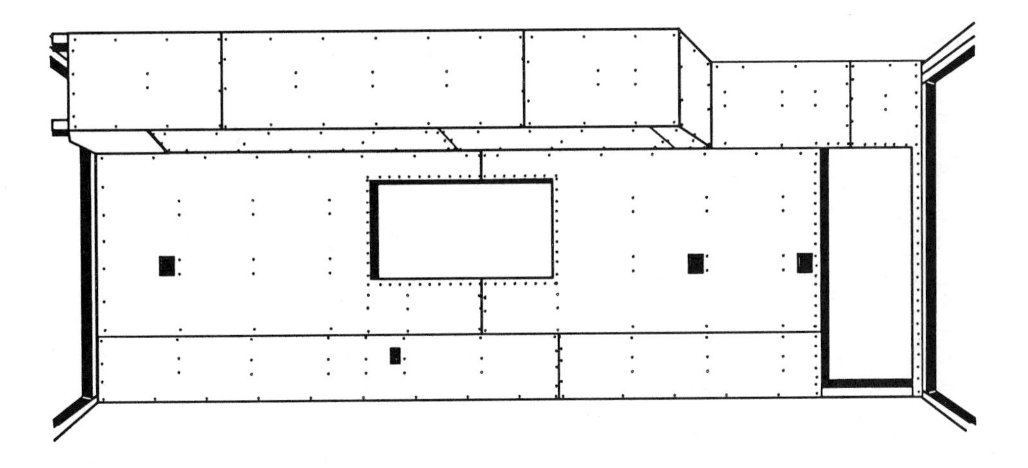

FIGURE 2–24 After nailing off the soffit, go back and check for loose spots, torn paper, and nails that may have missed the studs.

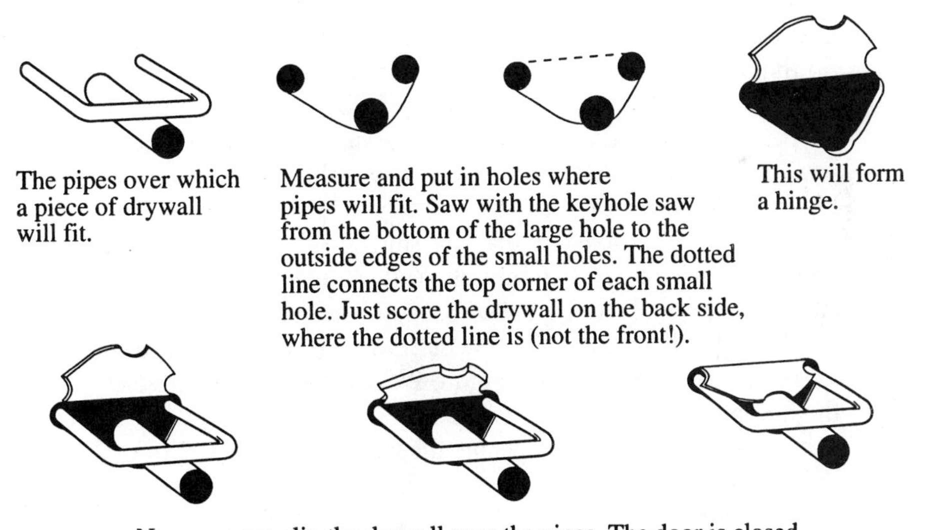

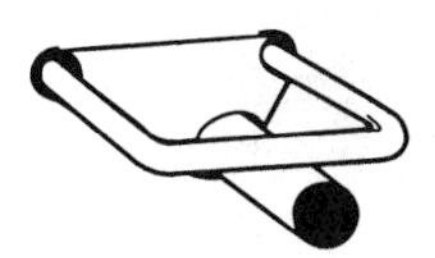

The closed trap door with only three small cuts showing on the front side of the board.

FIGURE 2–25 How to make a trap door

Hanging Stairwells and Cathedral Walls

Two more types of walls require special hanging methods: the stairwell wall and the high wall in a room with a cathedral ceiling.

HANGING A STAIRWELL WALL

Most building codes require up to ¾-inch fire-rated drywall in stairwells and under stairwells. Be sure to check building codes in your area. In addition to this heavier drywall, there are three other problems you will encounter when you hang a stairwell wall.

First, the stairs go down the wall at an angle, so the drywall will have to be cut at an angle. Figure 2–26 shows where the upstairs wall and the downstairs wall join. No matter how good the framer is, these walls almost always sit in or out from each other.

If you hang the wall in the normal way, the second row of the drywall will be right on this joint. This is probably the hardest joint for a finisher to fix, but there is a simple way to alleviate the problem. When you cut the board for the first row, rip the board in half and hang the half-size sheet. If you do this, the second row does not go all the way down to the problem area. The third row of drywall will cover this area, and the edge of the board will be away from the problem area. When you hang the half sheet, remember to put the cut edge up next to the ceiling. Figure 2–26 shows the half sheet and how it is hung.

The second problem is that the studs on the top wall will not usually match up to the studs on the bottom wall. You will have to put a stud in the wall so the end of the drywall can be nailed properly. (See Figures 2–27 and 2–28.)

After you hang the third row of drywall, you will run into the third problem: angle cut. The illustration in Figure 2–29 shows how to use the T-square to find the first point for the angle cut. Hold the T-square against the bottom of the last upper row of hung drywall, keeping the lip tight against it. (Notice that the T-square has a lip on the top piece that keeps it from moving as you cut the board.) Move the T-square over until it stops against the stairs. Measure from the side edge of the hung board to this point. Mark a corresponding point, Point A, on the bottom of the board to be cut. Now measure from the bottom of the upper board to the point at which the stairs begin. Mark a corresponding point, Point B, on the board to be cut. Now measure from the bottom outside edge of the upper board to the floor. Mark a corresponding point, Point C, on the board to be cut. Finally, draw a line connecting the points in order. Follow this line for the cut. (See Figures 2–29 through 2–31.)

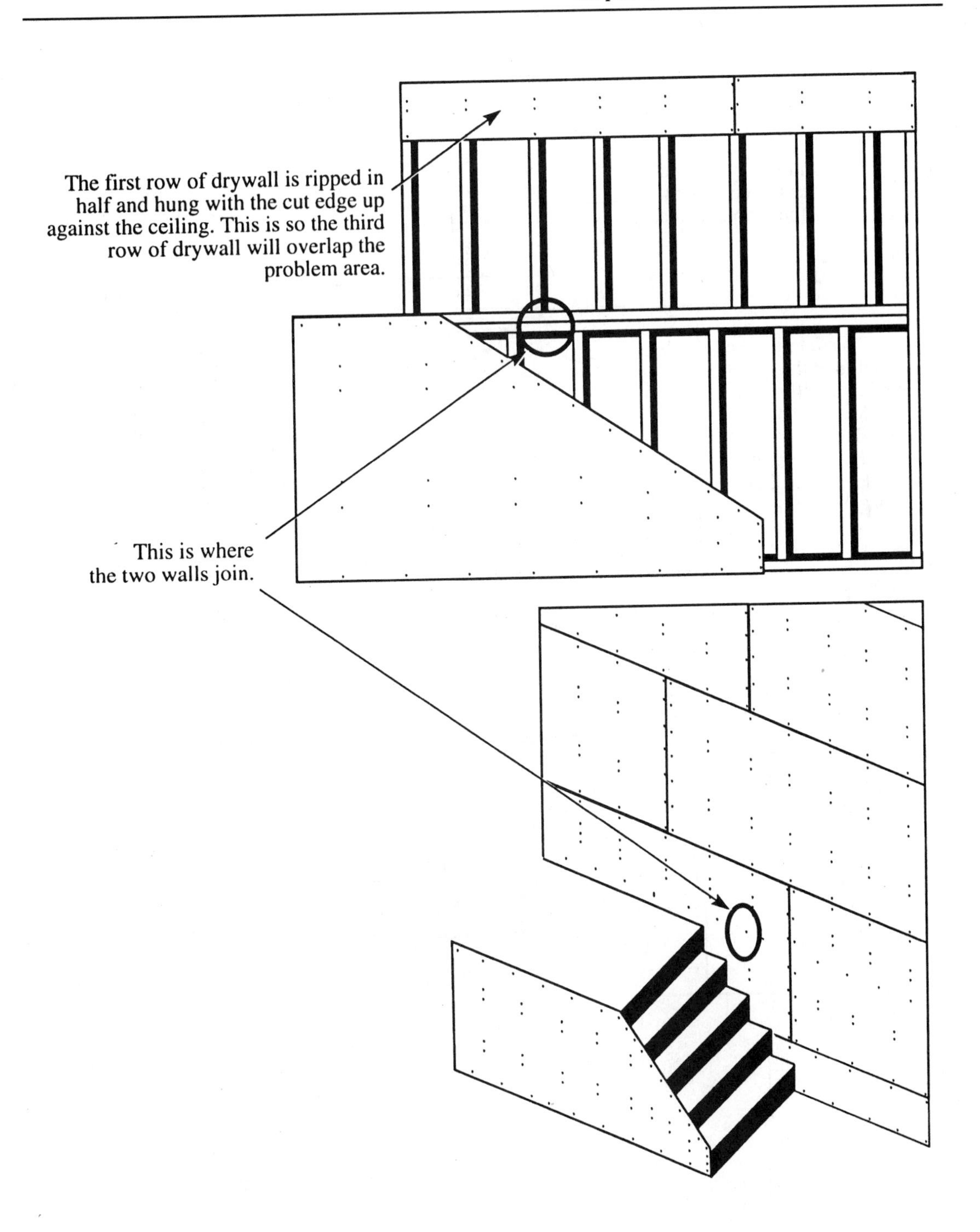
The first row of drywall is ripped in half and hung with the cut edge up against the ceiling. This is so the third row of drywall will overlap the problem area.
This is where the two walls join.

FIGURE 2–26

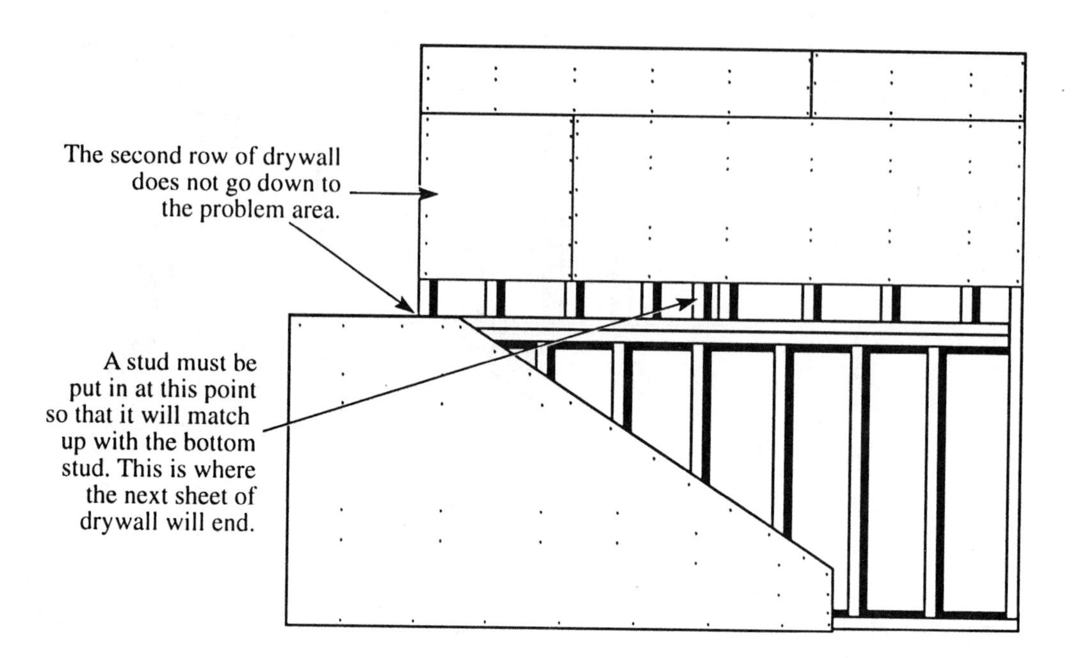

FIGURE 2–27

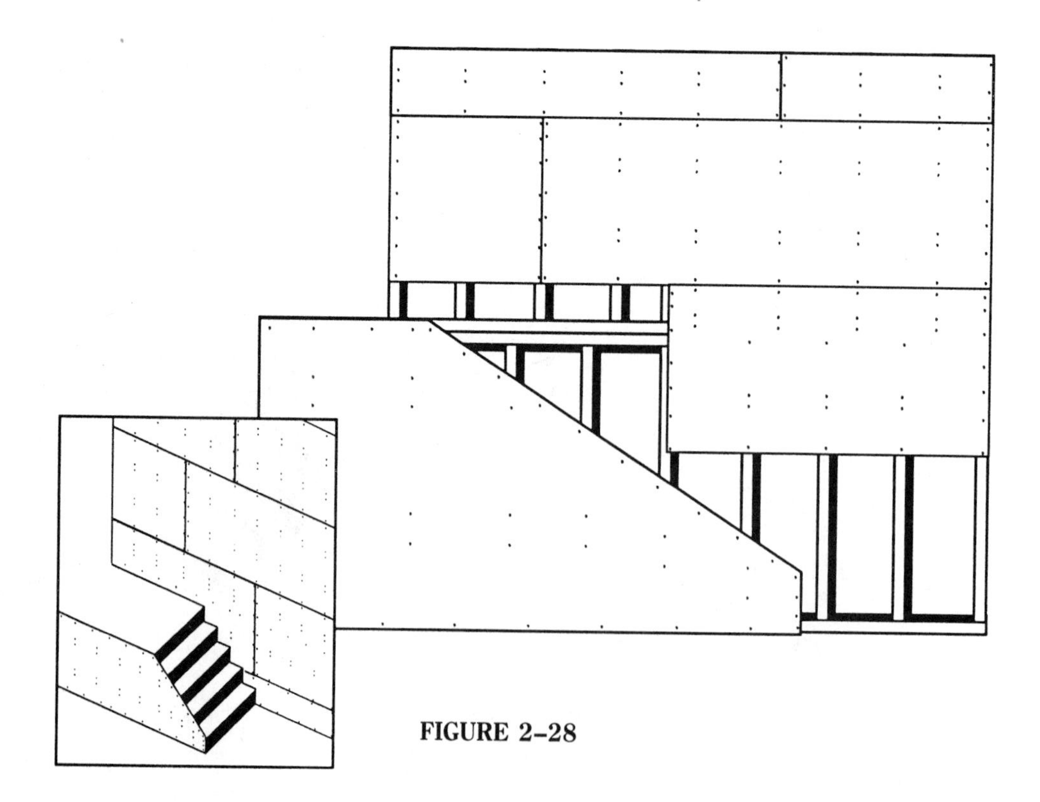

FIGURE 2–28

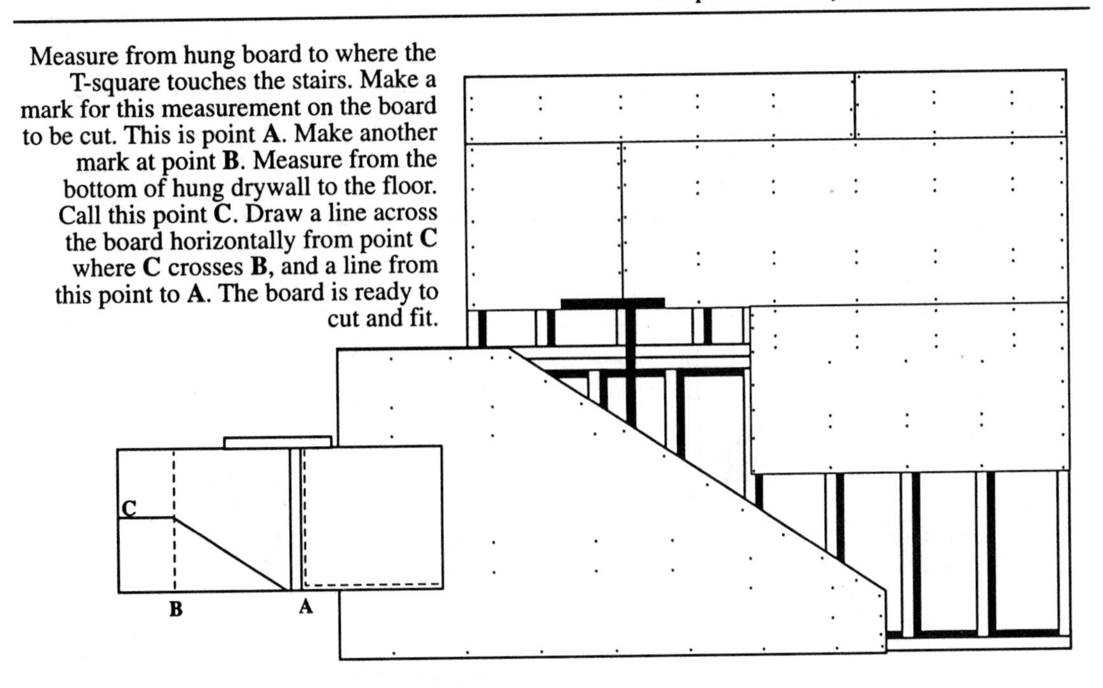

FIGURE 2–29 After marking the board, it is ready for hanging.

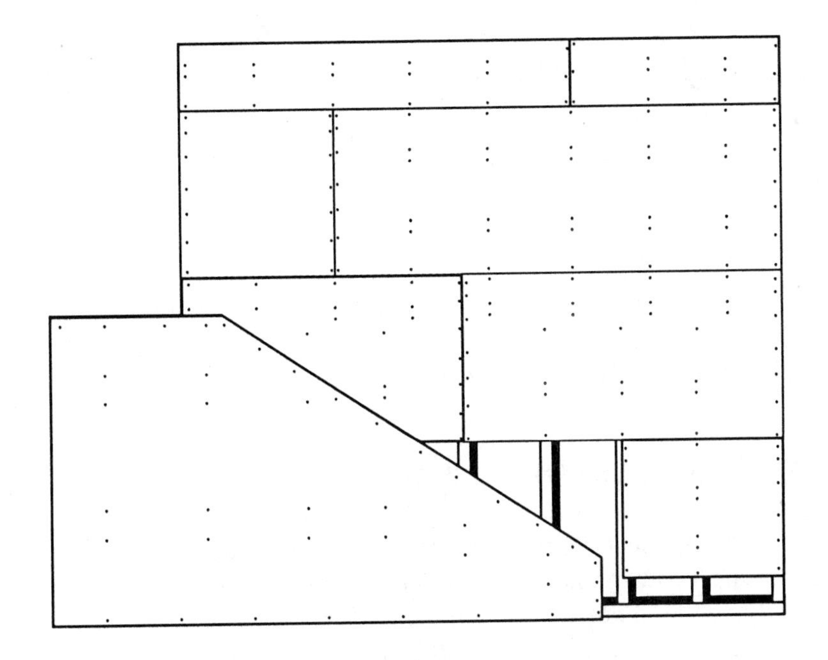

FIGURE 2–30

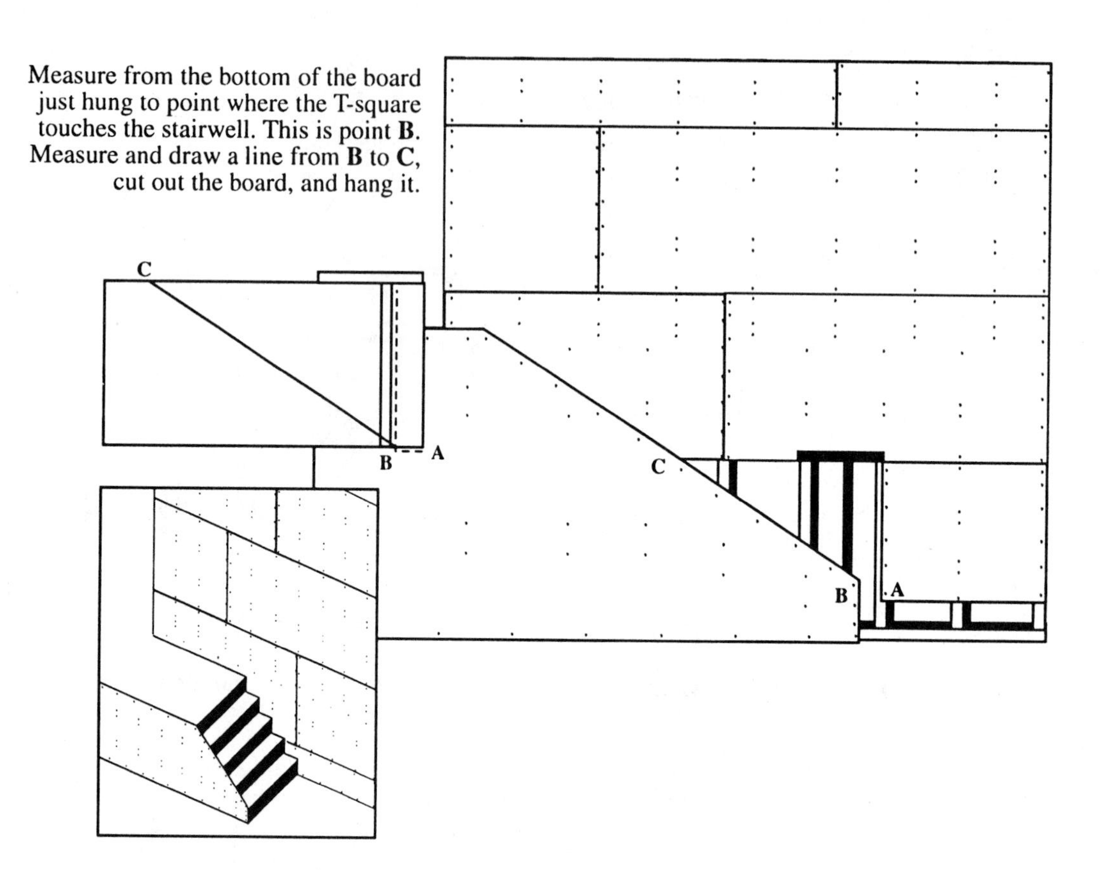

FIGURE 2–31

To cut the board for the stairwell angle, use your utility knife and score along the line connecting B and C. Now you can lift the board up and cut this piece off. The board is now ready to hang.

HANGING CATHEDRAL WALLS

The angle cuts for the cathedral walls will be done with the same method, except that the T-square will be pointing up instead of down. The cathedral wall also will be hung with a board ripped in half, but you will start the board at the bottom of the wall and go up. You also will have to put a stud in this wall to match the end of the board. Figures 2–32 through 2–39 illustrate how to hang cathedral walls.

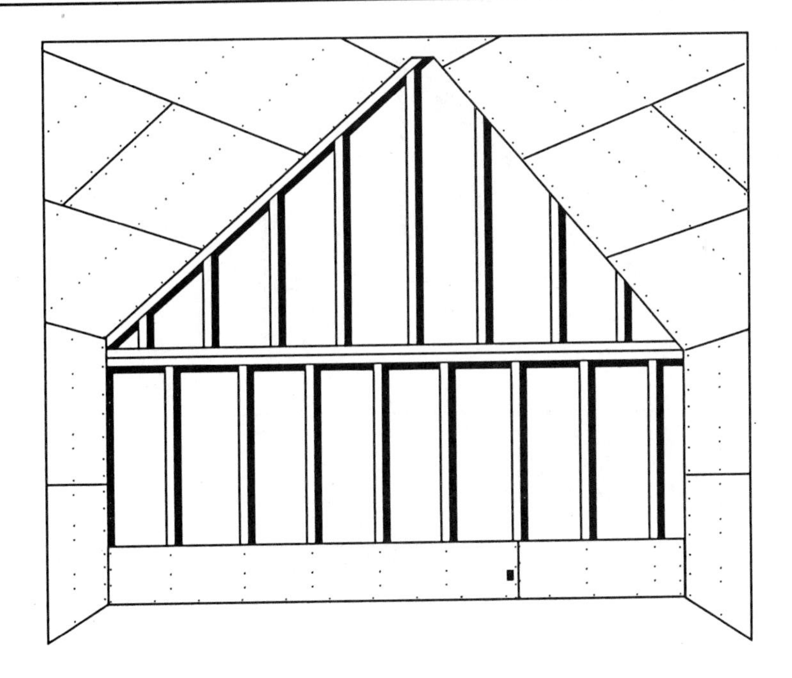

FIGURE 2–32

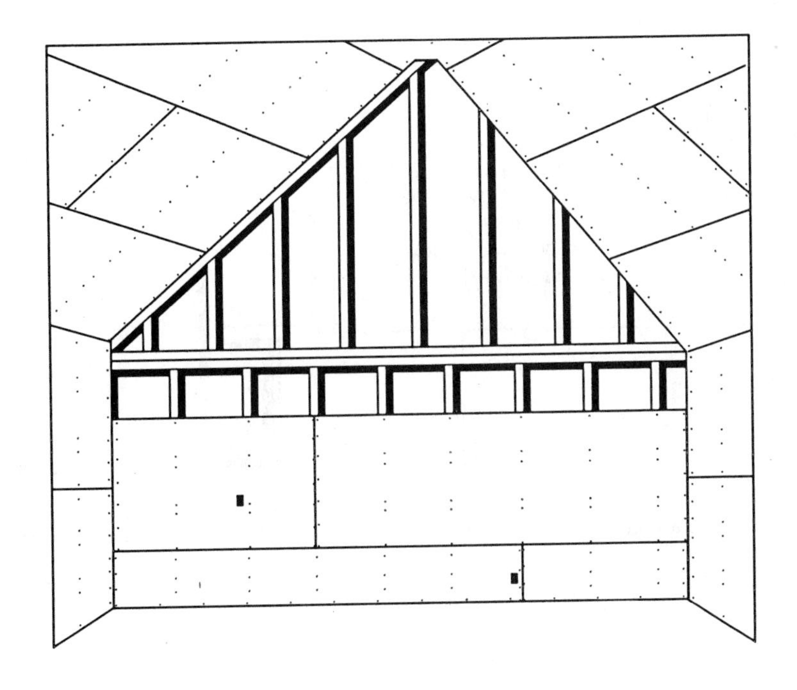

FIGURE 2–33

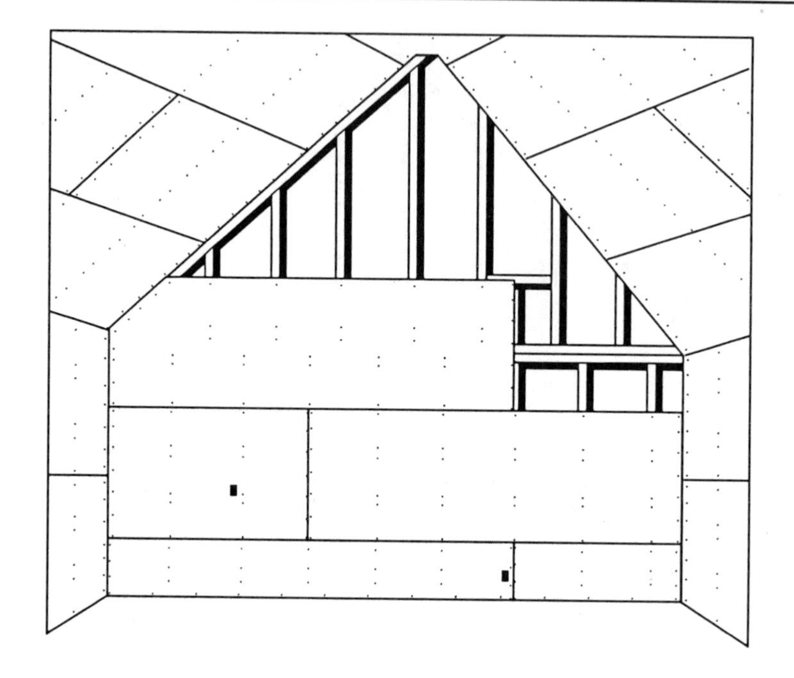

FIGURE 2–34

Put the end of the T-square up against the ceiling and at the top of the drywall board as at *right*. This is point **A**. Now measure from the bottom of the T-square to the wall, then up to **C**. Draw a line from **A** to **C**, and cut the drywall accordingly.

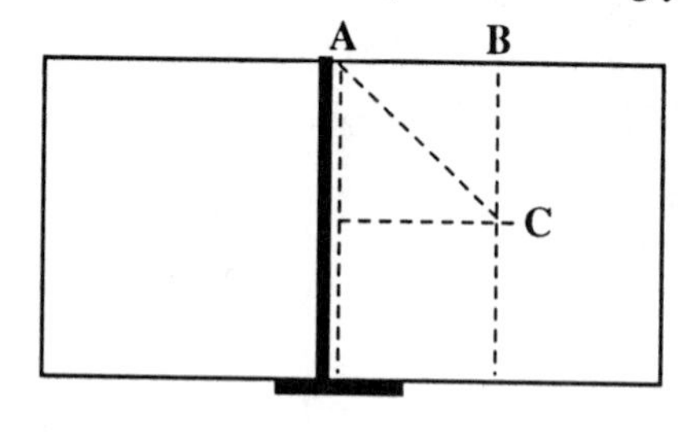

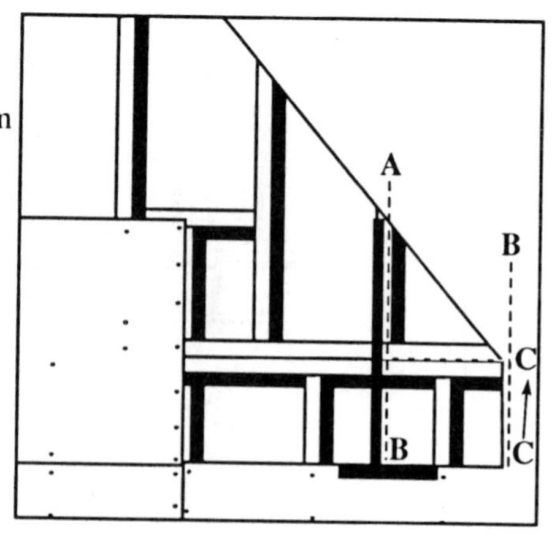

FIGURE 2–35

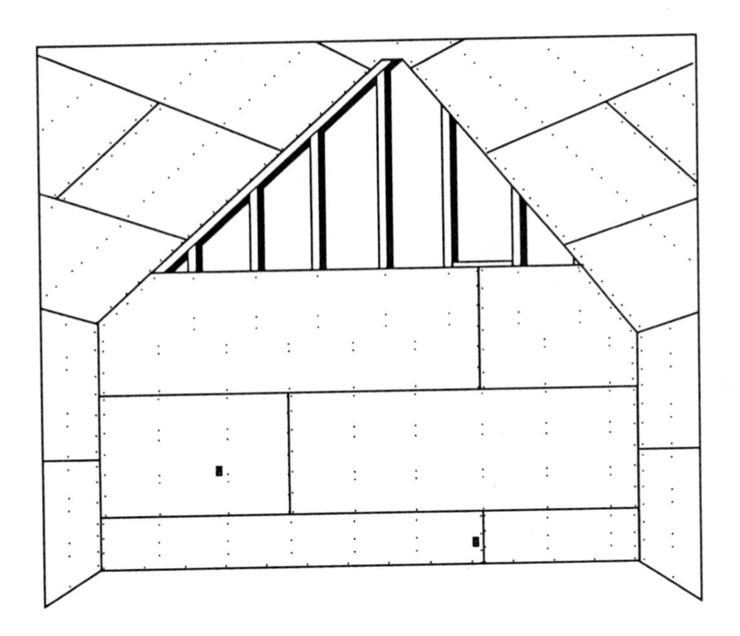

FIGURE 2–36

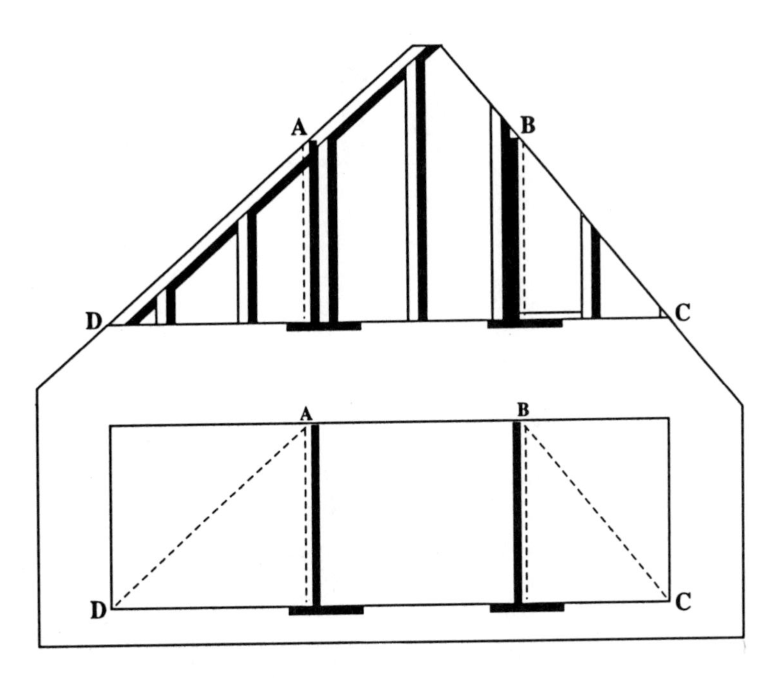

FIGURE 2–37 First measure across the bottom to get the length of the board you will be using. Determine Points A and B by using the T-square. Draw a line from A to D, and B to C. Cut the board accordingly and hang it.

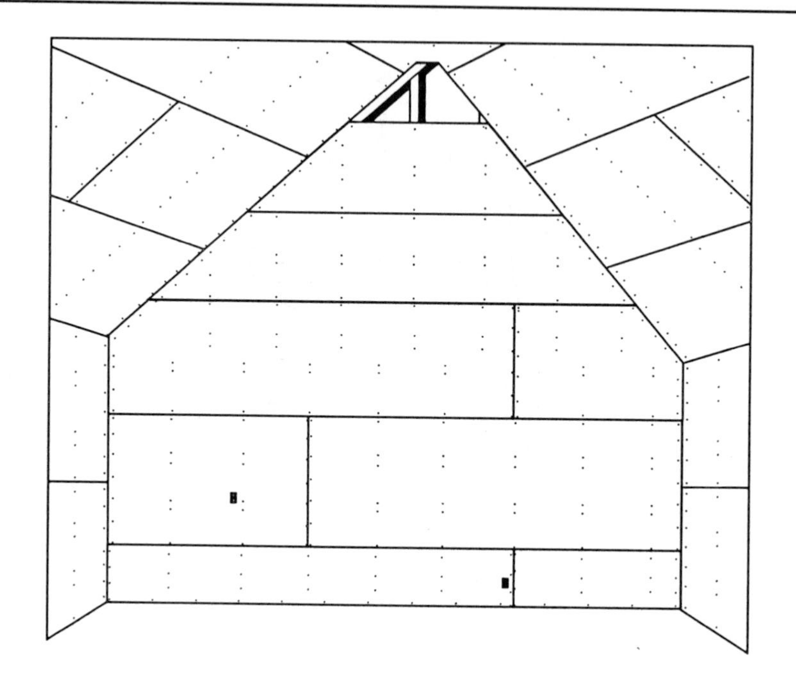

FIGURE 2–38

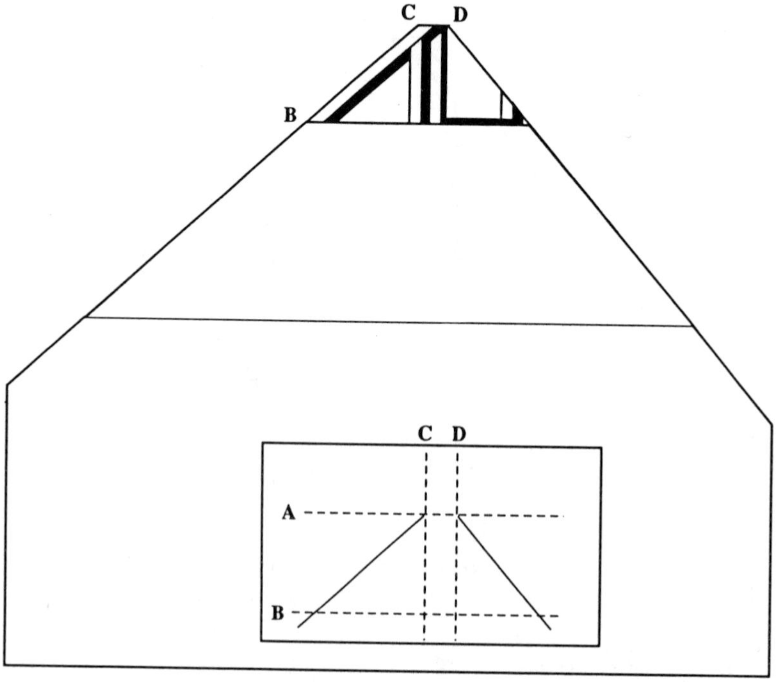

C D

B

C D

A

B

FIGURE 2–39

Hanging Round Walls

On the following page you will see an illustration of a typical round wall. Drywall that is ½ inch thick would not bend around such a wall without breaking. To hang a round wall, use two layers of drywall ¼ inch thick. This thinner board will bend a little, but if it doesn't bend enough, use one of the following methods to bend it more.

When a scrap piece of drywall is left leaning against a wall overnight, the piece will be bowed by the next morning. This is because of the moisture in the air. To bend the drywall, therefore, lay it across two sawhorses in the evening, and place a weight in the middle. By morning, the drywall will be bowed enough for you to hang it on the wall without breaking it (Figure 2–40).

A quicker but somewhat tricky method is to wet the board down. A problem that sometimes occurs with this method is that the paper is loosened from the inner plaster, causing blisters in the board.

A round wall is hung the same as any other wall, so there should not be any problems. When you hang the wall, make sure that the butt joints are away from the curvature of the wall for a better fit. When a round wall is hung, the butt joints

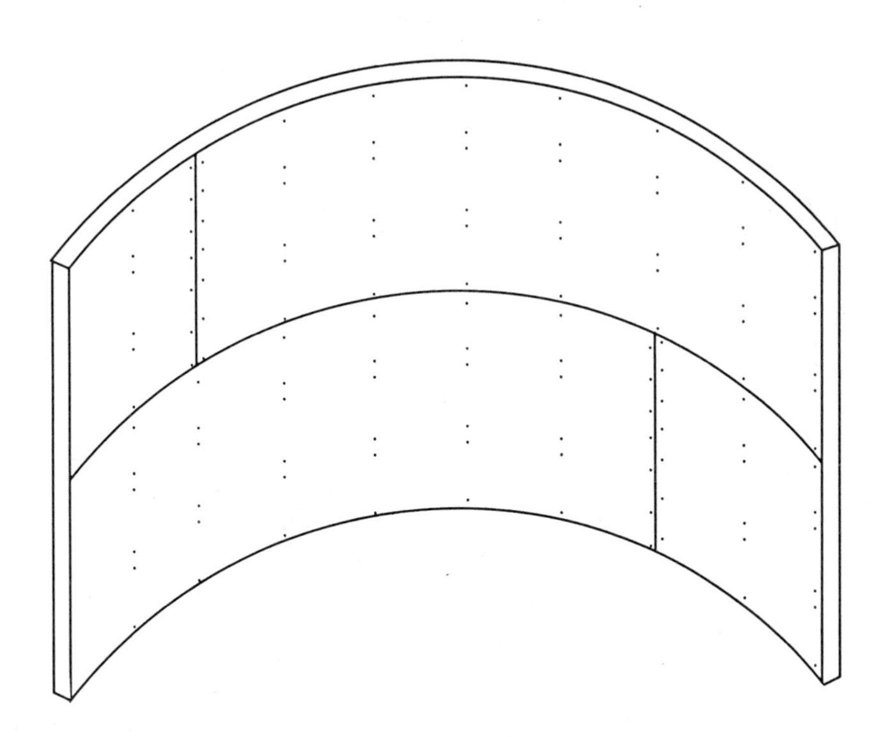

FIGURE 2–40

of the first layer of drywall should not be on the same stud as the first. You will be able to nail the stud only on its edge, as it will stand at an angle to the board (Figure 2–41).

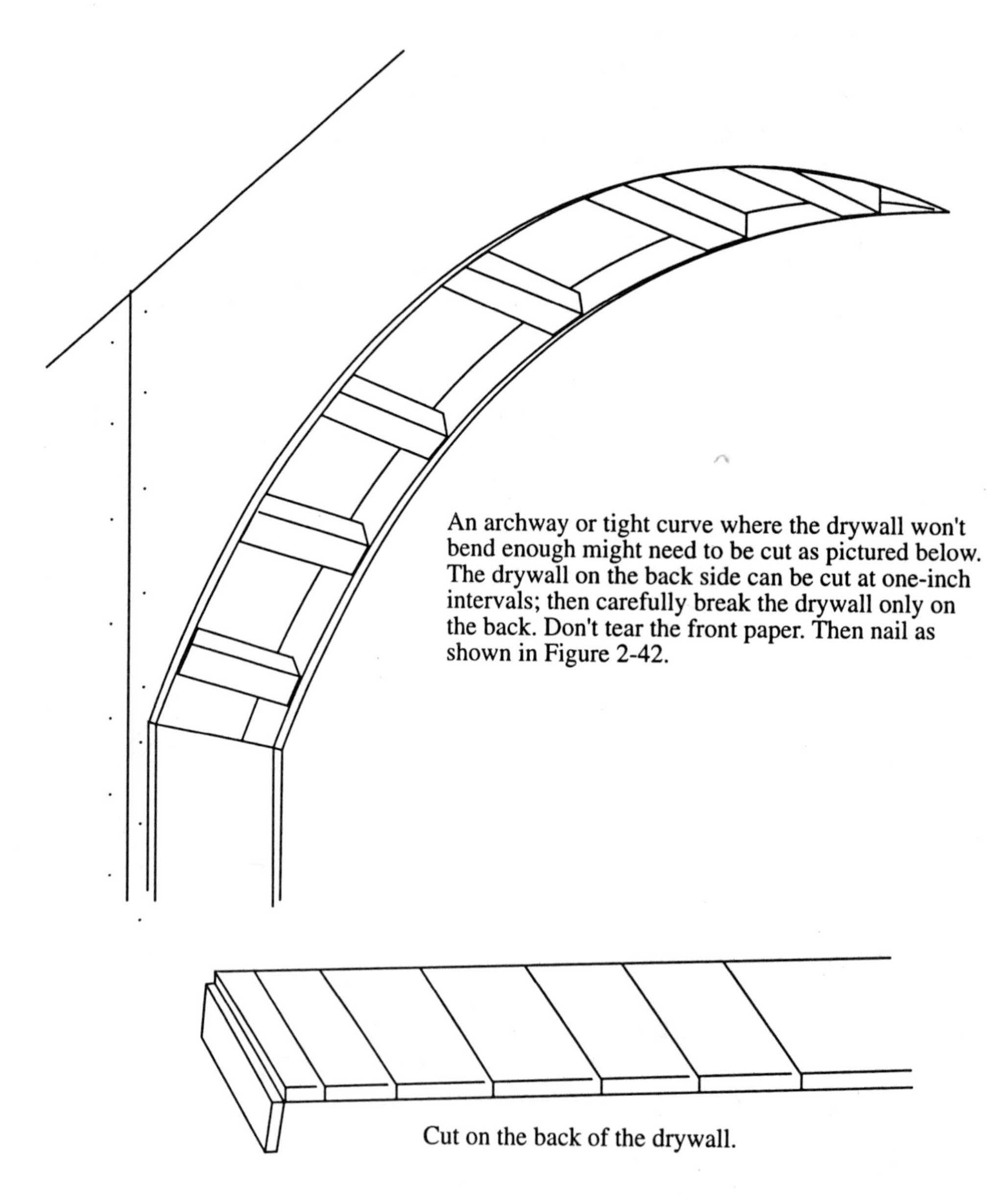

FIGURE 2–41 Do not align the butt joints of the first and second layers, and never put a butt joint on the curve. Place it as much to the side as possible.

An archway or a tighter curve may need to be cut on the back at one-inch intervals as shown in Figures 2–42 through 2–44. Any metal corner bead needed for such a tight curve also can be cut at one-inch intervals on one side only, as shown in Figure 2–44.

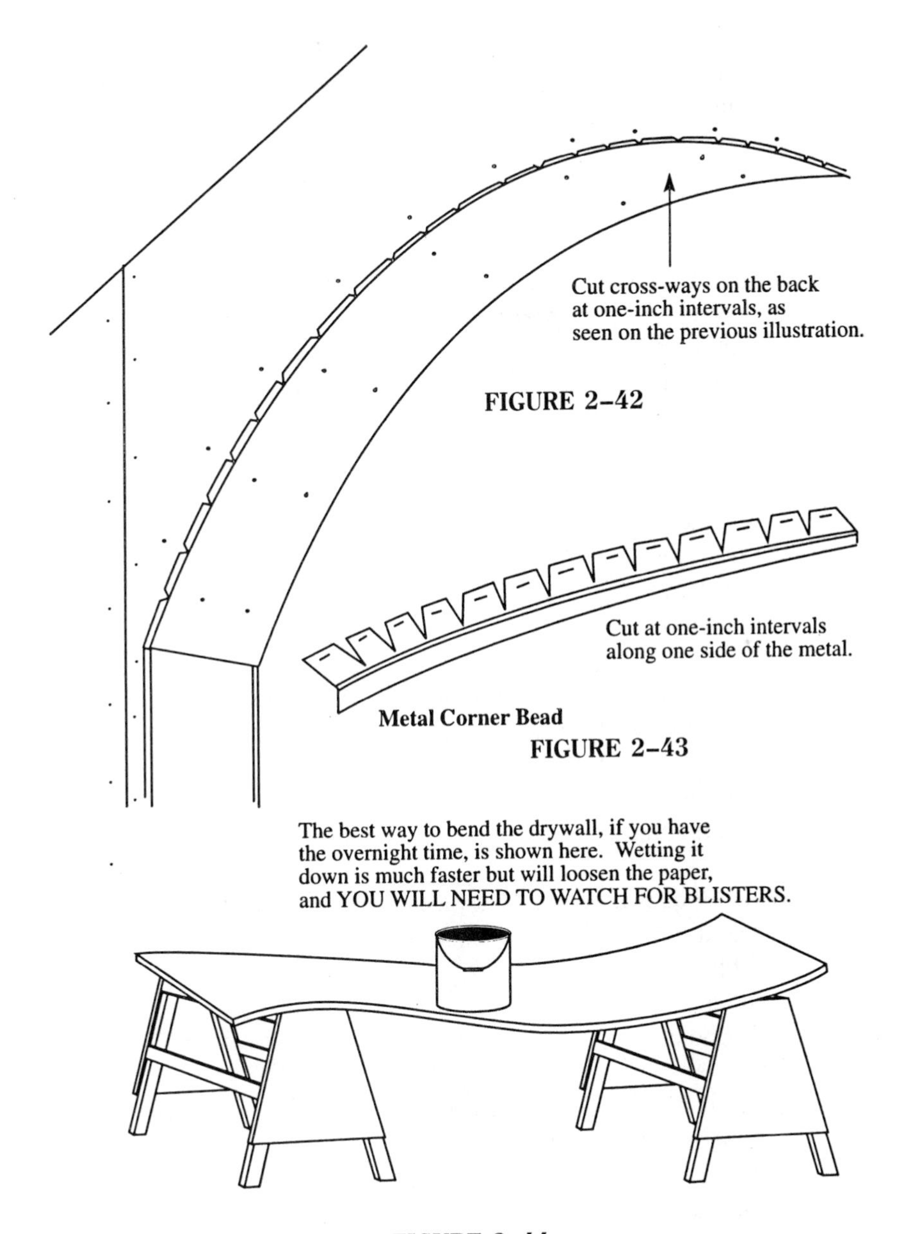

FIGURE 2–42

FIGURE 2–43

FIGURE 2–44

Questions

HANGING CEILINGS

1. What is the first thing to do when you are going to hang a ceiling?
a. Measure from the side to the last joist within the span of drywall.
b. Check the house for square corners.
c. Mark the ceiling joists.
d. Place the benches where you will be using them.

2. In which part of the house should you start hanging drywall? Why?
a. The back of the house, in order to get in practice for the living room.
b. The closets, in order to get the hard part over with first.
c. The back of the house, so by the time you get to the living room you will have used the excess drywall and you can hang the entire room easily.
d. Hang all the big sheets throughout the house and then hang the little pieces.

3. What should be hung first?
a. All the big sheets
b. All the walls
c. The ceiling
d. All the bottom sheets

4. In which direction should drywall be hung on the ceiling?
a. Opposite to the joists
b. Parallel with the joists
c. Either way
d. Alternating directions

5. Which tool is used to cut a piece of drywall in half?
a. Handsaw
b. Utility knife
c. Jigsaw
d. Keyhole saw

6. When hanging the ceiling, what is the best procedure to follow?
a. Line up butt joints in a straight line.
b. Hang butt joints perpendicular to joist.
c. Stagger butt joints.
d. Hang factory edges parallel to joist.

7. When hanging a closet, what is the best procedure to follow?
a. Hang the closets last, using any small pieces that are left.
b. Cut new boards to avoid unsightly appearance.
c. Use scrap pieces but not little pieces.
d. Don't worry about closets because nobody sees them.

8. After hanging a board, what should you do?
a. Sweep the floor.
b. Tape it so it will look neat.
c. Check nails or screws, and pull out any that missed the stud.
d. Admire a job well done.

9. If a screw didn't go in far enough and is sticking out above the drywall surface, what should you do?
a. Hammer it in.
b. Use the hand screwdriver to screw it in deeper.
c. Use some pliers to pull it out.
d. Use the hammer to pull it out.

10. After pulling out a nail or screw, what should you do?
a. Put in three more to take its place.
b. Tap in any paper that might have been pulled out.
c. Caulk it immediately so it will be airtight.
d. Coat it with joint compound so nobody will know.

11. When hanging the first board on the ceiling, and when the walls are not square, what should you do?
a. Place the drywall tight to the outside wall.
b. Place the drywall so it is out of line a little to each wall.
c. Hang the drywall square with the joist. The side walls will not be square.
d. Either way, it doesn't matter.

12. When cutting a piece of drywall and the measurement is 63 inches, the drywall should be cut at
a. 62¾ inches
b. 62½ inches
c. 63 inches
d. 63¼ inches

13. How many nails should be used to hang ceilings?
  a. Two sets of two per joist in the field
  b. Three sets of two per joist in the field
  c. One every twelve inches per joist in the field
  d. One in the middle of the field

14. When hanging ½ inch drywall on the ceiling, the ends usually are nailed
  a. every eight inches
  b. every sixteen inches
  c. every seven inches
  d. every twelve inches

HANGING WALLS

15. When hanging the walls, what is the best procedure to follow?
  a. Hang the bottom boards first.
  b. Hang the top boards first.
  c. Hang the one closest to the window.
  d. Hang the one closest to the door.

16. The nail or screw should be
  a. dimpled slightly under the drywall surface.
  b. even with the surface.
  c. sunken at least ¼ inch.
  d. on top of the drywall surface.

17. Before putting the top board in place, you should
  a. take a break.
  b. mark where the studs are.
  c. move the toe jack in place.
  d. start a row of nails along the top of the board.

18. When cutting a thin strip of drywall to fill a crack, what is the best procedure to follow?
  a. Use a small hammer to nail it.
  b. Cut the board from a piece that has the factory edge because it's stronger.
  c. Use a saw to cut a strip.
  d. Use screws to install it.

19. When hanging walls, the ends of drywall should be nailed
a. twelve inches on center.
b. seven inches on center.
c. eight inches on center.
d. sixteen inches on center.

20. When hanging walls, you should nail
a. three sets of two nails twelve inches on center.
b. one set of two nails in the center of field.
c. one nail in the center of field.
d. two sets of two nails sixteen inches on center.

21. When hanging the bottom wallboard, you should use the ________ to hold the board off the floor and up to the top piece of drywall.
a. clincher
b. toe jack
c. hammer
d. T-square

22. What is the best way to measure for a receptacle box on the bottom piece of drywall?
a. From the bottom of the top board to the top and bottom of the receptacle box
b. From the top and bottom of the receptacle box to the bottom of the drywall board above
c. To the right and left sides of the box from the wall
d. To the top of the box from the bottom of the top piece of drywall, and to the bottom of the box from the floor

Questions

HANGING WALLS WITH OPENINGS

1. What is the picture framing method?
a. A method of hanging drywall up to a window and then cutting a piece around it.
b. A method of hanging drywall across windows and doors and then cutting out the openings.
c. A method of cutting pieces of drywall 18 inches by 22 inches.
d. A method of cutting drywall six to eight inches past the side of the window.

2. When using the header method, the hanger should
   a. hang all ceiling pieces first.
   b. hang up to the window and cut a header piece on the top.
   c. hang drywall past the side of the window or door at least six to eight inches.
   d. hang all bottom pieces on the walls first.

3. When using the picture framing method, the hanger should
   a. measure from the ceiling to the floor for first measurement.
   b. nail all around the window before sawing it out.
   c. use the clincher along the baseboard.
   d. tap the drywall over the top of the doorway so the excess drywall will fall off.

4. An electric tool used for cutting drywall around windows and doors is the
   a. drywall jack.
   b. clincher.
   c. router.
   d. rocker.

5. If the windows are going to have metal corner bead on them, the drywall edges need to be
   a. nailed with two rows of nails.
   b. rasped to take off uneven edges.
   c. beveled to a smooth edge.
   d. painted with a sticky substance that will hold the corner bead.

HANGING KITCHEN WALLS

6. What is a trap door?
   a. A small peephole so you can see into another room.
   b. A hiding area under the stairwell.
   c. A cutting method the hanger uses to do away with big holes between pipes.
   d. A doorway that can be filled in with drywall and needs very little tape.

7. The most important hanger rule is:
   a. Hang the soffit last.
   b. Don't forget your measurements.
   c. Butt joint to butt joint, factory edge to factory edge.
   d. Drive your nails in two at the same time.

8. When hanging the soffit,
  a. cut according to length. Width doesn't need to be measured, as the excess will be cut off even with the edge.
  b. measure each piece precisely.
  c. use no more than five pieces to a soffit.
  d. use twice as many nails to be sure that the drywall stays in place.

HANGING STAIRWELLS AND CATHEDRAL WALLS

9. The first piece of drywall hung on a stairwell wall should be
  a. the first sheet at the top of the wall.
  b. a two-foot rip at the top of the wall with factory edge on the down side.
  c. a two-foot rip at the top of the wall with the cut edge on the down side.
  d. a two-foot rip at the bottom of the wall.

10. The first piece of drywall hung on a cathedral wall should be
  a. a two-foot rip on the top of the wall with the cut edge up.
  b. a two-foot rip on the top of the wall with the factory edge up.
  c. a two-foot rip on the bottom of the wall with the factory edge up.
  d. a two-foot rip on the bottom of the wall with the cut edge up.

11. The problem area on the stairwell wall is the point at which
  a. the top step comes into the floor.
  b. the ceiling joins the wall.
  c. the bottom step comes into the floor.
  d. the two floors' framing comes together.

12. Which tool is most often used for an angle cut piece of drywall filling in the stairwell or cathedral wall?
  a. Clincher
  b. Drywall jack
  c. T-square
  d. Toe jack

13. For stairwells, what kind of drywall is required by most building codes?
  a. Water-resistant drywall
  b. ½-inch drywall
  c. ⅝ or ¾ inch fire rated drywall
  d. One-inch plasterboard

HANGING ROUND WALLS

14. Generally, what kind of drywall is used for round walls if ½-inch drywall is code?
  a. ½-inch drywall
  b. Two layers of ¼-inch drywall
  c. One layer of ¼-inch drywall
  d. Two layers of ½-inch drywall

15. What is the best method of bending drywall to fit a tight curve in a wall?
  a. Use an iron to heat it up.
  b. Cut little strips.
  c. Water it down.
  d. Lay it across two sawhorses all night.

16. What is the best way to treat drywall for an archway or a tight curve?
  a. Heat it up with a hair dryer.
  b. Cut it at one-inch intervals on the surface.
  c. Cut it at one-inch intervals on the back side.
  d. Use a vise to bend it.

Chapter 3
Metal Trim and Corner Bead

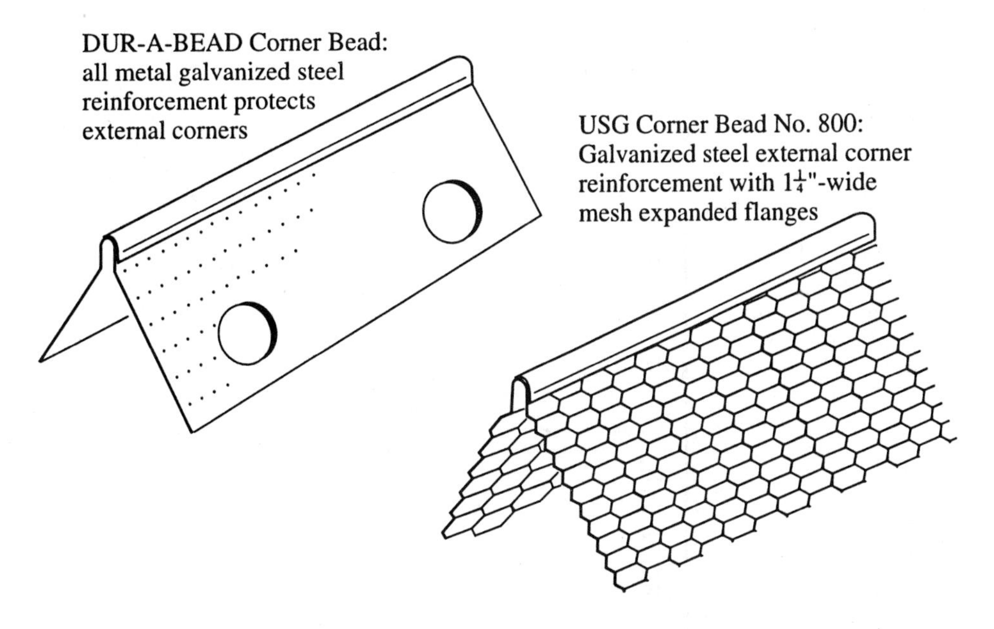

FIGURE 3–1 Two types of corner bead ***(Courtesy of U.S. Gypsum Co.)***

Corner bead is a strip of metal that has a 90° bend in it. The strip is usually eight to ten feet long. It's made in different widths. The most commonly used is 1¼ inch. (See Figure 3–1.)

The edge of the corner bead sticks out enough so that when the bead is nailed to the wall and then covered (floated) with joint compound, the metal will be covered. This is done so the corner will have a hard edge, but it will not show when the wall is painted.

Corner bead is used not only for wall corners but also for window and door frames in place of wood. Figure 3–2 shows how to apply the bead to regular corners, and Figure 3–3 shows how to apply the bead to window and door openings.

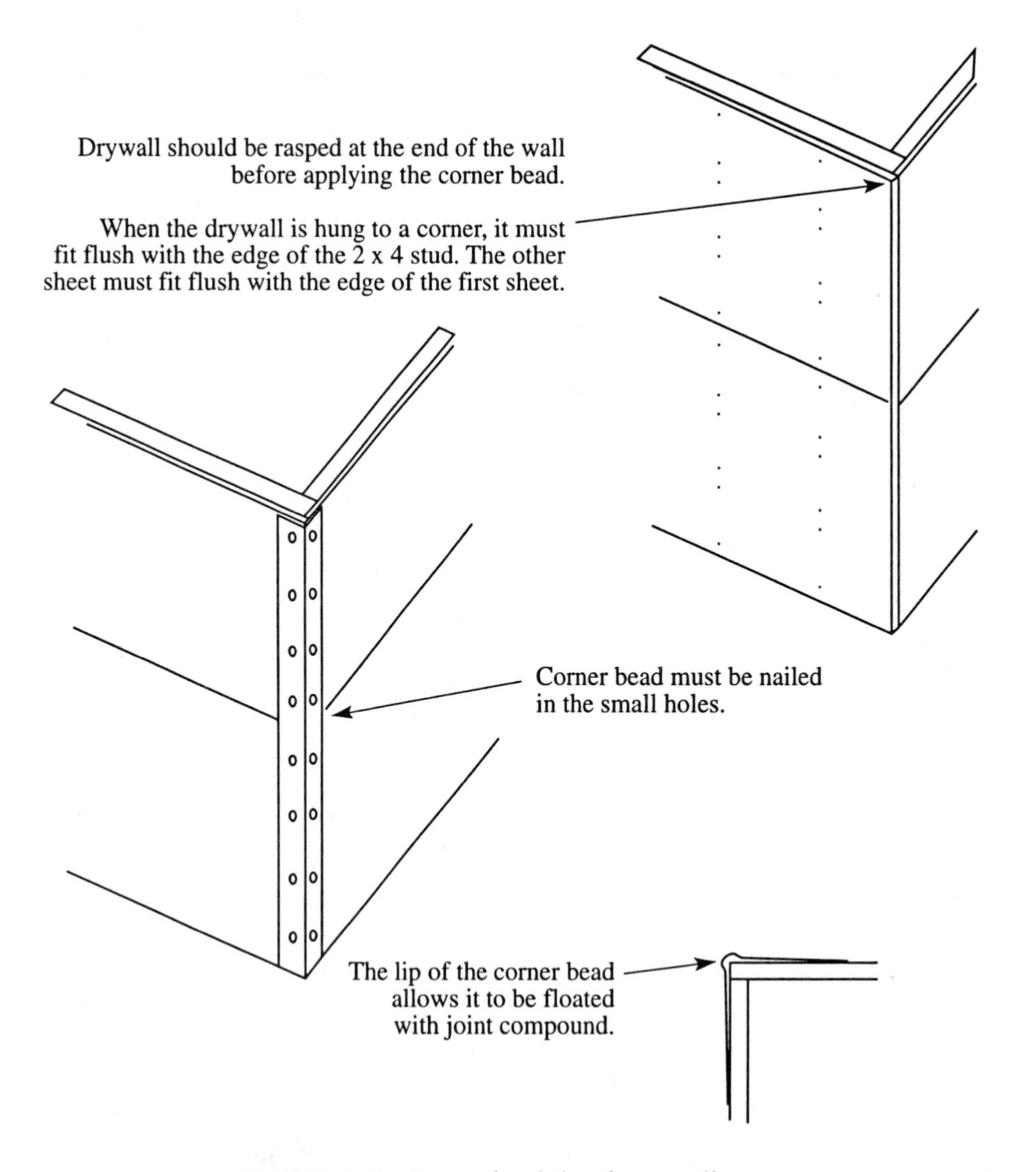

FIGURE 3–2 Corner bead details on wall corners

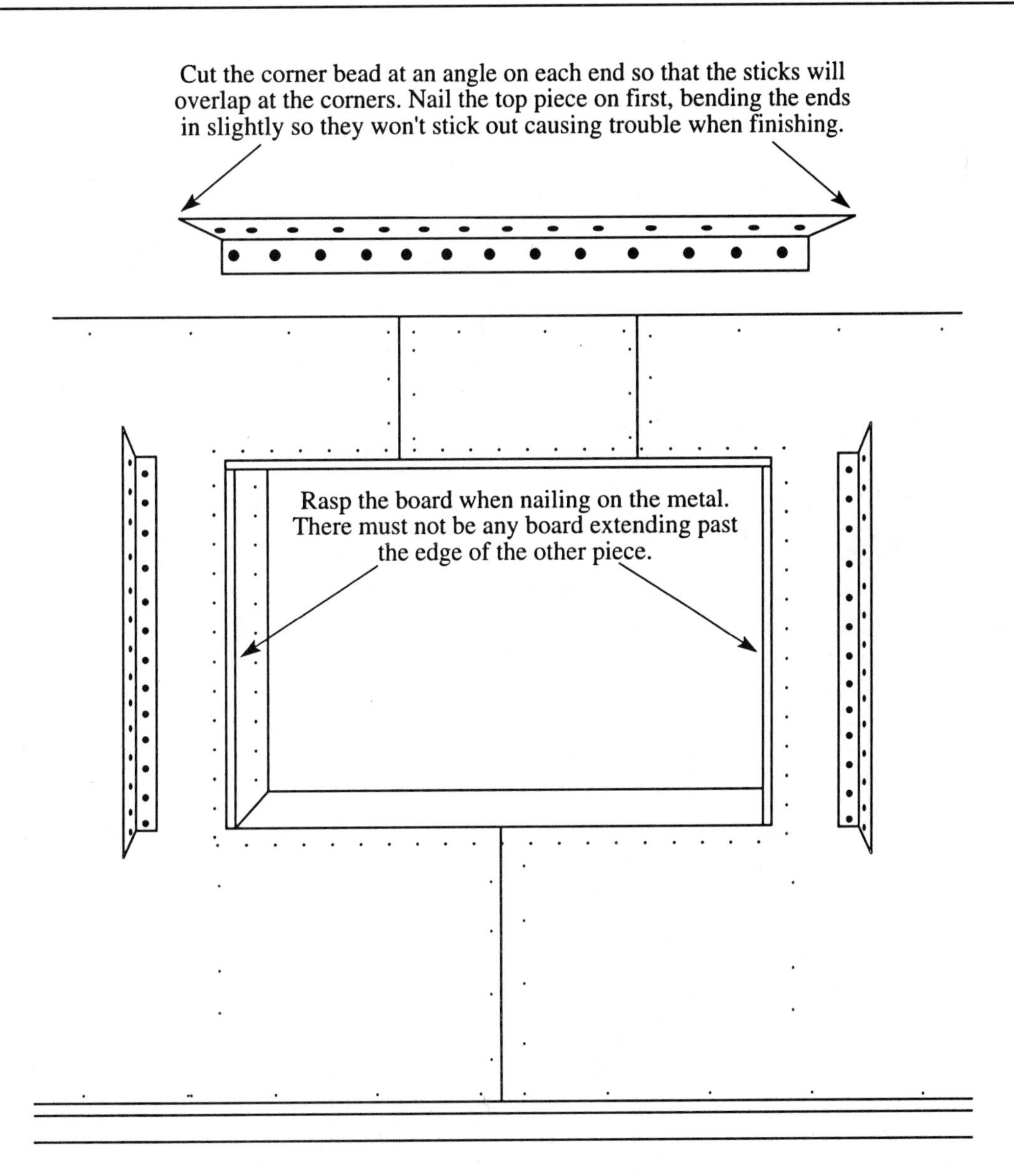

FIGURE 3–3 Corner bead details on windows

APPLYING THE CORNER BEAD

Before hanging drywall on the inside of a window, you must rasp the drywall around the edge of the window. If the drywall goes past the window edge, it will pull the corner bead out of line, and the corner will not be square. It's important before you apply the corner bead that you check all the corners. Make sure that one drywall edge is not sticking out past the edge of another. Unless the corner joint is smooth and square, the corner bead will go on crooked.

Corner bead is difficult to apply correctly and requires care. If it's done incorrectly, the bead won't get covered when joint compound is floated over it. When applying the bead to a corner, put pressure against the bead as you nail it. Start nailing in the center of the bead and nail all the way to one end. Then nail the other end. Each nail in a pair should be directly opposite the other, and the bead should be nailed about every twelve inches. Any loose part of the bead must be nailed down.

When using the clincher or screw attachment, follow the same procedure.

The corner bead on a soffit is nailed the same way as the other corners, but there is usually a corner of the soffit that uses three pieces of bead joining together from three different directions. These corner pieces are cut as shown in Figure 3–4.

Sometimes a builder will use plywood to cover the soffit. Most hangers will nail just anywhere, believing that it is acceptable to nail into the plywood. It is not. The plywood bounces when you drive a nail into it. This keeps the nail from holding tight. Even if the soffit is covered with plywood, you must place the nails in the stud. You will be able to tell where the studs are because the plywood will be nailed there.

Some corners are less or greater than 90°, so regular corner bead will not work on them. The finisher will have to use what is called flex bead. Such corners are called bastard angles. (See Figure 3–5.)

If you come upon a circular opening or archway that requires corner bead, cut the bead at one-inch intervals along one side of the angle so it can be bent around the opening. Refer to Figures 2–42 through 2–44.

A plastic corner bead is available now for corners that are not square. If you cannot find it, the angle of a piece of metal bead can be made wider by fitting a one-inch piece of pipe inside the metal corner bead. Tap it with a hammer until the angle is the desired size.

Another convenient new product is the bullnose corner bead. This gives a rounded-off look. This metal is put on in almost the same way as regular corner bead except, of course, the angle cuts are much harder to make. Flannery, Inc., also sells two metal pieces that help match the corners so they can be finished properly. See Figures 3–6 and 3–7.

Other Metals You Should Know About

Expansion Joints or Control Joints

Usually, twenty feet or more of wall space requires expansion joints. These joints are designed to relieve stress in much the same way as expansion joints in cement do so.

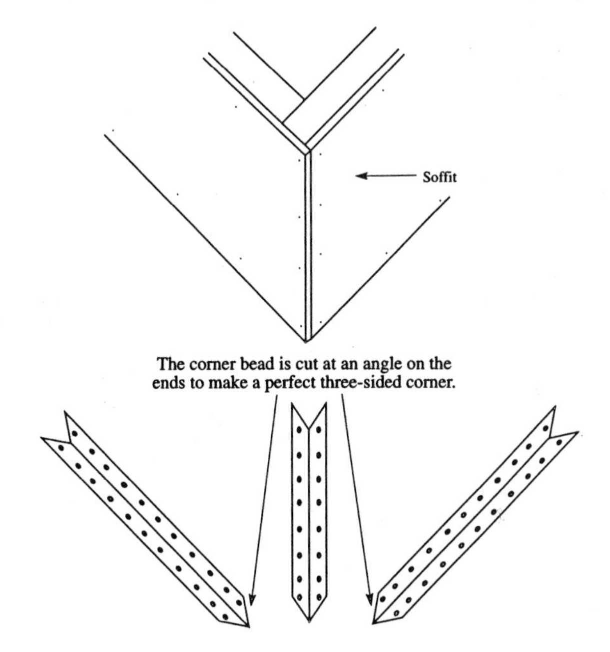

FIGURE 3–4 Corner bead details on 3-way corner

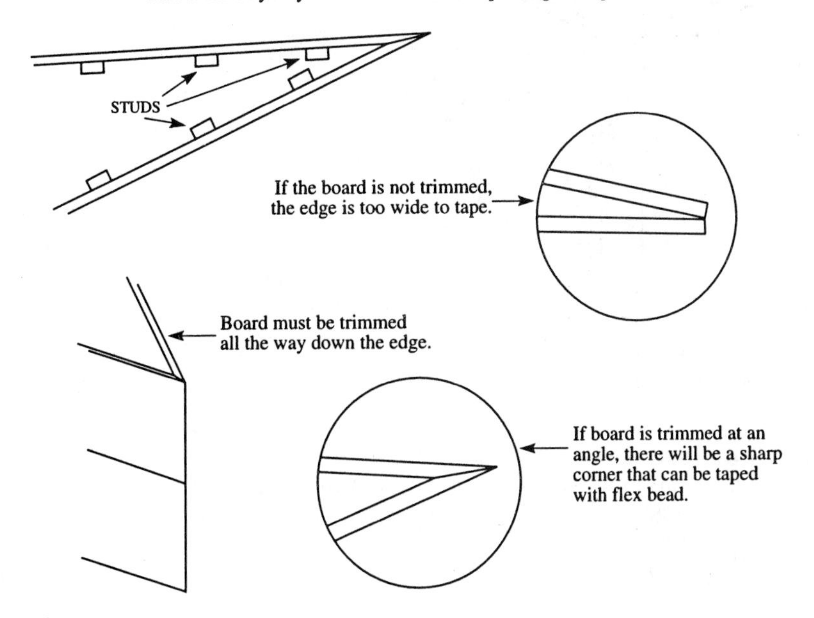

FIGURE 3–5 Preparing bastard angles for flex bead

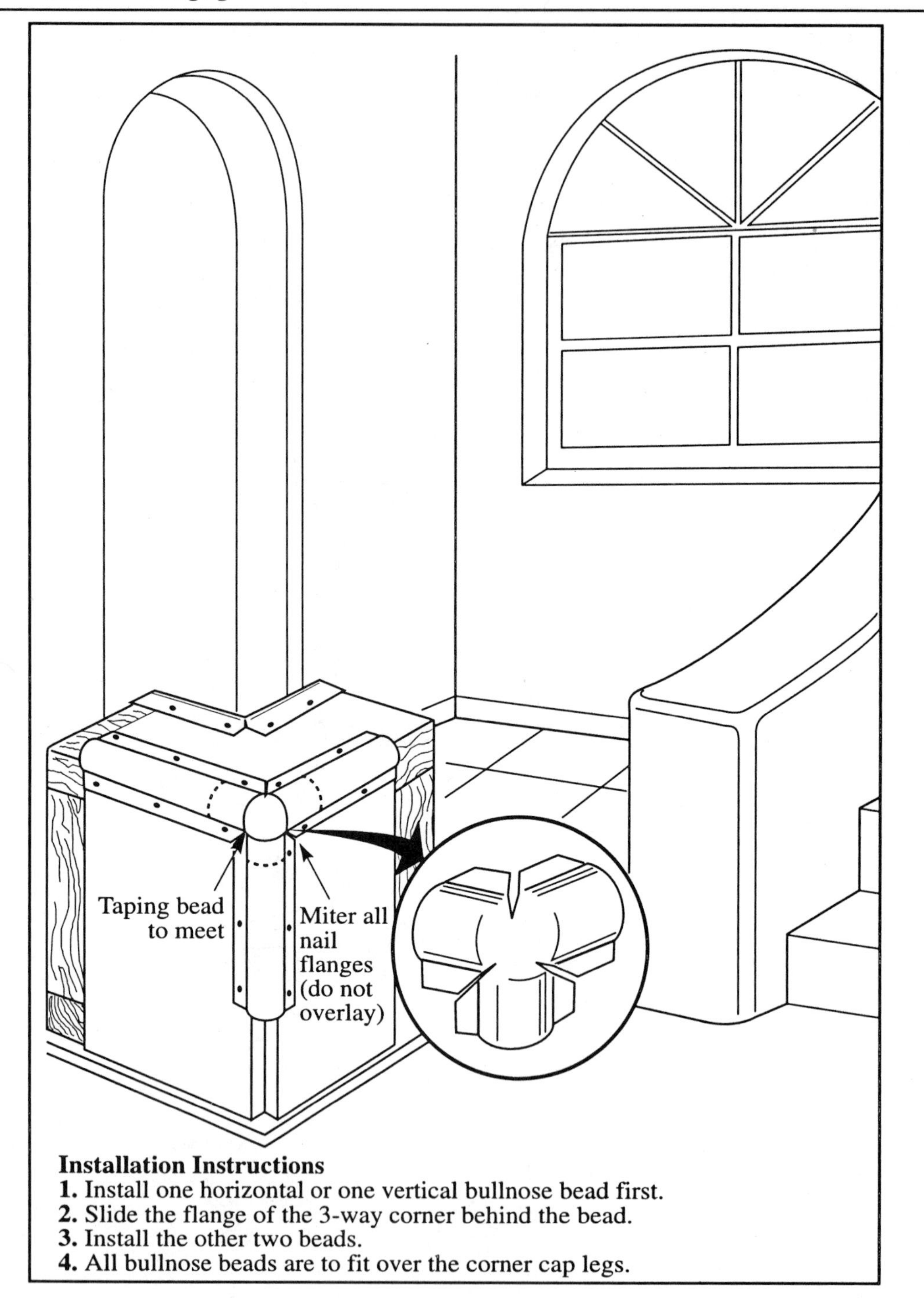

FIGURE 3–6 Bullnose corner bead, the new look (*Courtesy Flannery, Inc., Pacoima, CA*)

CUTTING THE MITER

1. For cutting miters in an archway, install the header bead first. The bead should extend from the framing on one side to the framing on the other side with a simple straight cut.
2. Cut a small piece of bead approximately 6" long to be used for a guide. With a pair of snips cut a half moon section out of each end as shown in the illustration, and trim to fit the header bead. When you have accomplished this, simply cut the two vertical beads to length and with the small guide, place it over the bead, and scribe the half moon shape. Cut on the line and nail the beads in place.

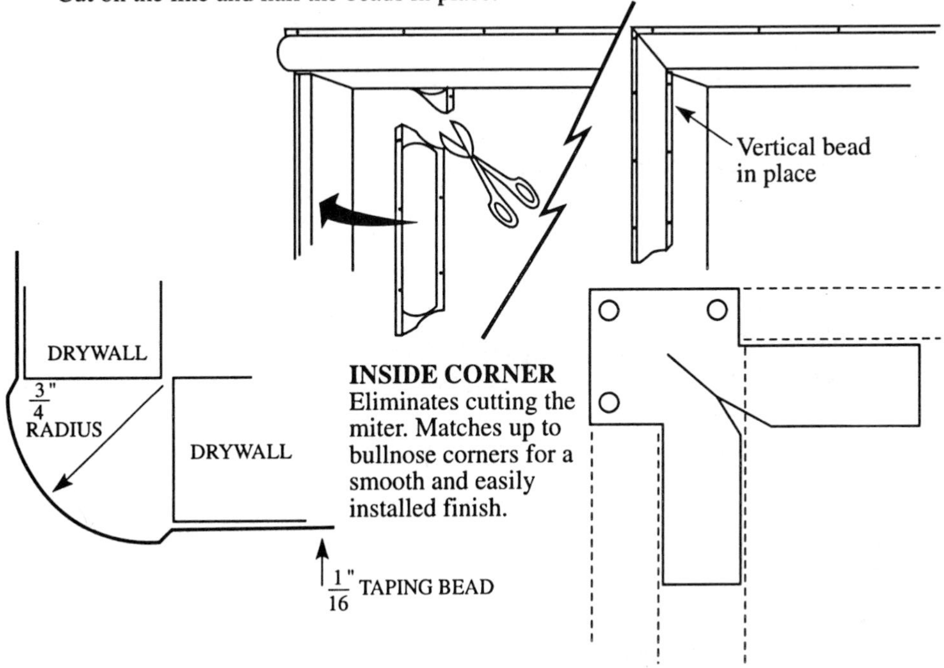

FIGURE 3–7 Bullnose corner bead (*Courtesy Flannery, Inc., Pacoima, CA*)

METAL FURRING CHANNEL

Metal furring channel can be used to build suspended drywall ceilings. It also can be used to furr a wall area, creating air space for soundproofing. This channel is used for many other things as well. (See Figure 3–8.)

METAL STUDS AND RUNNERS

Metal studs and runners are used in the metal framing industry. You will see metal framing on most commercial job sites. Metal framing will affect your work as a hanger or a finisher. When you use the screw gun, remember to let the gun do

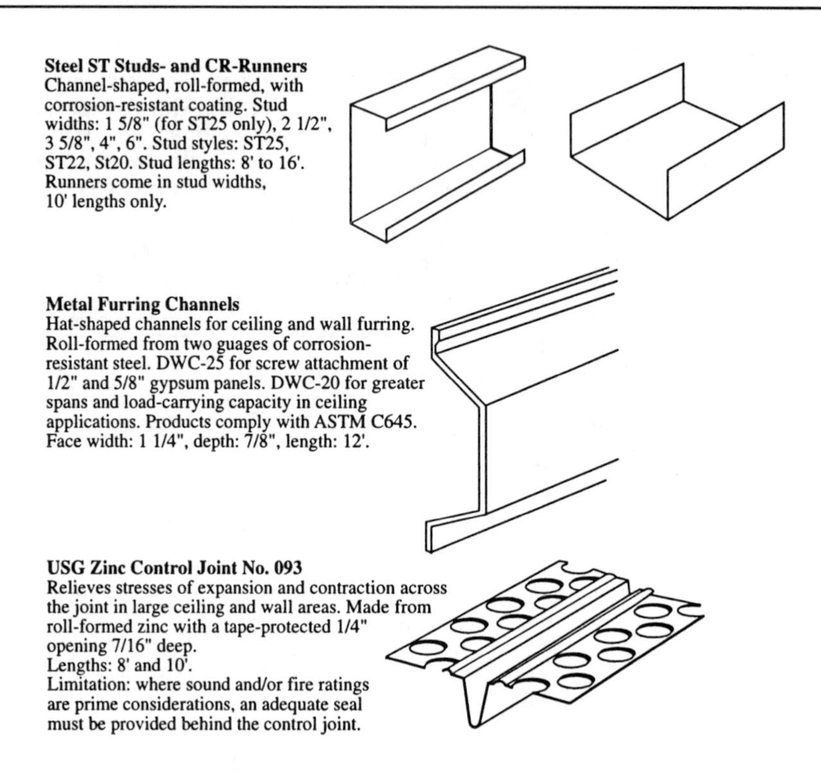

FIGURE 3–8 Studs and runners, metal furring channel, and control joints. (*Courtesy Unimast, Inc.*)

the work. If you push in too much when driving the screws, the studs will twist; this in turn twists the drywall. The problems caused by twisting the studs usually aren't noticed until you start finishing. Even though the recess is filled and smoothed out, the edge of the recess is showing and it may be difficult to figure out the reasons for this. If you take a long piece of metal and place it across the wall, you will understand the problem more clearly (Figure 3–9).

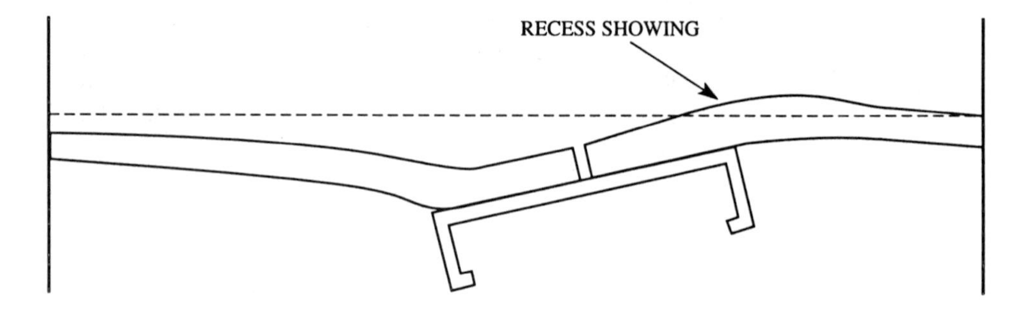

FIGURE 3–9 Sometimes these joints take in the entire piece of drywall to break the section out far enough to hide the joint.

Questions

METAL TRIM AND CORNER BEAD

1. What is corner bead?
a. Fiberglass tape used for corners
b. Metal trim that gives a square look when finished
c. Colorful plastic that snaps on the corners
d. Rubber trim that protects the corner

2. What is bullnose corner bead?
a. Colorful plastic rounded trim
b. Metal rounded corner trim
c. Fiberglass tape trim
d. Rubber trim that protects the corners

3. What is a control joint used for?
a. To stop joint compound from cracking
b. To stop the wall from swaying
c. To relieve stress
d. To keep metal studs from twisting

4. A drywall suspended ceiling might be constructed of
a. control joints.
b. studs.
c. concrete.
d. metal furring channels.

5. For what kind of construction are metal studs commonly used?
a. Residential
b. Commercial
c. Duplexes
d. Residential and duplexes

Chapter 4
Drywall Repair and Shortcuts

Shortcut Procedures

Repairing Drywall

Hot Patches

Repair work, such as fixing a hole in the drywall, is sometimes necessary. One way to fix a hole is to cut out the drywall from stud to stud and nail another piece in its place. This is a difficult and time-consuming procedure. A better, faster, and easier way to do the repair is called *hot patch.*

If there is a hole in the wall, draw a square around it. Keep the square as small as you can but go past the edge of the hole. Saw this square out. Cut a piece of board two inches bigger than the hole in the wall. Score the board on the back to the size of the hole, and then pull it loose from the patch. You want to end up with a piece of drywall the size of the hole, but you want the paper on the front of it two inches bigger. This is a hot patch. The paper on the front keeps the patch from falling into the hole and also takes the place of drywall tape. All the finisher has to do is spread joint compound around the hole, place the hot patch in the hole, and wipe down the paper as if it were tape. After it is finished, the patch will be as strong as the original board. (Refer to Hot Patch, Figure 6–13).

POPPED NAILS

Another problem that you will run into is popped nails. When you look at the drywall, you might notice small round areas sticking out from the board. If you press against the board, the area will move. This indicates that a nail has popped. A nail pops because the board was not held tight to the stud as it was nailed. The nail might have been dimpled, but there was a space between the board and the stud. The solution to this problem is to renail the area, but push the board up tight to the stud as you nail.

Sometimes the insulation is covering the stud and, when the board is nailed, the nails will pop. Another possibility is that the hanger did not sweep the house out before hanging the drywall. Any trash behind the board would keep the board away from the wall when it is nailed.

Hanging Shortcuts

If you plan on hanging the walls only in your own house, then speed is of no real concern. But if you plan on making drywall installation your life's work, then speed matters. Hanging drywall can be a lucrative trade, but speed is essential. The methods explained so far are the basics. Here are some shortcuts that, coupled with experience, will help make you a quicker and more efficient hanger.

MARKING JOISTS

When you go through the house to mark the ceiling joists, use neither a pencil to mark nor a bench to stand on. Simply take a hatchet and make a chop mark under each joist. This way, you can reach the ceiling without getting up and down off the bench—the hatchet handle is long enough to reach the ceiling easily.

NAILING

Nailing consumes more time than any other phase of hanging. Almost all beginning hangers will hit a nail eight to ten times. Try to hit the nail only three times: once to start it, once to sink it, and a last time to dimple it. Speed will come only with experience, but there is a way to speed up your nailing now. Take a small box of nails home with you. As you watch television, grab a handful of nails and practice with them. Bring the nail into position for nailing without the use of the other hand. You will be surprised how much faster you are within a week.

When hanging the top board on a wall, always start the nails along the top first. A few of these nails may be knocked out or fall out before you get the board completely hung. These nails need to be replaced. Most hangers would stop what they are doing, get a bench to stand on, and renail. To save some time, drop a nail on the floor, hold the hatchet by its head, and let the end of the handle drop down onto the nail. The sharp head of the nail will stick in the wooden handle. Reach up with the hatchet and start the nail, pull the handle away and the nail will stay in the board. Now you can drive the nail in quickly.

MEASUREMENTS

Another time-consuming phase of drywall installation is making measurements. When you measure for a board, you should take all measurements for that board and mark them on the scrap piece. If you forget a measurement and have to go back to the room and measure again, you're wasting a lot of time. It will take a lot of practice before you will be able to take four or five measurements and cut the board without forgetting half the measurements. Until then, pick a piece of scrap drywall and write them down. Then you can put the scrap piece on top of the stack of drywall and refer to it as you cut the drywall board.

When you are hanging drywall on the walls, the board is hung horizontally. However, if an area is less than 48 inches wide, the board should be hung vertically.

This is a good way to hang closets. The problem is getting the board through an opening only 82 inches high. To solve this problem, score all the way across the board on the back side, bend it, bring it into the closet, and then unfold it. Now you can nail it up, and if you are careful, the score line won't even have to be finished later.

Each time you cut a board, try to figure where the cut-off piece can be used. Otherwise, you might run out of usable board and end up with a huge pile of useless scraps. A lot of the end pieces can be used in hallways and in closets.

CUTTING DRYWALL

With practice a T-square is unnecessary to cut drywall. Use a tape measure and a knife instead. Draw a line with your pencil, then cut it with your knife. This will be slower than using a T-square, but after you have used the pencil for a while, you will become skilled enough to use the knife in its place.

When cutting a hole out for a water pipe, make the center points on the board, and use the keyhole saw to knock them out. If you look at the keyhole saw, you will see a long round wooden handle with a small shorter piece of metal at the front end of it. This is the perfect size for smaller pipes, and the handle is good for the big pipes. Make sure to knock the saw all the way through the board for the larger pipes.

SYSTEMS

Use a system in hanging. Give each person a job to do. When you walk into a house, one person should start marking ceiling joists while another begins sweeping the house so you don't stumble over any trash. A third person could be taking measurements in preparation for hanging. Work out a system and stick to it so it becomes a habit. Be efficient!

Questions

DRYWALL REPAIR AND SHORTCUTS

1. What is a hot patch?
   a. A hole covered with metal
   b. A hole taped and coated with quick set
   c. A hole covered with a heated tape
   d. A patch cut out of drywall with two extra inches of paper all around

2. What causes a popped nail?
a. A person pulling against the drywall
b. Failure to hold the drywall against the stud when hammering the nail
c. Earthquakes
d. Failure to hammer the nail in far enough

3. If you don't have a pencil, how else can you mark a joist?
a. Drive a nail there.
b. Use some chalk.
c. Use the hatchet to make a chop mark.
d. Put some joint compound on the wall.

4. Why do you put a row of nails along the top of the drywall that fits on the top of the wall area?
a. So you can hold the board with one arm and drive the nail with the hammer
b. So the butt joints fit tighter together
c. So the factory edges will be straight
d. To avoid using the toe jack

5. Why would you write measurements on a small piece of drywall?
a. So you can count how many cuts you made
b. So you can count them and figure your drywall footage
c. To avoid having to take the measurements again
d. So you can figure how much joint compound you will need to finish the job

6. How do you get a piece of drywall 96 inches high into a closet that has a door 82 inches high?
a. Cut it in half.
b. Score it along the front about 20 inches down and bend it back.
c. Score it along the back about 20 inches down and bend it forward.
d. Bend it far enough to fit through the door.

7. To cut a hole for a shower area pipe, one of the best tools is a
a. drywall knife.
b. hammer.
c. keyhole saw.
d. jigsaw.

Part 2
Finishing

Chapter 5
Drywall Finishing Materials and Tools

Introduction to Finishing

Finisher, taper, floater, and *mudder* are all names for the person who puts the finishing touches on wall construction. The process itself is best described as *finishing,* since that is what it does: it finishes the wall in preparation for the final covering (paint, texture, paper, or paneling). The goal of finishing is to cover all cracks and crevices in the wall and create a flat surface ready to receive a final covering.

Finishing is an art that has been handed down through many generations. It is usually learned on the job, through demonstration, and until now, there have been no books to reinforce knowledge for the beginner. Although technology has advanced in recent years, many finishing methods and techniques have not. Thus, if you learn from a hand-finisher who uses traditional procedures, you risk learning to finish incorrectly.

Originally, the recessed edges on drywall were constructed to allow room for the recess to be taped and covered with joint compound and remain flat. Many years ago, joint compound would shrink a lot, so the finisher would completely fill the recess and put the tape on top of the board. As it dried, the plaster would shrink and pull the tape back into the recess. Then, when the drywall was covered with a second coat of joint compound, it would finish out flat. In recent years, however, technology has produced higher-quality joint compound, which shrinks very little, if at all. Thus, finishers who use old procedures with new materials make joints that bulge out from the wall and must be treated as butt joints.

This section of the book is an introduction to the art of finishing.

Finishing Materials

Here are the basic materials you will need to finish your walls. They are available at most hardware and drywall stores. Many other materials are available, and more are added to the market all the time. As you learn the trade, you may wish to try other materials as well.

JOINT COMPOUND (PLASTER BASE)

After drywall is hung, large cracks and crevices might remain in the joints. These need to be prefilled and smoothed over. Joint compound is used for this task. Finishing joint compound contains a glue that makes it adhere to the reinforcing tape. When applied correctly, joint compound gives a smooth and straight finish to the wall. Joint compound generally comes premixed in boxes and buckets, but you can also buy it in powdered form.

TAPE

All cracks filled with joint compound (as well as small, nonfilled cracks) must be covered with reinforcing tape (usually called Perfa tape). If these filled cracks are not covered with tape, the joint compound will crack as the house settles and shifts. Tape usually comes in 250- and 500-foot rolls, about two inches wide. It can also be purchased in circles (to slip over pipes), and in squares (to fit around light boxes), allowing for tight fit. A self-adhesive fiberglass mesh tape is also available. Many people find it easier to use, but it is rather expensive.

CORNER BEAD

Corner bead is a V-shaped metal strip that fits on 90° corners. Highly resistant to wear and tear, it gives more solid reinforcement than paper does. When used to frame windows and doors, it provides a neat, sculpted look. In a house that has wood studs, corner bead framing must be nailed on or put on with a clincher (see Figure 1–7) or screw attachment.

FLEX BEAD

Flex bead is tape with two parallel metal strips sealed lengthwise down the center, providing strength and flexibility. It is used for rounded fur downs and bastard corners (non-90° angles).

L BEAD

L bead is an L-shaped strip made of metal, plastic, or papered metal. It is put on the edge of drywall where it fits against metal, concrete, or even acoustic ceilings. In houses, it is used inside windows as a sweat strip to prevent moisture from damaging the drywall and causing deterioration. Papered metal L bead is also used as corner bead in places that regular corner bead would have to be mudded for application.

JOINT COMPOUNDS

The three main types of joint compounds are taping, topping, and all-purpose. Taping joint compound is used for taping and first coat. Topping joint compound is used only for second and finish coats. All-purpose joint compound is used for taping, first coat, second coat, and finish coat. When you are starting out, all-purpose joint compound is the best one to use. You can use taping compound for a finishing coat, but it will be hard to sand. You *cannot* use topping compound for taping and first coat because it is very soft, doesn't hold together well, and crumbles easily if it gets wet.

A product called Plus 3 is a joint compound that is lightweight (about 35% lighter) and shrinks less than other brands. It is good for textures, and it also sands well.

Quick set joint compound is a product you will use often. Because its drying time is short, quick set (Durabond is one brand name) is used on jobs that need to be finished quickly. It sets like cement, doesn't shrink, and can even take a second coat while it's wet. It comes in powder form, and you mix it yourself. United States Gypsum Company puts out a product that weighs 25% less than other quick set joint compounds, and, unlike older versions, it can be sanded easily. You may choose from the following set-up times for lightweight quick sets: 20–30 minutes, 30–60 minutes, 60–120 minutes, 180–360 minutes, and 240–360 minutes. Quick set sets solid and enables the finisher to tape, coat, recoat, and finish a job in one day. (United States Gypsum Company products are also known as sheetrock.)

Finishing Tools

There is a vast array of tools on the market. Here are some of the most useful ones. But look around for yourself—you may find others that you'd like better.

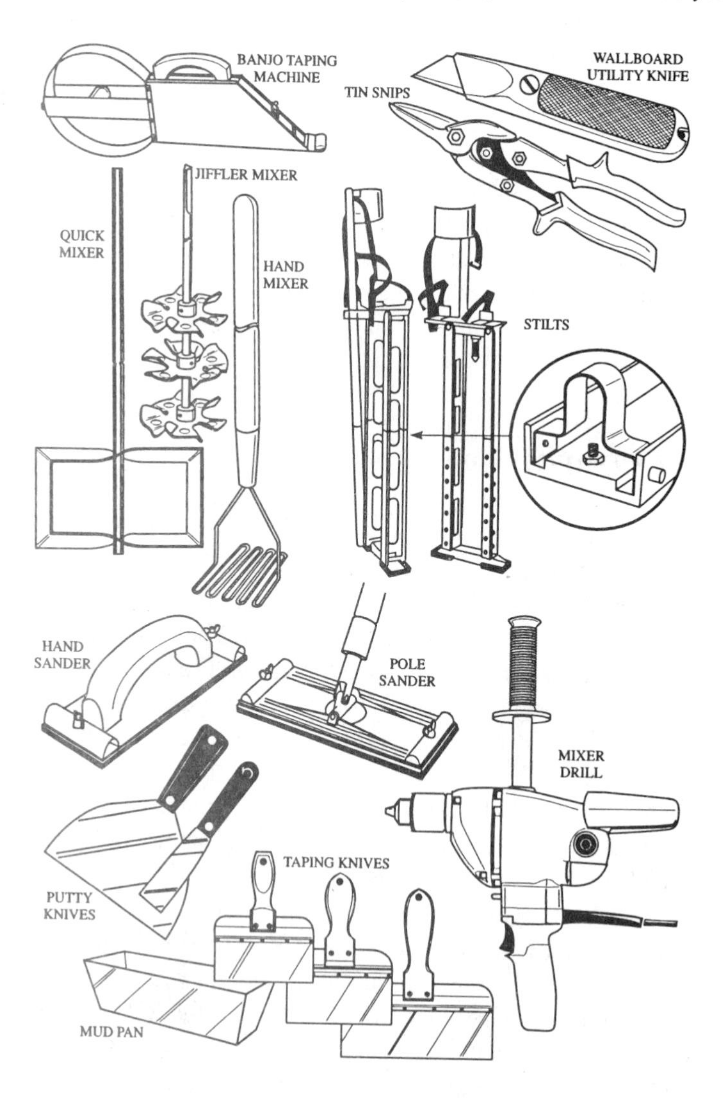

FIGURE 5–1 Finishing tools

PANS

You'll need some pans to hold the joint compound while you are using it. The size you choose will depend on the size of the knife you're using. They come in metal or plastic. You will find that plastic is more comfortable in the winter.

TAPE AND PAN HOLDER

If you will be taping by hand and working on stilts or scaffolding, you may find a tape and pan holder helpful. It fits easily on a belt.

TAPE CREASER

A tape creaser is handy for taping corners because it folds the tape as it feeds it out. This allows you to put the tape directly into a corner. You can get the same results if you run the tape through your hand, as shown in Figure 5-2.

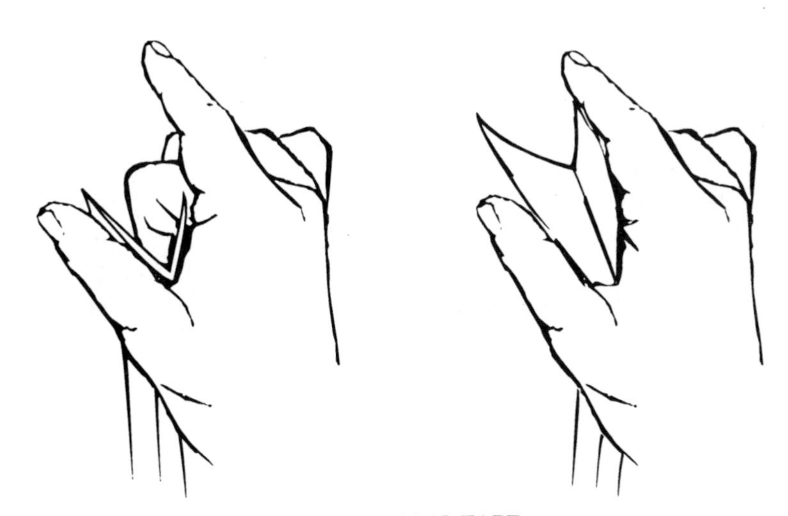

CREASING TAPE

To fold the tape for angles, you can thread it through a tape creaser tool or simply pull it through your hand in this fashion.

Hold your hand around the tape as shown in the figure on the left, then close your thumb and pull the tape through your hand as shown on the right. Be careful not to cut your hand. This method is much faster and requires no tools.

FIGURE 5-2

BANJO

The banjo tool speeds up the process of taping. It precoats the tape with joint compound as you lay the tape down, allowing you to put the tape directly on the wall. This tool is further explained in Chapter 6.

HAND MIXER

The hand mixer looks like a giant potato masher; it's used to thin and dilute joint compound according to the particular job. For bigger jobs, you can get a paddle mixer, which attaches to an electric drill, making it easier to mix the joint compound.

KNIVES

Knives come in sizes ranging from one inch to 24 inches long. Each has its use, as you will see.

HAMMER

A drywall finisher shouldn't have to carry a hammer, but you may find it necessary anyway because you will occasionally find nails that haven't been driven far enough into the drywall. A drywall hatchet it the most useful type, though, because the hatchet part can be used for opening various containers, such as joint compound buckets. The head of this type of hammer is rounded to dimple the drywall without cutting into the paper.

CLINCHER

The clincher is a piece of metal bent to 90° with two sharp protruding edges. It is used for putting corner bead on corners. You simply place the protruding edges of the tool on the corner bead and strike the clincher with a mallet. It will push a little piece of the corner bead's edge back into the drywall. Repeat this up and down the corner bead. Check building codes in your area. Some areas require that you use screws.

STILTS

Stilts save you time and money. With stilts, you can do ceiling work without the time-consuming hassle of moving around scaffolding and boards. Contrary to popular belief, walking on them isn't at all difficult. They are made to extend to different heights, and springs on them adjust to the way you walk. However, some states do not allow them.

TIN SNIPS

You will be using these to cut metal corner bead to suit your needs.

RASP

A rasp is a very strong file-like device used to shave off excess edges of drywall that may protrude on some corners.

UTILITY KNIFE

A solid utility knife is useful around for cutting drywall and other items.

POWER MIXER

The power mixer is, of course, a large drill with a paddle that fits on it. It is used to mix joint compound.

HAND SANDER

The hand sander allows close control and enables you to feel what you are sanding. For instance, you can tell if a butt joint is rounded, if metal is not filled square, and if you have ripples at the bottom of a butt joint.

POLE SANDER

The pole sander allows you to reach the ceiling and other high areas. It works best on flat areas. If you have a bad butt joint, you might want to check it by hand.

Questions

DRYWALL FINISHING TOOLS AND MATERIALS

1. What is a finisher's function?
a. To cover the cracks with tape
b. To tape and cover with joint compound
c. To camouflage bad areas with texture
d. To make the drywall surface flat and free from imperfections, so it is ready for paint or coverings

2. What is the purpose of a recess beveled edge on drywall?
a. It helps in determining which way the drywall is hung.
b. It is designed for the tape to be set beneath the surface and covered with joint compound.
c. It is a strong area that holds nails better.
d. The edge is stronger, so it doesn't break when it is being moved.

3. What is the purpose of paper tape?
a. To make the joint compound stronger
b. To soak up moisture
c. To allow movement in the wall without cracking of the joint compound
d. To hold the joint compound in the cracks

4. What is quick set used for?
a. Texture
b. To speed up the process when time is short
c. To help paint adhere
d. To finish bathrooms and damp areas

5. What are the three types of joint compound?
a. taping, topping, and all-purpose
b. taping, quick set, and topping
c. texture, quick set, and topping
d. all-purpose, quick set, and topping

6. What is topping best used for?
a. Taping
b. First coat
c. Second and finish coats
d. Texture

7. What is a banjo used for?
a. First coat
b. Taping
c. Spotting nails
d. Playing music

8. What is a clincher used for?
a. To reinforce butt joints
b. To fasten tape on corners
c. To fasten corner bead on corners
d. To put covers on receptacle boxes

Chapter 6
Drywall Finishing

The Four Basic Joints

FLAT JOINTS

Drywall is made with two beveled edges. When the beveled edges of two pieces of drywall come together, they form what is called a *flat joint* (it isn't really flat; see Figure 6–1). Flat joints are the easiest of all joints to finish because the recess that is formed is about ⅛ inch. This leaves plenty of room to embed the tape, cover it with joint compound, and still end up with a flat wall. However, if a stud is out of line or the hangers made a mistake, it's the finisher's job to straighten it out.

BUTT JOINTS

Butt joints rarely are found perfectly flush (see Figure 6–1). One board usually will sit slightly higher than the other, creating a high side and a low side. Bad butt joints are the most difficult to cover. With no beveled edge to set tape into, the tape has to sit on top of the board, with joint compound layered over that. Thus, bad butt joints cannot be made completely flat no matter what you do, but you can camouflage it to look flat.

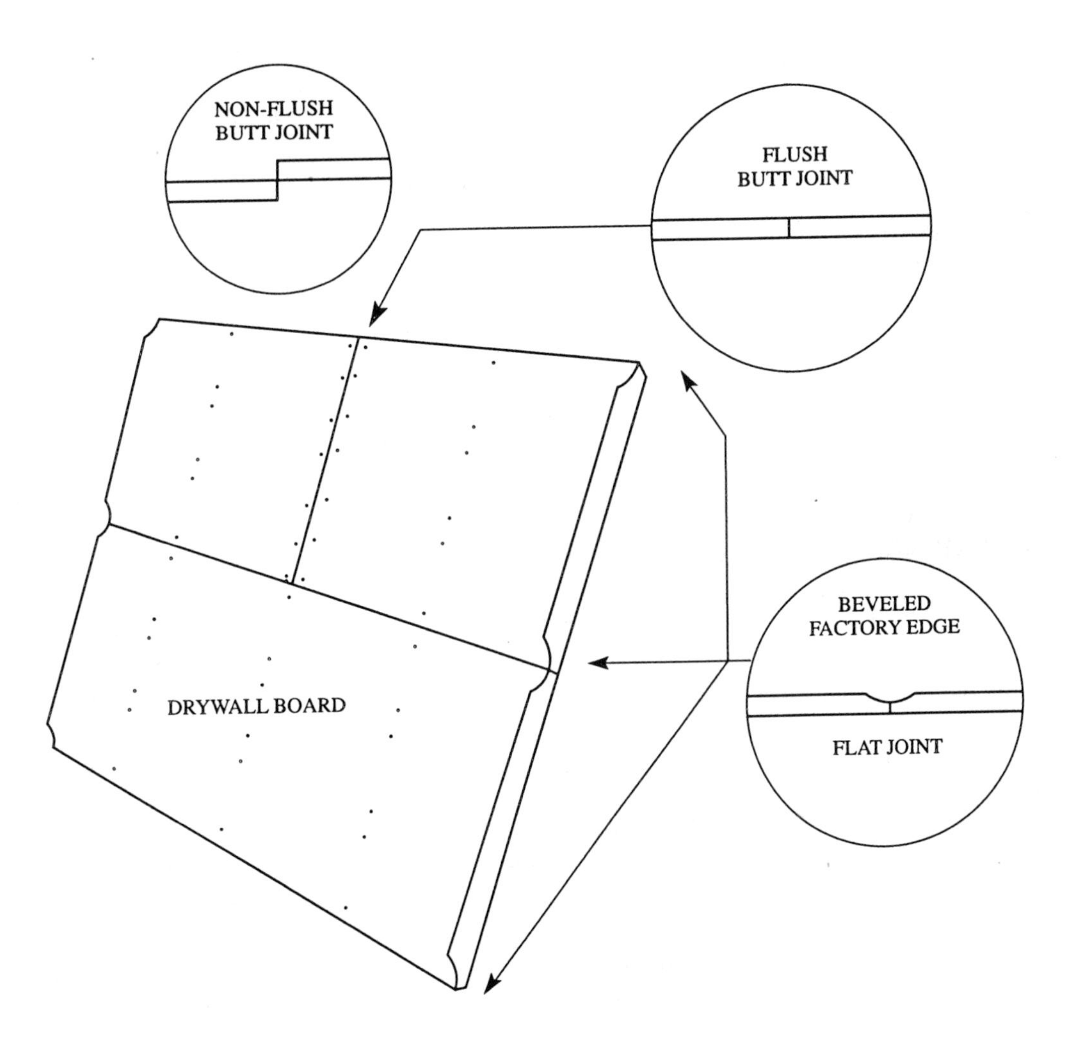

FIGURE 6–1 Butt joint and flat joint cross section

ANGLES

The corners are very seldom taped square even by people trained in this field. If the tape is rounded, it will need to be finished with thick mud to look square. Too much mud will later crack. I will explain later in taping.

METAL OR CORNER BEAD

To save money on wood, builders are using more metal for framing windows and doors. Metal requires a lot of joint compound and is frequently shallow. Special care should be taken when coating windows and doors because it looks cheap when they are not square.

BASTARD ANGLES AND JOINTS

The term bastard angle refers to any joint that does not form a 90° angle. They take special attention which will be explained during each phase of this book.

PREPARING THE JOB FOR TAPING

Before you even get your tools and materials unloaded, check the house to make sure all boards are nailed off tight and all metal is on. Check to see if the job can be completed. If any boards are hung improperly, you will have to make two or three extra trips back after you finish to fix it. This is what finishers call *punch out,* things to fix after the job is done. Punch out wastes time and money; my motto is "Knock out punch out."

Once you decide to go ahead with the job, make sure you have enough tools and materials to finish. Put them in a central location that can be reached easily from all over the house. Use this location as a work area. Since someone will be working on the ceiling in this room, check this room first and arrange the tools on the floor directly under one board. This will make it easier for the person on stilts to reach the ceiling joints.

Then go through the rest of the house, checking it carefully. Pick a starting point and follow the wall all the way through the house. Anywhere the board is broken or cracked, pull it off and prefill it. It will never finish properly if it's loose and moves at all. Remember, the house will be settling. Often, the drywall has been pried with something, and the edge is broken. Tear the paper off and prefill it. Check all butt joints. Bad butt joints should be prefilled. Receptacle boxes (the holes through which the wires are threaded) should be prefilled with joint compound along the edge that needs repairing. Make them strong enough to hold when the outlet cover goes on. Receptacle boxes are sometimes forced when they are covered with drywall. Maybe a wire doesn't fit right under the drywall. Sometimes a hanger puts the drywall on and nails it tight. Then it cracks behind the board. The paper may not be broken on the surface, but it needs to be taken out and repaired. Dig out the broken drywall and prefill it so it can be taped later on. Prefill any big cracks. (See Figures 6–2 through 6–4.)

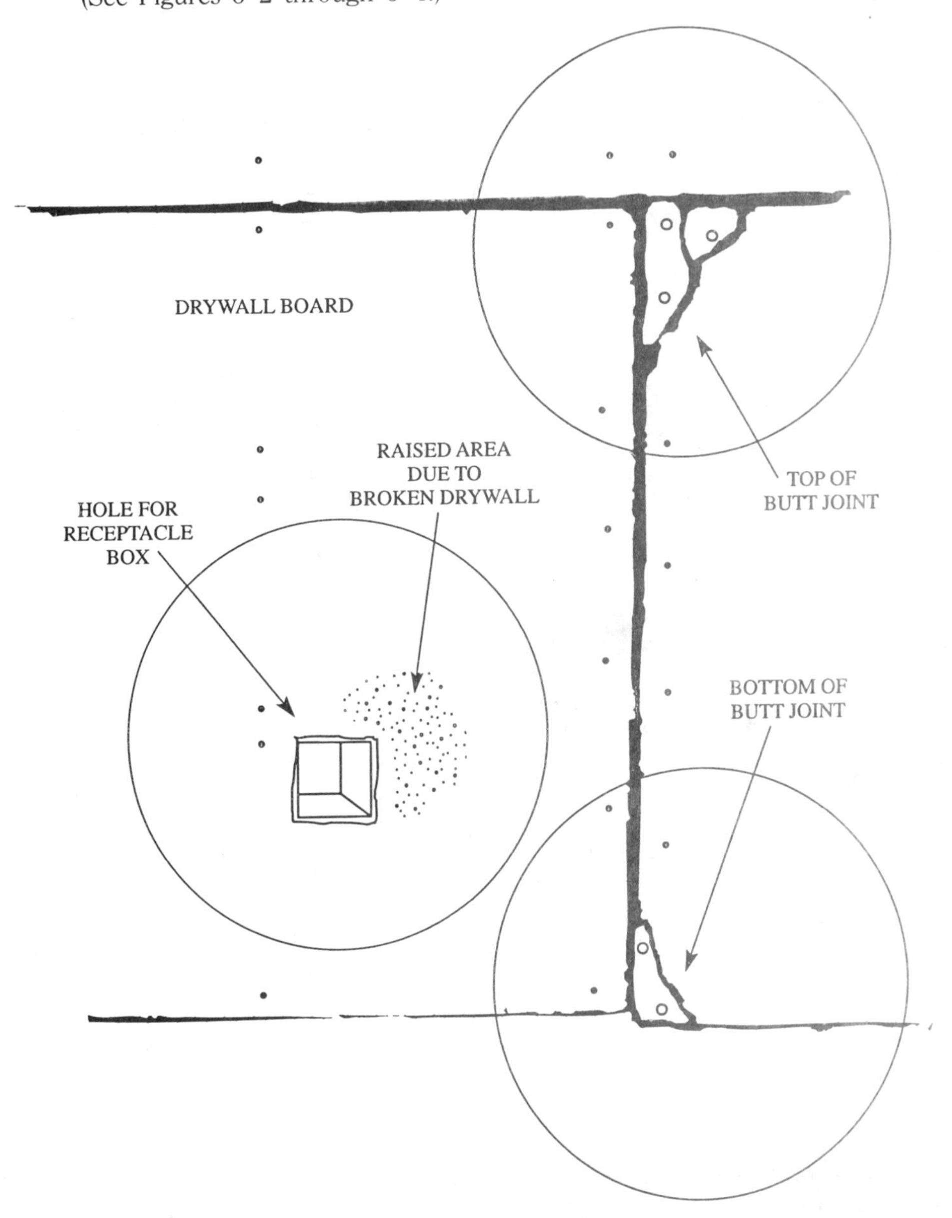

FIGURE 6–2 The receptacle box shows a soft spot where the board has been broken underneath. The drywall immediately around it must be cut out and repaired. Hangers often break the corners of drywall, especially at butt joints. Remove broken board and fill the hole with joint compound.

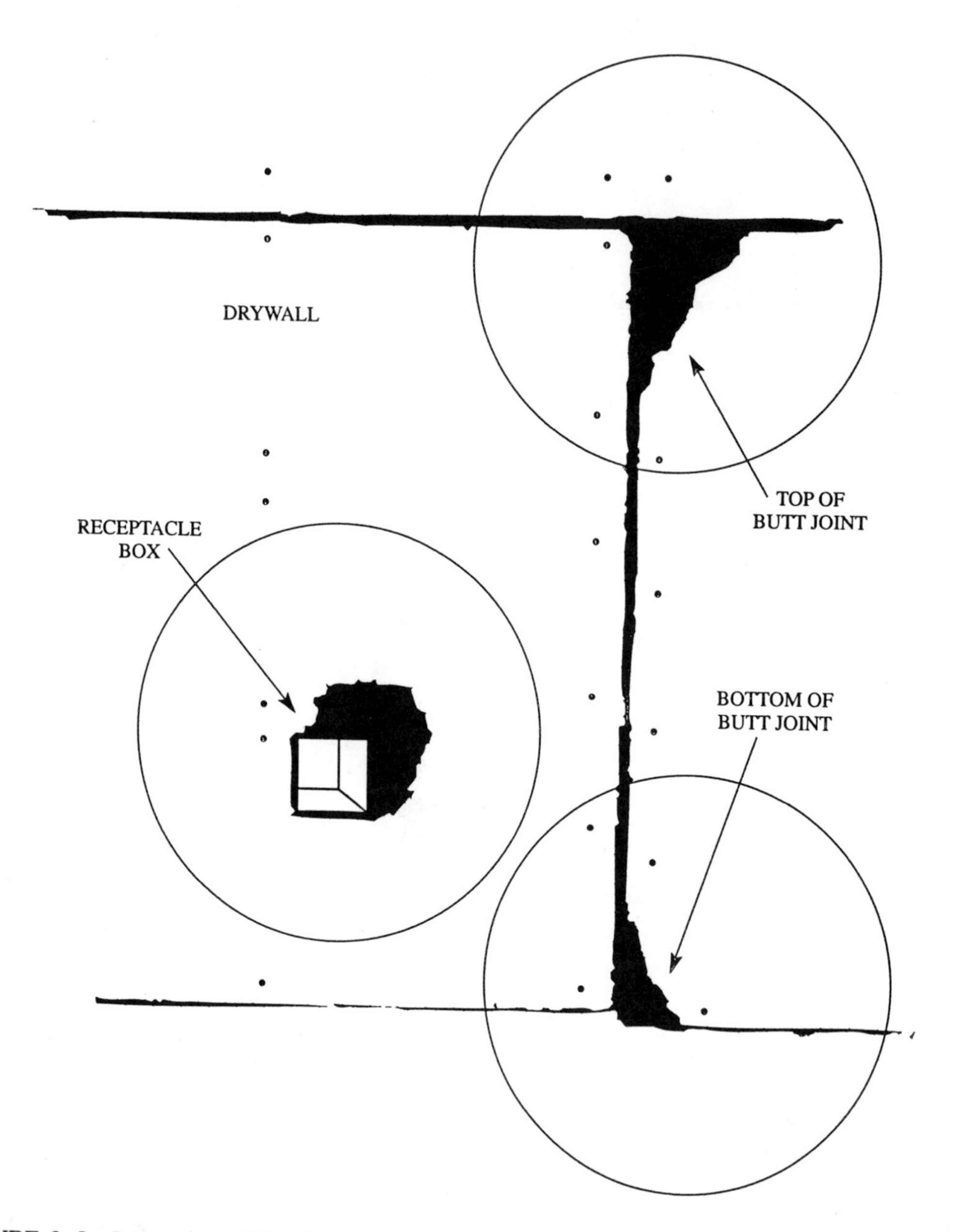

FIGURE 6–3 Loose drywall has been removed from the receptacle box. If the hole is too big and the joint compound falls behind the wall, place tape across the hole and push it in a little to act as a holder for the joint compound.

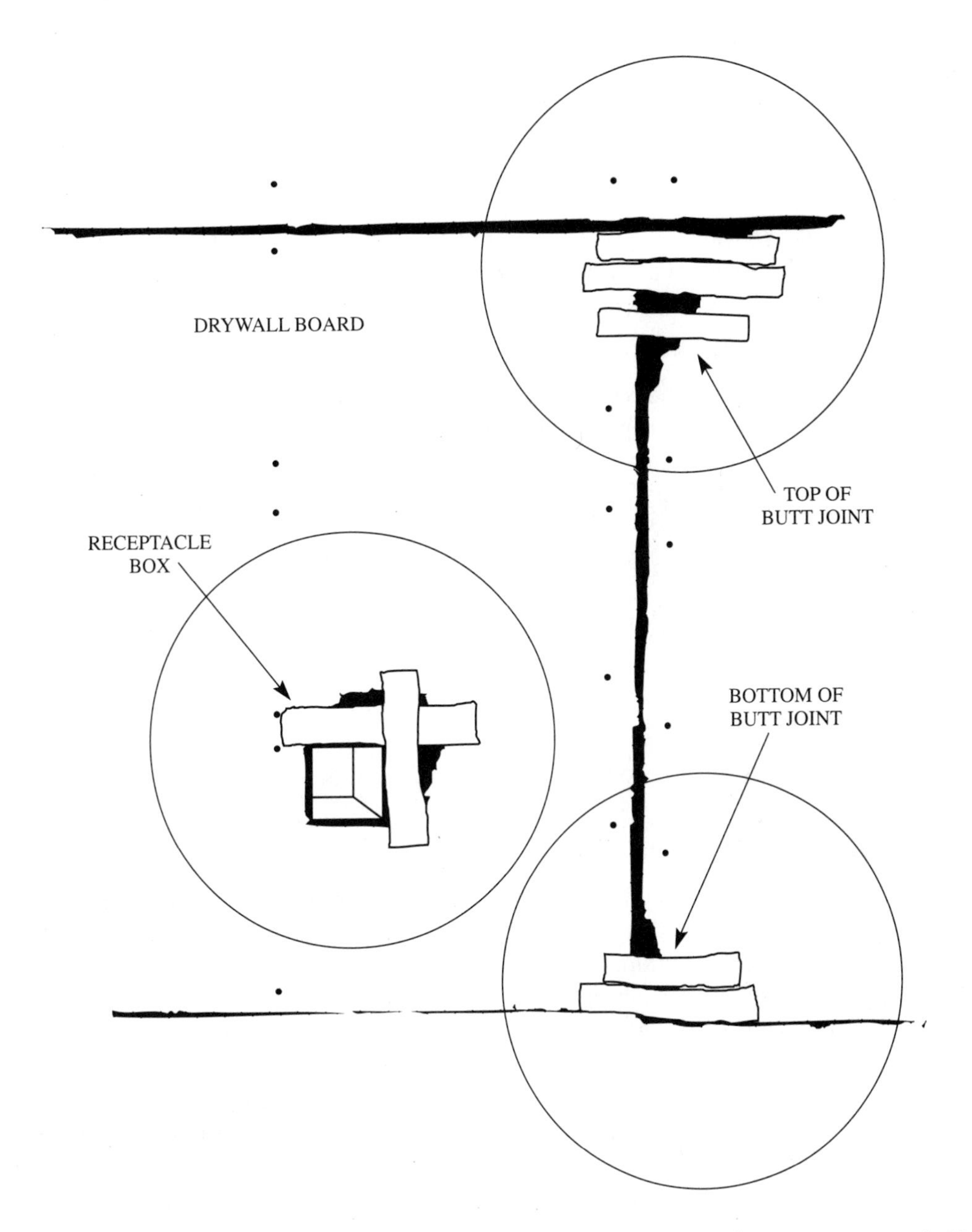

FIGURE 6–4 The receptacle box has been taped to act as a holder for the joint compound. If the joint compound still won't stay in place, use more tape on top of it to hold it in.

TAPING

TAPING ORDER

When you tape, you should use a four-, five-, or six-inch knife, and you should tape the room in an orderly and efficient manner.

Butts and Headers

Headers are the vertical joints over doors and windows. In a house, butts includes all vertical joints except the corners. These are all joints that are not made by factory (beveled) edges. These are all taped and coated like butt joints. When taping, always do butts and headers first, since they require the most joint compound and drying time.

Flat Joints

Flat joints are those that are made by factory (beveled) edges. These are taped second.

Angles

Angles are the corners. They should be taped third.

Receptacle Boxes, Etc.

Receptacle boxes, switch boxes, metal, pipes, and the like should be taped last.

If you tape in this order, you will gain speed and efficiency. Also, your chances of forgetting something are minimized. Remember, you want to work as fast as you can but still do the job right. If you work too fast, you'll do sloppy work, and it will slow you down during the following steps of the process. Any joint compound that goes on where it doesn't belong will have to come off sooner or later.

There are three ways to tape. The first is to do it by hand, the second is to use a banjo (which is much faster), and the third is to use the automatic taping tools. The third method is for the professional. I will explain hand taping and the banjo as I describe each kind of joint.

TAPING BY HAND

Work with joint compound straight out of the box, or as thick as possible. Never spread the joint compound too far in advance of putting the tape on and wiping it down. The reason for this is that when the joint compound starts to dry, it doesn't stick as well. It also leaves air pockets, which develop into blisters. Spread the joint compound along a joint. Place the tape on top and use the knife to smooth the tape, leaving the tape smoothed out on top of the joint compound.

USING THE BANJO OR TAPING TOOL

The banjo is fairly inexpensive at about $85.00. If cared for properly, it will last indefinitely. This tool can be filled with joint compound with tape threaded through it. When you pull the tape out the end, it is already covered on one side with joint compound. This makes taping twice as fast.

Taping tools must be watched carefully when you're first learning to use them. If you run low on joint compound and you're not aware of it, you can have pieces of tape with no joint compound on them. This will leave blisters. So as the joint compound runs low, you will need to watch the joint compound-coated side of the tape as it comes out of the banjo.

Joint compound for the banjo should be diluted with water so it will pass through the tool more easily. However, if it's too thin, it will drip on the floor as you tape, making quite a mess. Depending on the type of joint compound used, you will have to adjust the amount of water to thin it just right.

TAPING BAD BUTTS AND HEADERS

As a result of your earlier preparations, all bad butt joints should now be prefilled. Now go ahead and spread more joint compound right over joint compound that's already there—even if it's not dry. You want only the thinnest layer of joint compound between the high side of the joint and the tape, because you're trying to make this as flush as possible. Make sure the tape is in contact with the joint compound, or it won't stick. The low side should be as smooth as possible, with the tape sitting on the built-up joint compound. When smoothing excess joint compound from under the tape, hold the knife in a laid-down position. (See Figure 6–5.) Hold the knife with light pressure on the high side of the joint, floating over the built-up low side so you don't pull any joint compound away from it. Don't put too much pressure on the high side or you will take too much joint compound out from under the tape and cause a blister. By laying the knife down, you can control the amount of joint compound taken from under the tape. The more the knife is held out at an angle, the more joint compound it will pull out.

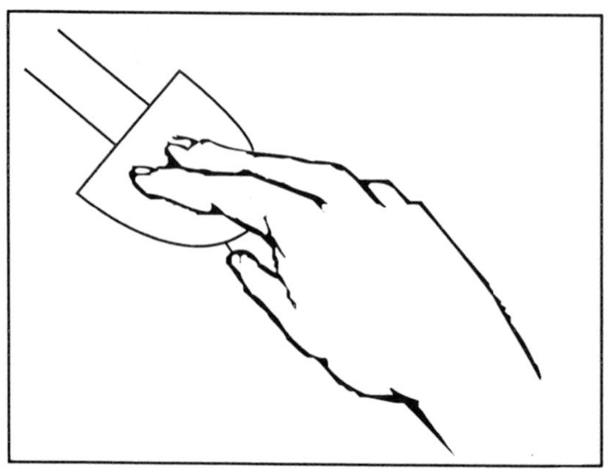

Lay the knife down so it doesn't take joint compound out from under the tape.

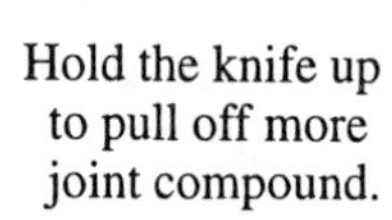

Hold the knife up to pull off more joint compound.

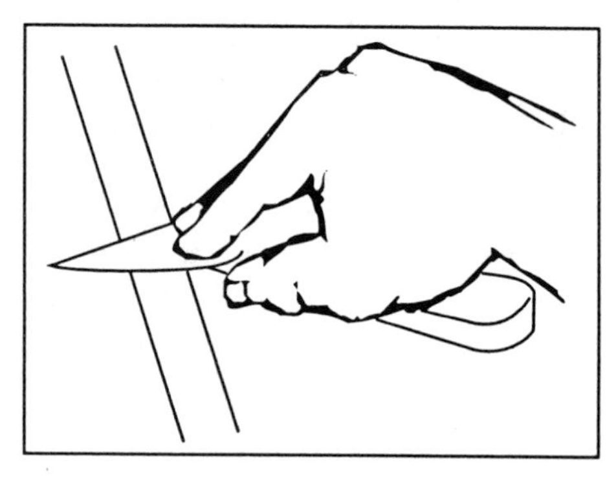

FIGURE 6–5 Knife positioning

USING THE TAPING TOOL TO TAPE BAD BUTTS

Bad butt joints must be prefilled before you use the banjo. The reason for this is that the banjo doesn't lay down enough joint compound to build with. Be extra careful wiping them down: because butts create such an uneven surface, they blister easily. It's easy to push out too much joint compound on the high spots. A knife will put even pressure on an uneven surface. Sometimes when the butt joint is bumpy and rough, it's better just to run your hand over the tape and press the joint compound into all low areas.

TAPING FLUSH BUTT JOINTS

Flush butt joints are rare, and they must be coated differently than bad butt joints. Remember that the tape should sit as close to the surface of the board as possible. This will make it easier to achieve a flush finish. You will probably have a few blisters before you find out how close you can get the tape. You need to build joint compound up on both sides of the tape in order to make it appear flush. (See Figure 6–6.)

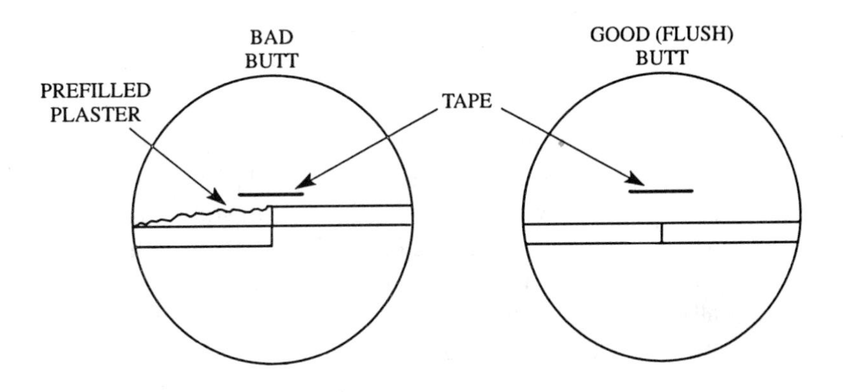

FIGURE 6–6 Taping butt joints

TAPING FLAT JOINTS BY HAND

If they are hung and taped right, flat joints are the easiest part of drywall finishing. Flat joints are those made by the beveled edges of the board. (See Figure 6–7).

Spread plenty of joint compound along the flat joints to secure the tape to the joint. When you roll out the tape, stretch it out, leaving no slack. Otherwise, you

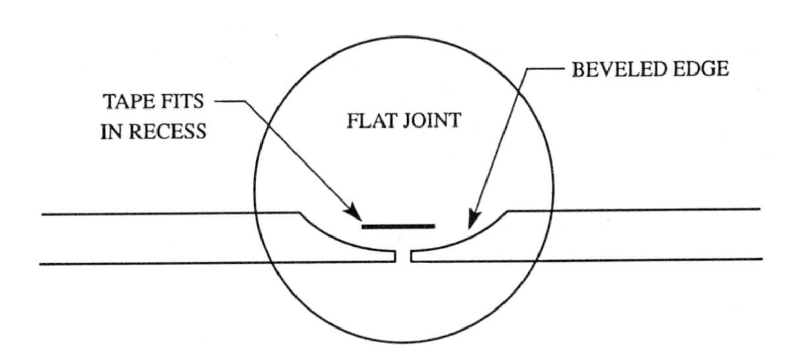

FIGURE 6–7 Taping flat joints

will end up with wrinkles when you start wiping the tape down. A four-inch knife is the best tool for pressing the tape inside the recess. You can use a six-inch knife, but it needs to be limber and you have to apply quite a bit of pressure on it to push it in deep. If the tape sits above the recess, the joint must be built round instead of flat, so be careful. For a better finish, make the best use of those beveled edges.

TAPING FLAT JOINTS WITH A TAPING TOOL

When taping flat joints with the banjo, hold the banjo by the handle at the top. Pull a few feet of tape out, and place the end of the tape on the flat joint at a starting place. Then run your hand over the tape to stick it to the joint, keeping pressure on the tape while pulling the banjo along with the other hand. Hold the tape tight so it doesn't slip. Repeat this all along the wall. When you reach the end of the wall and are ready to cut the tape, hold the cutting blade against the tape and twist. The blade will cut easily if it is kept sharp. When taping with the banjo, you don't have to worry about having too much joint compound in the recess, as the tape will fit nicely into it. You can use a six-inch knife quite comfortably.

TAPING ANGLES OR CORNERS BY HAND

For taping angles or corners by hand, a four-inch knife is recommended because of the straighter edge on the side of the knife. Many finishers make their own knives for corners, cutting the sides of regular knives so they are straight.

Because you turn your knife around to put joint compound on the wall, you might forget which corner of the knife to put the joint compound on. Put joint compound on the left corner of the knife to coat the right side of the angle, and on the right corner for the left side of the angle.

Spreading joint compound on the first side of the angle is easy. When spreading the second side, though, be careful not to let the side of the knife scrape the joint compound off the first side. Otherwise, you will have a blister where there's no joint compound. When spreading joint compound on the second side, hold the knife down flat, tilting it sideways away from the adjacent wall. This way, only the corner of the knife will be working in the center. (See Figure 6–8).

Wiping down corner tape can also create problems. Use a four-inch knife because the side of the knife is straighter and helps prevent pushing the tape back into any cracks. Holding the knife out straight from the wall helps make the corner square. If a corner is rounded, it has to be built up thick with joint compound to make it look square. This buildup of joint compound will begin to crack as the house settles.

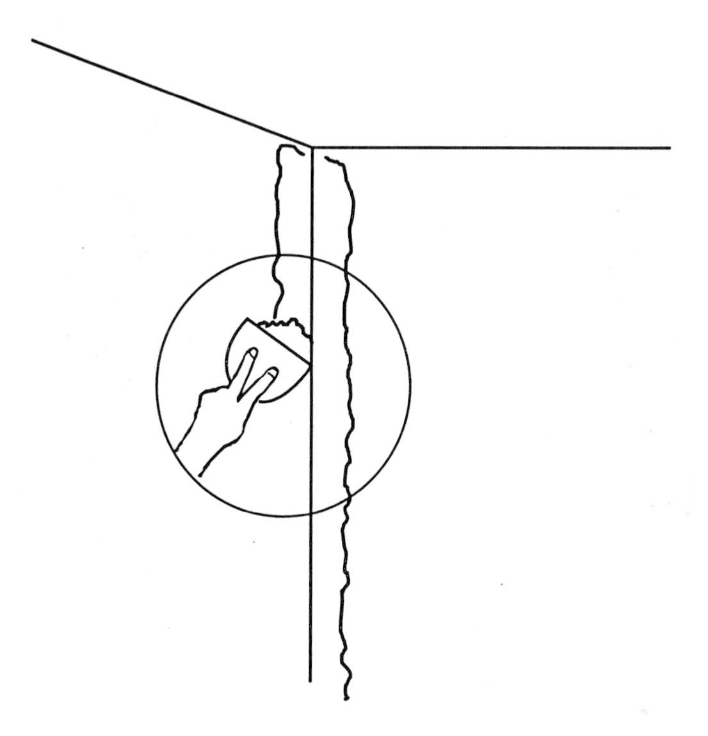

FIGURE 6–8 Spreading joint compound on angles

To fold the tape for angles, you can thread it through a tape creaser tool, or you can simply pull it through your hand, as shown in Figure 6–9.

TAPING ANGLES WITH TAPING TOOLS

Hold the banjo by the side handle (there should be a cloth handle through which you can slide your hand). Pull out some tape and push it into the corner, running your fingers down the center to stick the tape well into the corner. As you do so, keep the tape pulled out tight, maintaining pressure on it. Continue pressing into the center. Pull the tape out another few feet and repeat the procedure. When you get to the floor, twist the blade to cut the tape. The tape should always be left an inch or so from the floor. You never know what kind of trim will go around the base, so tape down as low as you can. Push the tape in tight the rest of the way to the floor. Then wipe it down with a four-inch knife.

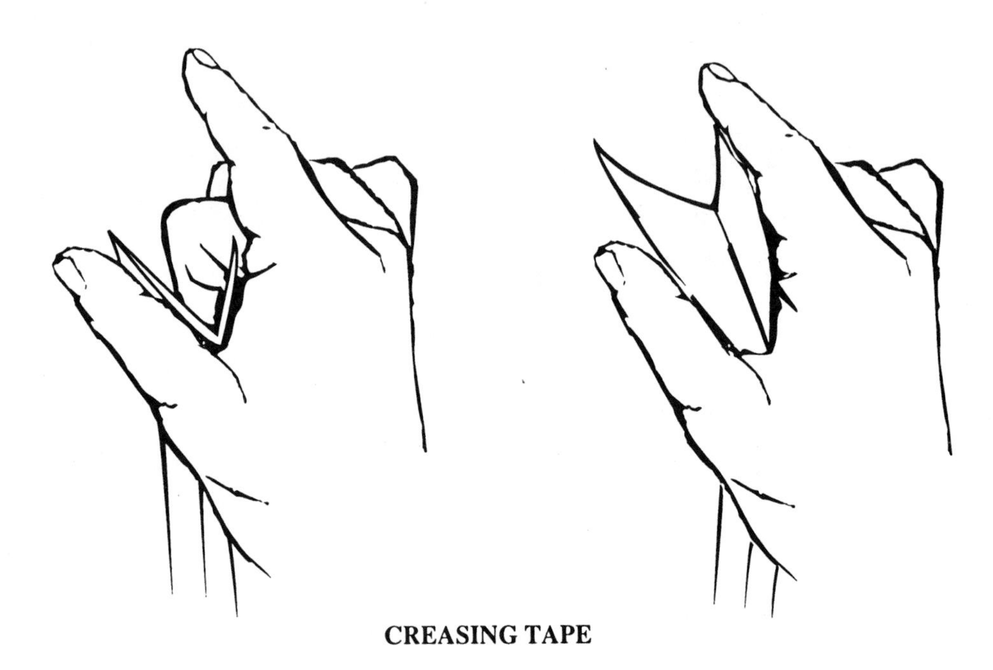

CREASING TAPE

FIGURE 6–9 To fold the tape for angles, thread it through a tape creaser tool, or simply pull it through your hand in this fashion: Hold your hand around the tape as shown. Close your thumb and pull the tape through your hand, taking care not to cut your hand.

TAPING CEILING ANGLES

Where different angles join (such as ceiling corners), be sure to get the tape all the way into the corners. Otherwise, you will leave a hole that will be visible from across the room. Merely pushing joint compound into the corner without taping it won't work because the joint compound will fall out of the hole. (See Figure 6–10).

BASTARD ANGLES, INSIDE AND OUTSIDE

A bastard angle is any angle that is other than 90°. It usually has a big crack because many hangers don't know how to shave the drywall to make it fit tight. These

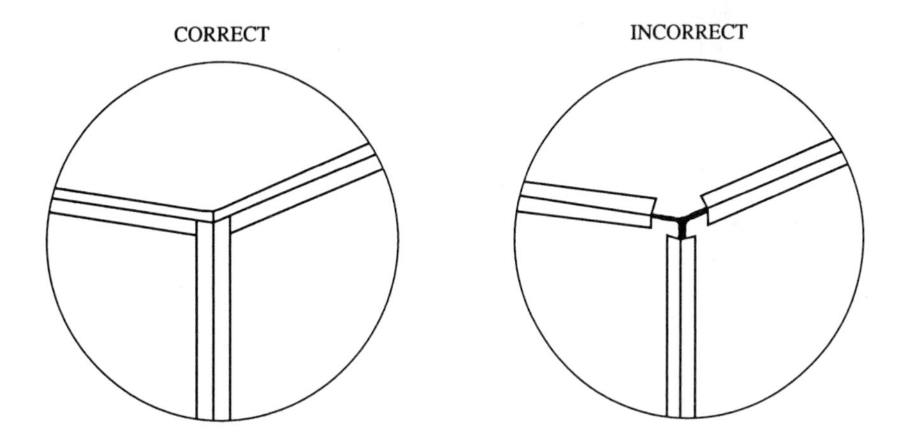

FIGURE 6–10 Taping ceiling angles

bad inside angles should already have been prefilled with joint compound when you prepared the job for taping. If it is a fairly straight angle, it can be taped in the usual way. If it has a deep side, prefill and flat tape it, and then apply an angle piece of tape. Take care to avoid pushing the tape into the deep crack. If the angle is crooked and has big pieces broken or cut out of it, you should use flex bead on it.

USING FLEX BEAD ON INSIDE CORNERS

To use flex bead, measure and cut the strip to the necessary length with tin snips. Crease it by folding it in the middle, keeping it as straight as possible. Spread on a lot of joint compound, place your creased flex bead in position, and wipe it down.

USING FLEX BEAD ON OUTSIDE CORNERS

Flex bead on an outside bastard corner is applied in the same way as it is on an inside corner, except that you must pinch the edge and check for straightness. Flex bead twists very easily, and if it isn't straight, it will adversely effect the appearance of the job. Flex bead also needs to be pinched out just enough to allow the joint compound to coat the angle and clear the tape. (See Figure 6–11.)

You might need to use metal corner bead. Corner bead comes only in a 90° angle. Here's how to bend it to the angle you need: Lay the corner bead on the floor, take a piece of one-inch pipe conduit about a foot long, place this inside the corner bead, and tap on it with a hammer until the bead is the desired angle. You

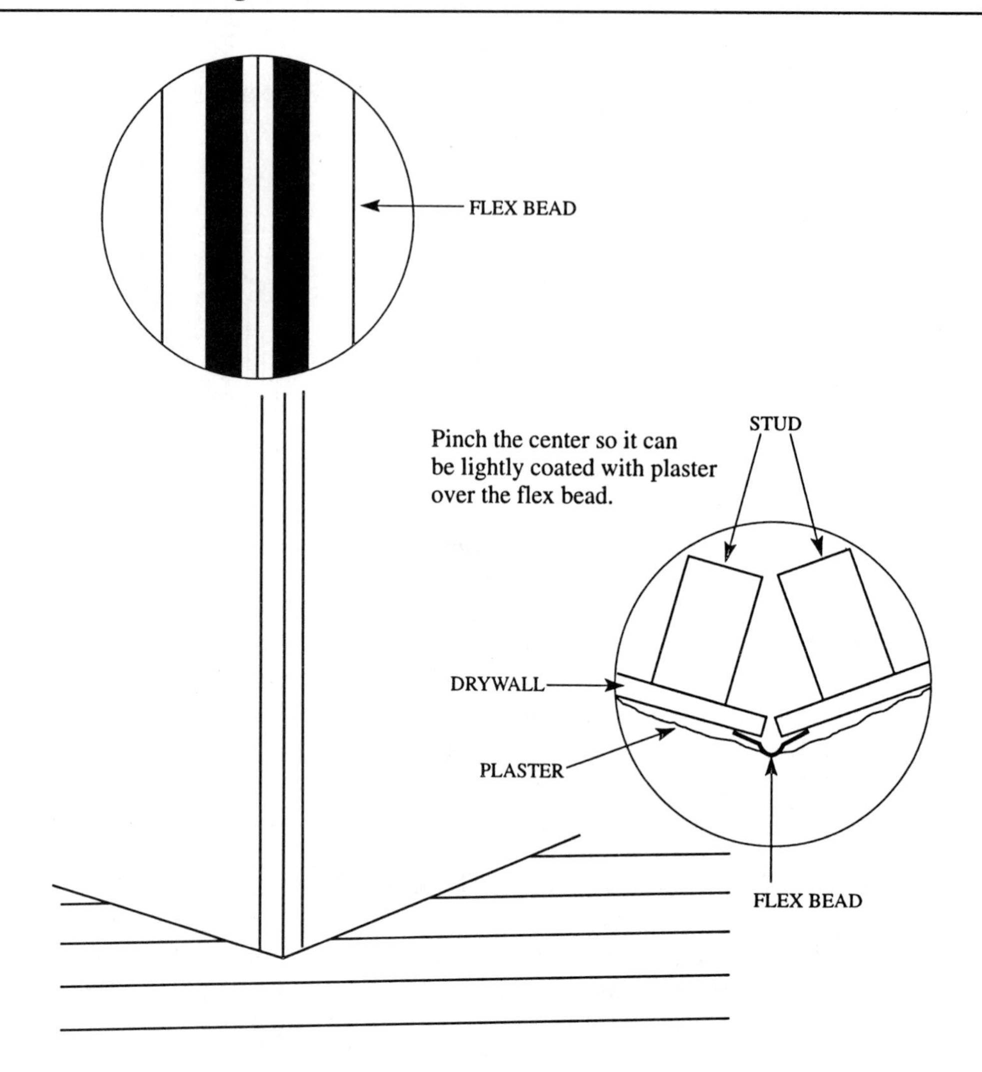

FIGURE 6–11 Flex bead

can use this metal on inside or outside bastard angles and corners. A flexible plastic corner bead is now available. You may find this easier to use.

TAPING RECEPTACLE BOXES

Receptacle boxes are difficult to get exact each time, and they are frequently missed by the hanger. If missed by more than a quarter inch, they should be taped, unless you know that the outlet covers will be big enough to cover the errors. If you don't know which outlet covers will be used, it's better to just go ahead and tape them. If you have to come back later and fix the job, it will cost you. Any broken board should have been repaired already. If the prefilled hole is three inches in diameter or bigger, it must be reinforced. A good-sized hole can be made as strong as the rest of the wall if it is done right. If a hole is bigger than about five inches across, it will need a hot patch.

When taping these holes, overlap the tape, making sure the back of the tape is coated with joint compound even over the hole. Tape at least three inches past the hole on each side to secure it well. Overlap the pieces of tape by at least half of the tape's width. When this is dry, you should be able to press the middle in just a little. When filled with joint compound and coated, it will be strong. If the hole is deep, it may need to be taped again to reinforce the joint compound. If you retape do it in the opposite direction for extra strength. (See Figure 6–12.)

THE HOT PATCH

The hot patch is a method used to fill and smooth holes in the drywall up to about a foot square. For ceilings, though, this method can be used only for small

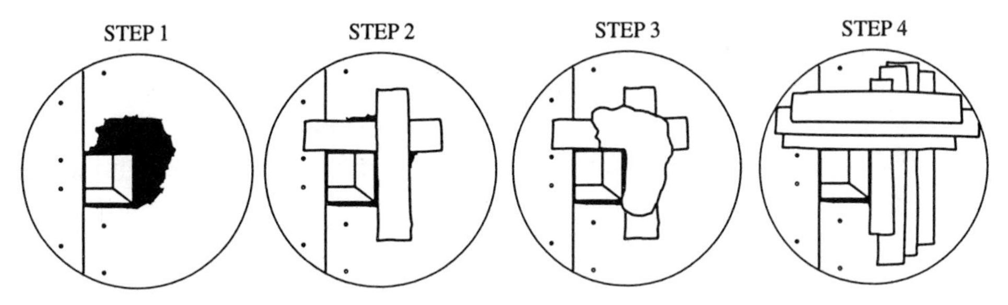

Taping the Receptacle Boxes With a Very Large Hole

STEP 1 Remove the drywall that has been broken.

STEP 2 Put only enough tape across the hole to hold in the joint compound that we are prefilling with.

STEP 3 Press the joint compound in the hole over the tape we have just put down.

STEP 4 Tape the entire problem area by overlapping the tape only half the width of the tape. This will make the area as strong as the regular board.

FIGURE 6–12 Taping receptacle boxes

holes because of the weight of the drywall used for the hot patch. On the walls, any hole bigger than a foot should be cut back to the stud. Then the drywall should be nailed or screwed into place.

To prepare a hot patch, follow this procedure: First, cut the hole out square with a utility knife. This is so you can measure it easily and cut a patch the right size. Cut out a piece of drywall larger than the hole, leaving about two extra inches all the way around. Turn the drywall so you are looking at the backside. Measure from each left and right side, come in two inches, and draw or score a line with your utility knife. Cut along the line and break the drywall along that line. Peel off the drywall, leaving the front paper intact. (See Figure 6–13.)

Now, score two inches in toward center, from the top and bottom, and peel these parts off the front paper. This piece of drywall should fit into the hole, with two inches of paper around it. Put joint compound all around the hole. If you have torn any paper from the front of the drywall, put joint compound under the paper to avoid a blister. Place the patch into the hole and wipe down the paper around the hole. If it is done right, the patch should be flush with the paper, and a light coat of joint compound will cover it neatly.

PLUGGING A HOLE

A hot patch is best because of its strength, but some holes are too big for this method. Sometimes hangers make receptacle boxes (light box holes) by mistake. Then they simply leave the cutout piece of drywall in the hole. To fix this, carefully remove the drywall plug and put a long piece of tape across the hole. Use as many pieces of tape as necessary. To hold the plug from falling through the wall, then push the plug into it. Then wipe down the tape on each side where it is showing, to prevent the plug from falling back into the wall. Now tape the front as if it were a receptacle box hole to cover. (See Figure 6–14.)

TAPING METAL CORNER BEAD AREAS

All corners inside windows and doorways need to be taped, or they will crack as the house settles. Outside corners that corner bead doesn't cover will also crack unless they have been cut correctly (See Chapter 3). Any hole in an outside corner should be taped, or the joint compound will crack and fall out.

You will also find places where the drywall wasn't cut right and the corner bead doesn't overlap. You can tape these places to help hold the metal. If the metal is solidly attached but is bent and doesn't fit tight to the drywall, it can be reinforced by taping. If the corner bead is left without reinforcement, it will move and crack

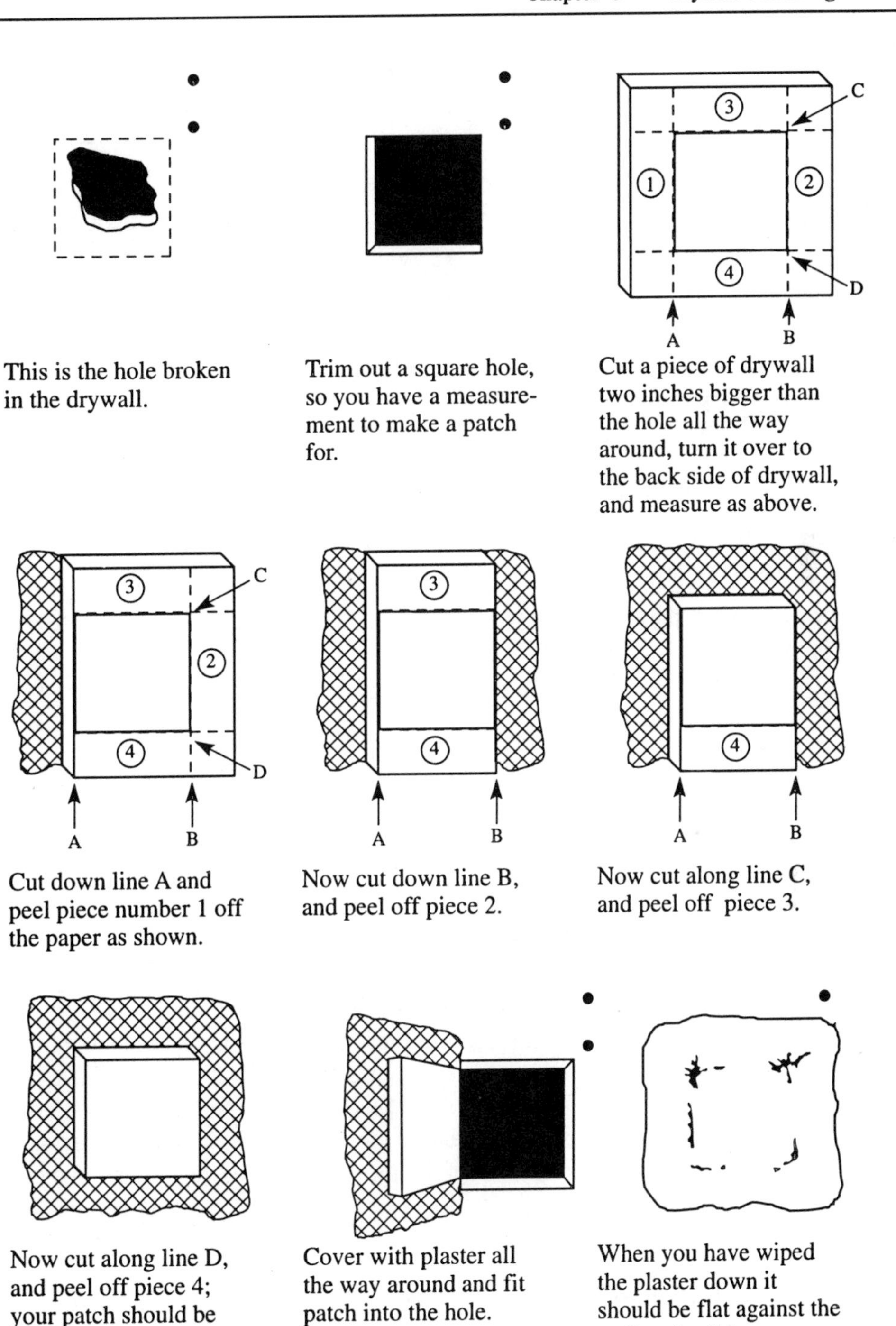

FIGURE 6–13 The hot patch

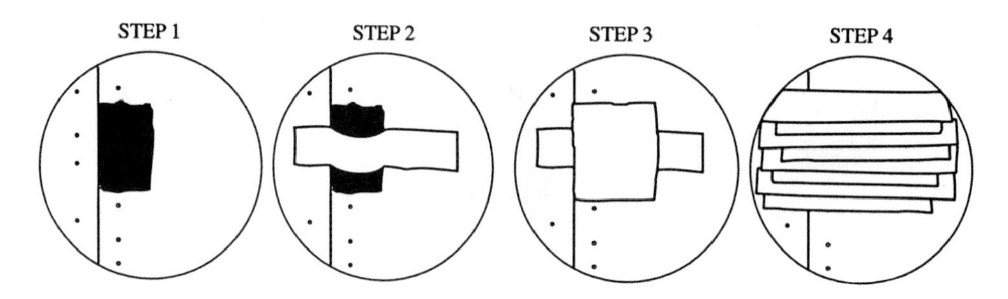

STEP 1 Here's a receptacle box cut out accidentally, in which the hanger has put a plug (piece of drywall).

STEP 2 Remove the plug carefully and put a piece of tape across the hole. Leave it long on each side, and leave slack in the hole part of the plug.

STEP 3 Push the plug back into the hole until it's flush with the wall. Tape the entire hole as if it were a patch.

STEP 4 Overlap the tape by at least half the width of the tape.

FIGURE 6–14 Plugging a hole

the joint compound. Since tape won't hold solidly, this should only be done for small areas. If the corner bead is not on tight or is otherwise faulty, it should be fixed. (See Figure 6–15.)

TAPING AROUND PIPES

Drywall around all pipes should be made airtight. Holes should be prefilled and taped. Round tape, which comes in sizes to fit all pipes, can be bought at a drywall supply store. It saves enough time to be worth buying. If you don't have round tape, you can make some by taking a short piece of tape and tearing out a hole the size of the pipe. If the pipe is big, take a piece of tape as large as necessary and tear out a half circle to fit each side of the pipe. You may need two or three pieces. (See Figure 6–16.)

TAPING AROUND BATHTUBS AND SHOWER UNITS

If the drywall doesn't fit in behind the shower unit, it needs to be taped. Some units have a lip, as shown in Figure 6–17. They should fit so the lip is under (or behind)

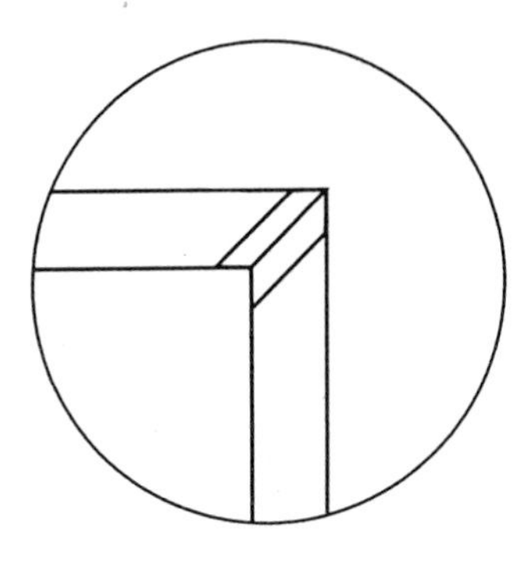

Tape inside windows and doors.

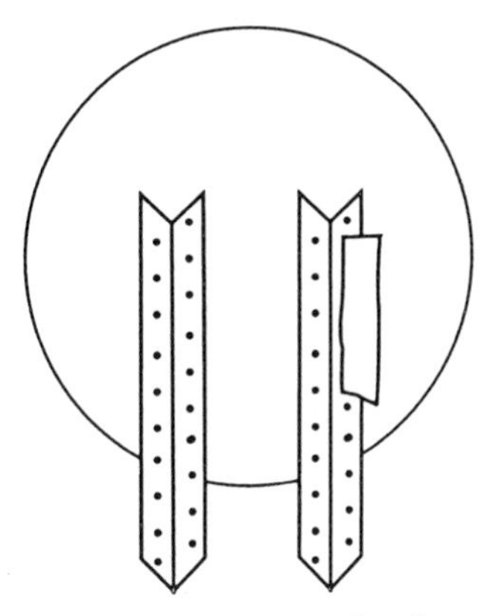

Tape along corner bead where it is needed.

FIGURE 6–15 Taping corner bead

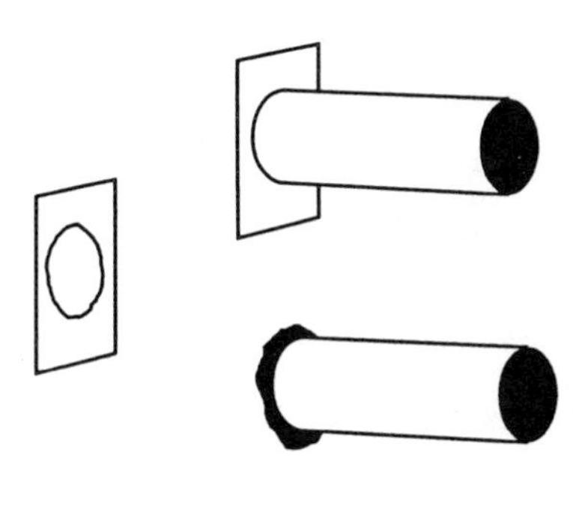

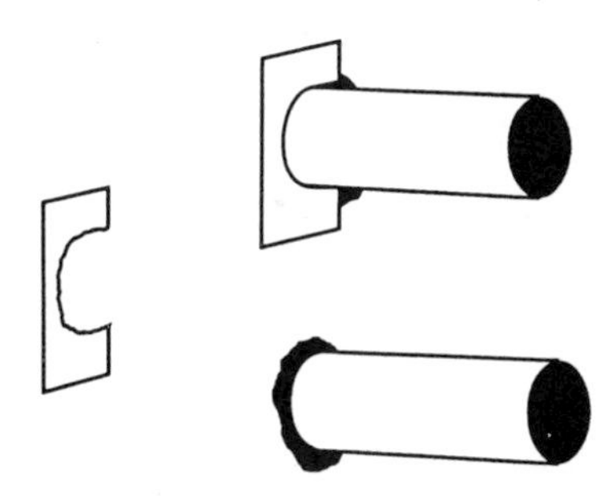

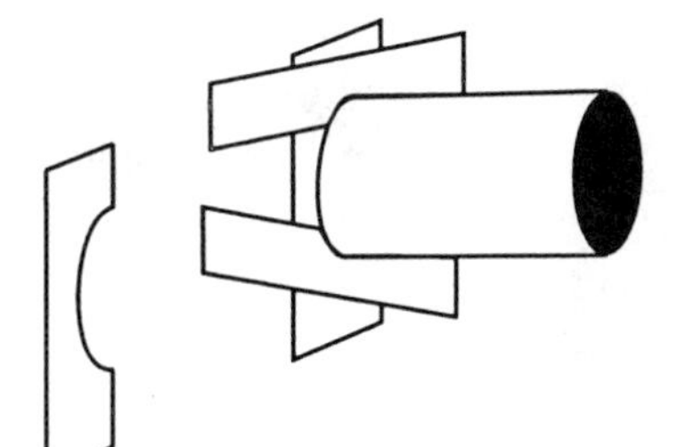

Drywall around pipes should be airtight. The easiest way to accomplish this is to tear the tape to form fit. Using circle tape with adjustable centers is worth the extra money and the time saved.

FIGURE 6–16 Taping around pipes

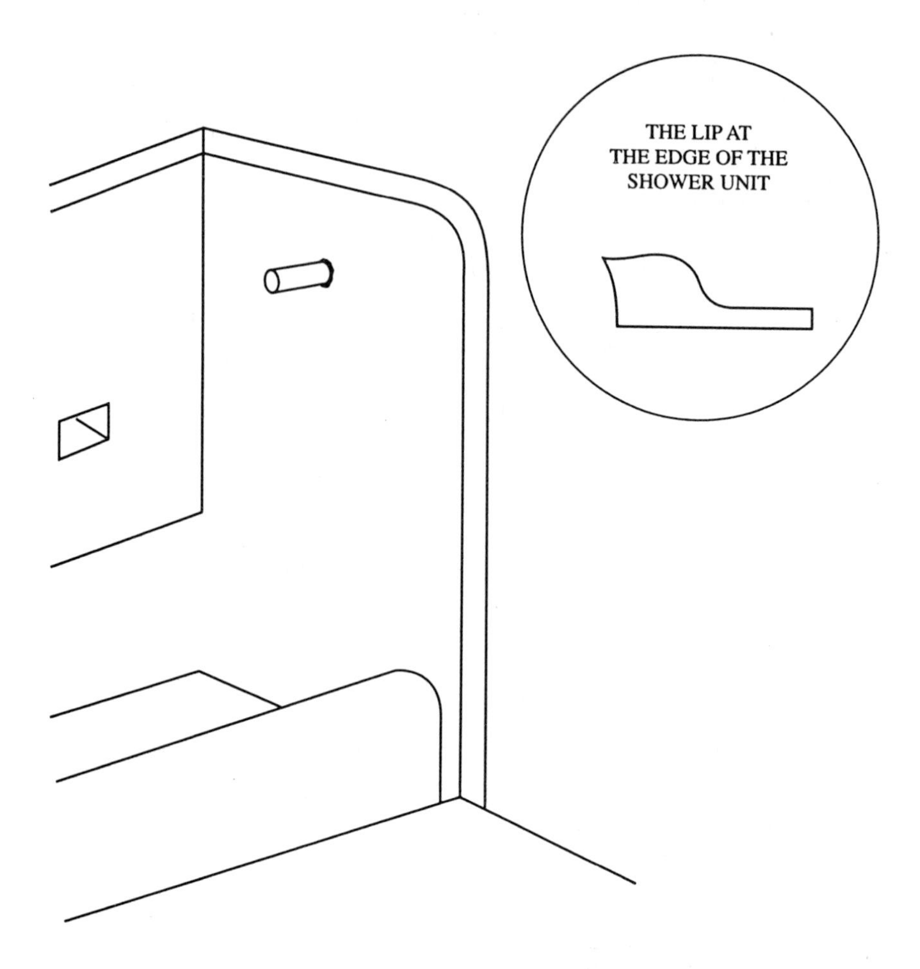

FIGURE 6–17 Taping a shower unit

the drywall, but sometimes it will be on top (in front) of the drywall. In any case, it needs to be filled and taped in airtight to the bathtub or shower unit.

CRACKS IN BOARD

Sometimes drywall gets cracked on the back as it's hung. Though the paper on the front side might not be broken or twisted, this area needs to be tapped. It won't finish properly if you merely coat it over.

NAILS AND SCREWS

For covering nail and screw holes, a seven- or eight-inch knife is better than a four-, five-, or six-inch one. The smaller knives are too stiff and will take off too much joint compound as you're covering the holes. The seven- and eight-inch knives are more limber and will leave more joint compound without creating an edge.

When taping a house, you should hammer all nails in if they are sticking out past the board. You should also coat all nails when taping. If the paper is broken where a nail or screw missed the stud and was pulled out, it should be coated now and hammered later. After it is coated with joint compound it stays in better, so hammer the paper the second time around. Spotting nails takes some practice. All two or three sets of nails should be coated with two strokes of the knife.

Hold the knife vertically with the blade facing you (see Figure 6–18). Put joint compound on the top corner of the knife. Place the knife at the bottom of the first set of nails and spread upward, keeping pressure on the bottom edge of the knife.

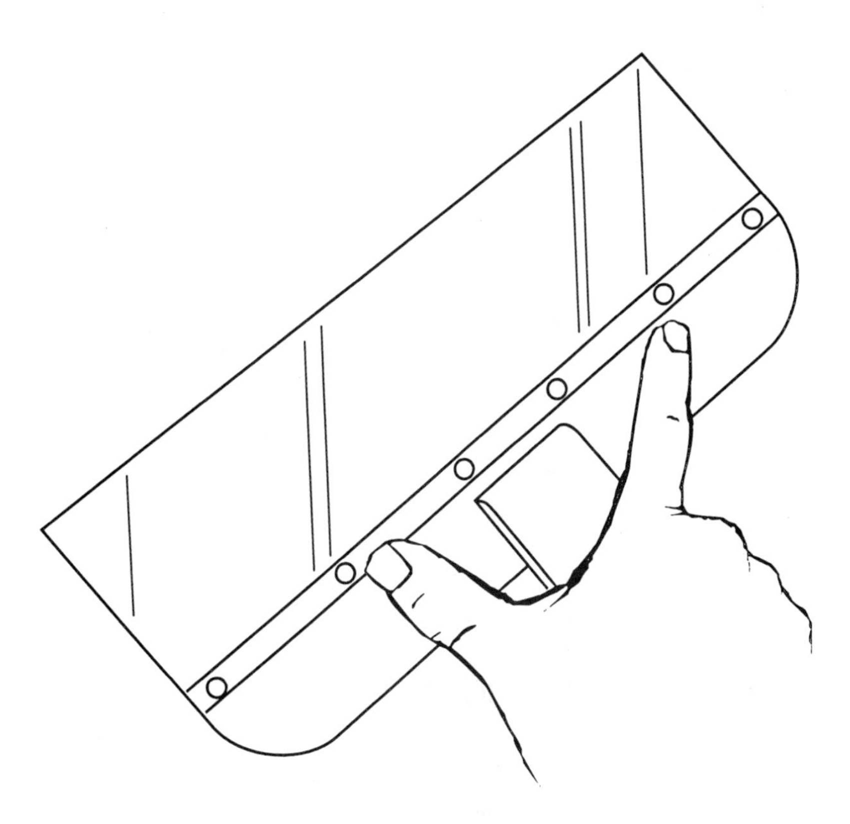

FIGURE 6–18 For maximum control, hold a seven- or eight-inch knife in this way.

When you reach the top, move the knife straight to one side, pulling it away from the joint compound, thus cleaning the joint compound from the edge of the blade. Now place the knife at the top of the joint compound you have just spread and pull straight down to remove any excess. In this way, you coat two or three sets of nails in one smooth action (see Figure 6–19).

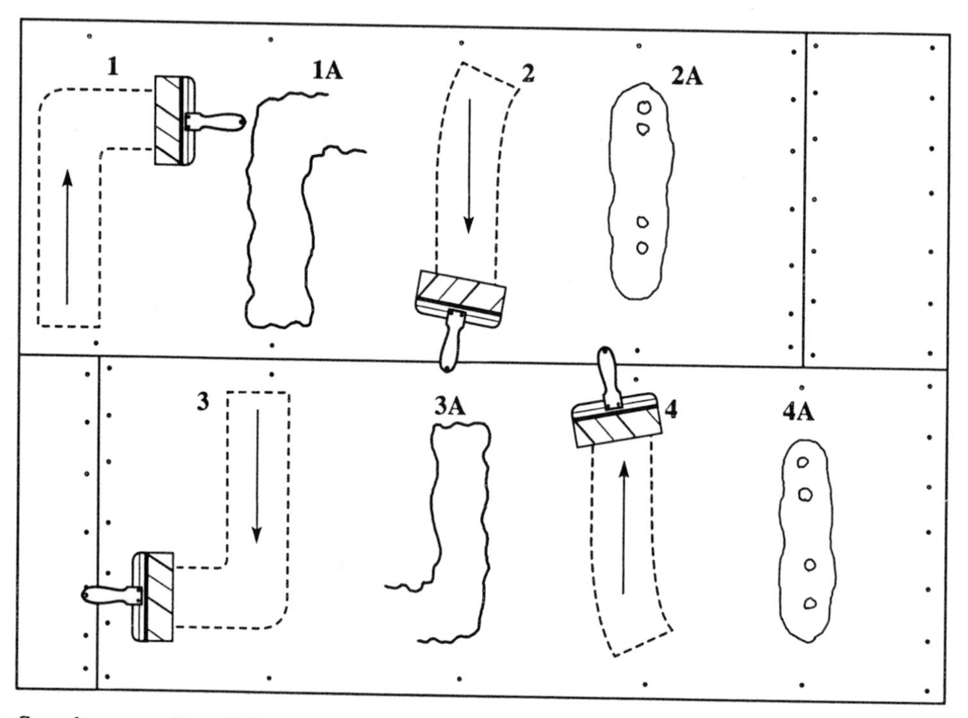

Step 1	Spread the knife with joint compound upward.
Step 1A	Joint compound is now spread over the nail area. Bring the knife off to the side, removing any excess joint compound from the knife.
Step 2	On the return trip, wipe joint compound from the wall.
Step 2A	You will now be able to see the nail holes filled with joint compound and no edges of joint compound on the wall.
Step 3	For the lower set of nails, spread the joint compound down the wall as shown.
Step 3A	You now have a layer of joint compound spread over the lower set of nails.
Step 4	With the return stroke, wipe joint compound from the wall.
Step 4A	Filled nail holes are visible.

FIGURE 6–19 Coating nails and screws in drywall

THE FIRST COAT

Applying the first coat is often called "bedding in." Some people consider taping the first coat, but in this book the first layer of joint compound placed over the tape will be called the first coat.

There are several ways to coat. The type of job you are doing will determine the best method. Time studies of the different ways to finish drywall have revealed the most efficient and effective methods.

A house that will have textured ceiling and walls needs only two coats. Quick set joint compound is a good choice for the first coat because it doesn't shrink.

A house that will have smooth walls needs three coats over bad butts and problem flats. The last coat is a very thin skim coat. Three coats can be done as fast as two because you don't have to spend time making the first two neat. Remember that the third coat will smooth any scratches or lines your knife might leave. If you have to build up a lot of joint compound and need to leave an edge, you still have two coats left to smooth it out.

A few terms need to be explained. These common practices should become habits.

FEATHER EDGE

When you spread joint compound over a joint or other area, run the knife along the edge of the joint compound, putting pressure on the *outside* edge of the joint compound. This blends the joint compound into the drywall without leaving a raised edge. This procedure is called *feather edge.*

BUILDING STRIP

A building strip is a strip of joint compound the width of the knife and feather edged on each side. It is useful for building a troublesome joint out farther.

THINGS TO WATCH FOR

Watch for ripples! Anytime you are spreading large amounts of joint compound, you will get ripples. They occur when you apply uneven pressure or tilt the knife slightly as you spread and work the joint compound. Many butt joints or trouble areas that require a lot of joint compound should be coated sideways for the third coat. Even if you think the joint is smooth, try this. You will see what I'm talking about. The area will show up like an X-ray as the joint compound begins to dry.

When coating butt joints, spread joint compound up to and across the adjacent flat joints, creating an overlapping effect.

When you are laying the first coat, the consistency of your joint compound should be as thick as possible. This minimizes shrinkage. (Less water, less shrinkage.)

If you are using quick set, keep it neat because it is difficult to sand. Quick set doesn't shrink, so when you are coating with it, don't build up the joints any more than necessary.

When using joint compound, build a little extra to allow for shrinkage. Some new joint compound products have very little shrinkage, so know the products you are using.

Where a flat joint meets an angle, coat the flat joint all the way into the center of the angle. You will still have to fill the beveled edge to the end of the wall. If the joint compound is wet when you coat the angle, cross right over the flat joint. Use a four-inch knife for the first coat and a five- or six-inch knife for the second coat. This way, the coats will overlap to the flat joint and fill completely. If you're coating the angle only once, be sure to fill it sufficiently.

For flat's and butt's first coat, use an eight-, ten-, or twelve-inch knife. For residential work with good hanging and tight joints, an eight-inch knife is fine. In commercial work with metal framing, the wider the joint the better, so a ten- or twelve-inch knife is recommended. If you are working for someone else, he or she might prefer a particular joint. Some architects, for example, will settle for nothing but a wide joint.

FIRST COATING BAD BUTT JOINTS

Butt joints are always coated first because they need extra drying time. Two basic methods are used to build a butt joint. Every butt is different. If you are just learning to be a finisher, you might wish to carry a yardstick with you. If you put the yardstick across the joint, you can see where the joint needs to be built up.

A bad joint often has a high side and a low side. Build it in from the high side, and then bring it in gradually to the low side. How far out you build it depends entirely on how bad the joint is. The joint might require a lot of build up to camouflage the bulge. If the joint comes in sharp, it will have a shadow. (See Figure 6–20.)

A twelve-inch knife is best for coating bad butt joints. Fill the knife with joint compound and start at the bottom of the joint with the edge of the knife running along the tape. Spread the joint compound as evenly as possible. Now spread the joint compound on the other side of the tape. Feather edge along the outside on the high side (just along the outside edge of the joint compound). With the knife laid down, smooth out the high side of the butt, leaving just enough joint compound to cover the drywall and the tape. Now feather edge the low side of the joint compound. Lay the knife down, smoothing from one end of joint compound to the other. If

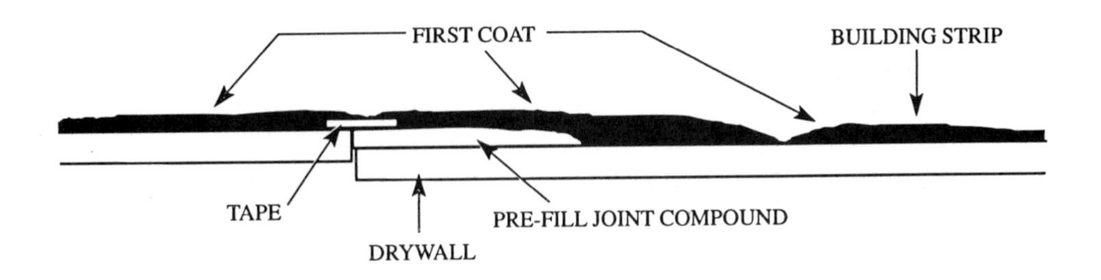

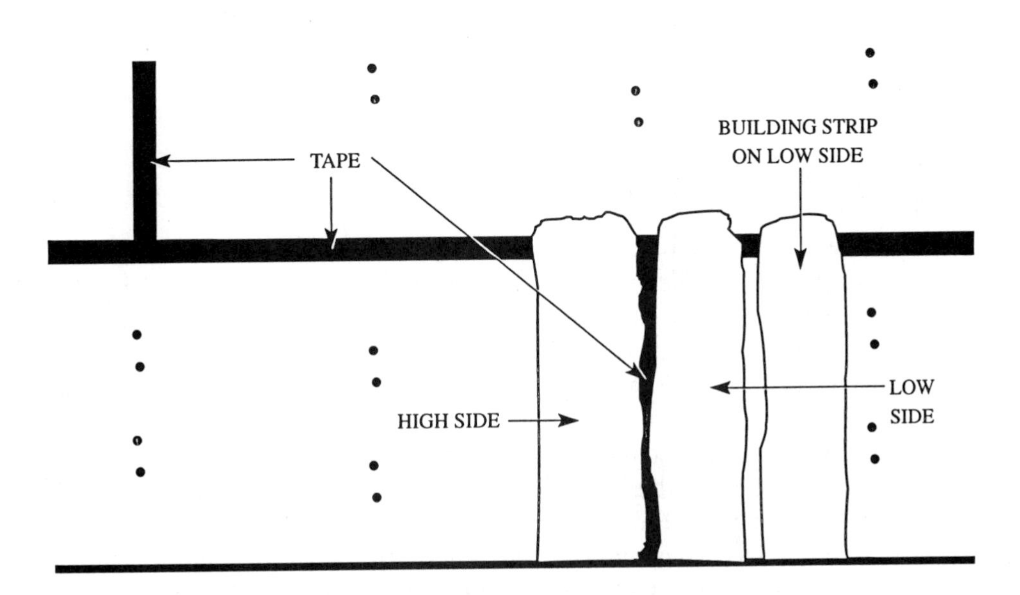

FIGURE 6–20 Applying the first coat to bad butt joints

you get the joint built right but leave an edge of joint compound along the side, don't worry about it. You can always cover it up with the second and third coats.

BUILDING STRIPS

If you have a really bad butt joint that needs more than twelve inches to build it out, you may have to use building strips to build it out farther. If so, spread joint compound along the side of the joint just coated. Feather edge on both sides and smooth it down the middle. Make as many of these building strips as necessary. The second coat will be built from the high spot of each strip. This will fill in the middle and make it flat. You can use building strips to build any wall any distance.

FIRST COATING HEADERS

Headers are short butt joints over doorways and windows. When coating a header, extend the joint right into the center of the angle along the ceiling. If the door frames are already on, it's troublesome to work around them, but if you take the time to keep the door frame clean, you will save time later. If you have a butt or header to coat over a framed door, you will coat the header in a horizontal direction; later, you might need to coat downward from the top corner.

FIRST COATING GOOD BUTT JOINTS

Because a good butt joint leaves the tape sitting above the board, it should be built up on each side of the tape. This spreads out the joint and makes it less noticeable. If a joint is built up too much, it will cast a shadow on one or both sides of the tape and be very noticeable. It's impossible to change the fact that the wall is built out around a joint, but it is possible to camouflage this buildup by keeping it as thin as possible.

Fill the knife with joint compound. Spread from one end of the tape to the other, keeping the edge of the knife along the tape. Now feather edge both sides of the joint compound. Lay the knife down and smooth the joint compound (The highest point of the joint compound should be just a little higher than the tape. It's best if the tape is covered slightly.) Now spread the other side. Feather edge only the outside and smooth it down. If the joint is built right but the tape is showing, don't worry—it will cover next time. If it's not built high enough, the tape will be difficult to cover with the second coat. (See Figure 6–21.)

JOINT COMPOUND SPREADING TECHNIQUES

Metal on the ends of walls is coated next because it requires a lot of joint compound and takes a long time to dry.

It's best to learn with an eight-inch knife. Use the joint compound straight from the box or mixed with a small amount of water. The less water you use, the less shrinkage you will get. The object of coating metal is to produce a square corner. If the metal isn't straight, you must build it straight with the joint compound. Sometimes the metal has a bow in it and needs to be built out around the bow.

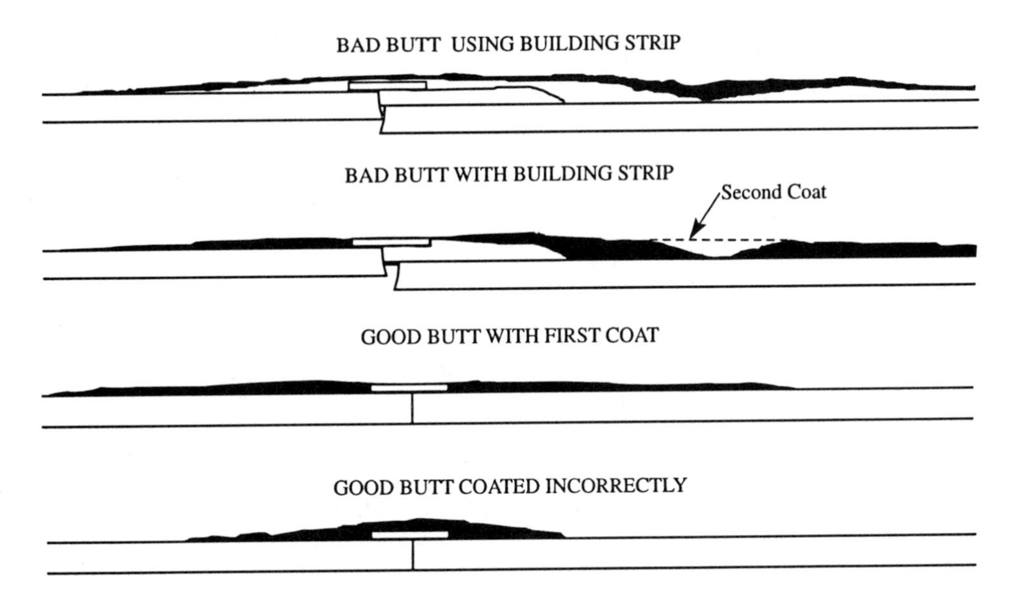

FIGURE 6–21 Coating butt joints

Almost all outside corners of windows and doors need to be built out so they have a square surface.

Most people coat metal a knife's-length at a time across the metal. Then they spread it out by running the knife straight down the metal. This procedure gives the inside of the metal too little joint compound and the outside too much. It's also a slow and difficult method.

Metal should be coated loosely. Too much pressure on a long knife bends it and gives an unsquare coat. Here's the best way to coat metal. Take a knife-full of joint compound and slap it across the width of the metal, scraping the joint compound onto the metal. Now you have a whole knife-full of joint compound at the top of the coating area. Place your knife above this joint compound and spread it down the metal, keeping pressure on the outside of the knife. As you pull downward, keep the knife's outside edge slightly in front, pushing the joint compound to the center where it is needed. Now take another knife-full of joint compound and slap it on the drywall about halfway down the drywall. As you bend down, spread the joint compound until you reach the bottom of the wall. When you get close to the floor, you will still have a lot of joint compound on the knife. Scrape the remaining joint compound off on the metal. Quickly turn the knife around and spread the joint compound evenly up to meet the joint compound just spread on the top half of the metal. The knife should be held in the same manner, with pressure on the outside and the outside edge ahead of the inside edge pushing the joint compound to the inside where it is needed. Now the entire stick of metal is filled with joint compound. Feather edge along the entire length of joint compound along the outside edge, then smooth the joint compound over by laying the knife down and running it over the surface.

COATING METAL ENDS AND DOORWAYS

When coating a doorway or other area with more than one side, spread joint compound on two adjoining sides before smoothing it down on the first side. Otherwise, you will create problems on the first side when you're spreading joint compound on the second side. When coating metal, slide a knife along the edge of the metal to take off excess joint compound. Don't use the blade of the knife because this procedure will dull or nick it. (See Figure 6–22.)

METAL WRAPPED WINDOWS

A six-inch knife is best for the inside of the window, and a ten- or twelve-inch one for the outside, as joint compound usually needs to be built around the corners.

Spread joint compound as shown in Figure 6–23, step 1. Fill areas 1, 2, 3, and 4 with joint compound, feather edge the outer side of the joint compound, holding pressure on the outside edge of the knife. Smooth the joint compound down from area 1A to area 2A by pulling the knife across the top. Keep pressure on the outside of the knife for support. Don't rest the other side of the knife against the metal. This is a difficult procedure, so when you're learning, it's best not to pull around the corners. Just pull straight across, as shown in step 2. (If you go around the corner, you must change pressure and direction, and this will adversely affect your control.) Now, place the knife above the top of the joint compound on the side of the window. Using the same technique, pull the knife from the top down the side of the window, as shown in step 3. The corners 1A and 2A in the picture almost always need to be built up. (Note that if the knife is resting against the metal edge, it will leave a dent where it goes from one piece of metal to the other.) Make sure the knife floats over these corners.

Now go back with a six-inch knife and smooth down the inside of the window. Hold the knife down so it will leave as much joint compound as possible. If you have metal inside the windows against the glass, do not cover the strip—it will only crack later. In a case like this, coat up to the metal or plastic sweat strip (see L bead, Chapter 5). If there is no sweat strip against the window and the drywall board doesn't fit tight against the window, it should be taped close enough so it can be caulked.

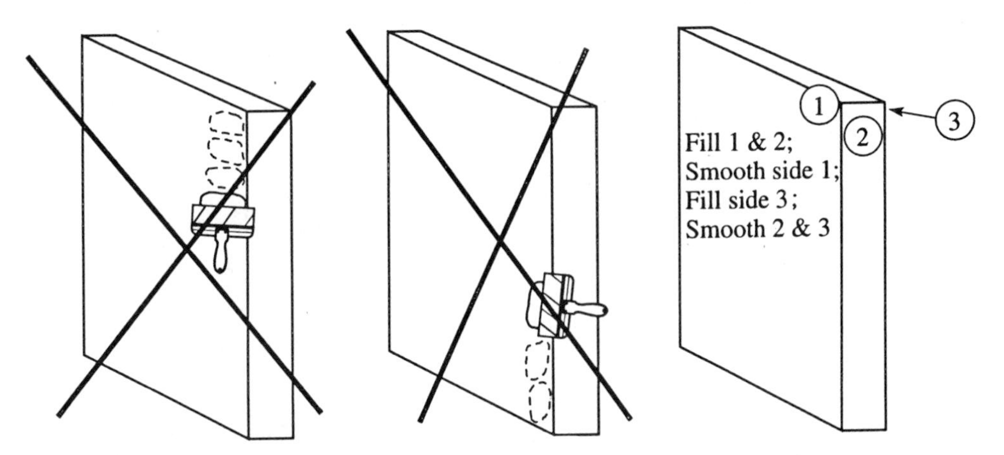

Do not apply joint compound by spreading it directly down the metal or one knife-full at a time. This is inefficient and time-consuming. Instead, go half way down from the top, then from the bottom up, as shown below.

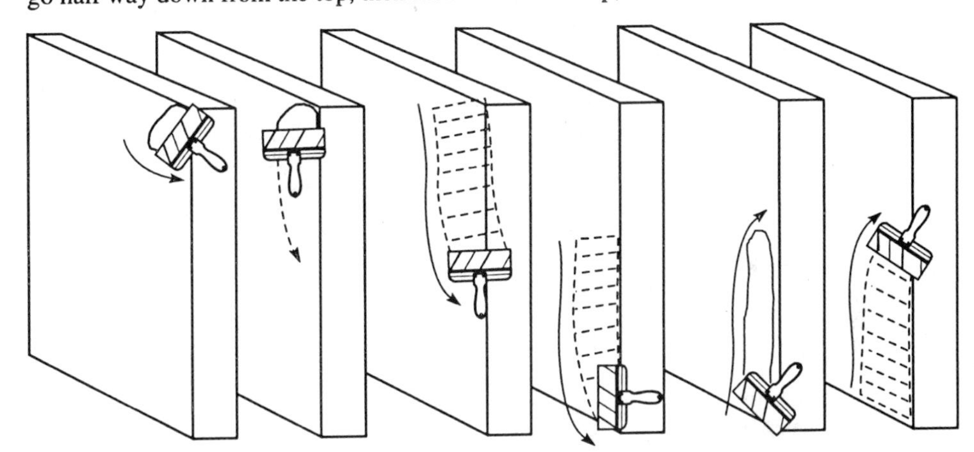

FIGURE 6–22 Applying joint compound to metal on wall ends

Some windows are not metaled all the way around, so they can have a sill attached. When coating the inside, coat all the way to the bottom of the sides. Make the corners square, neat, and clean of joint compound. Now continue at step 4. Fill sides 5 and 6. Feather edge and smooth down, as shown in step 5. If there is no windowsill, proceed to the bottom side. If there is a windowsill, proceed as in the center bottom picture. Make sure you blend in the bottom corner.

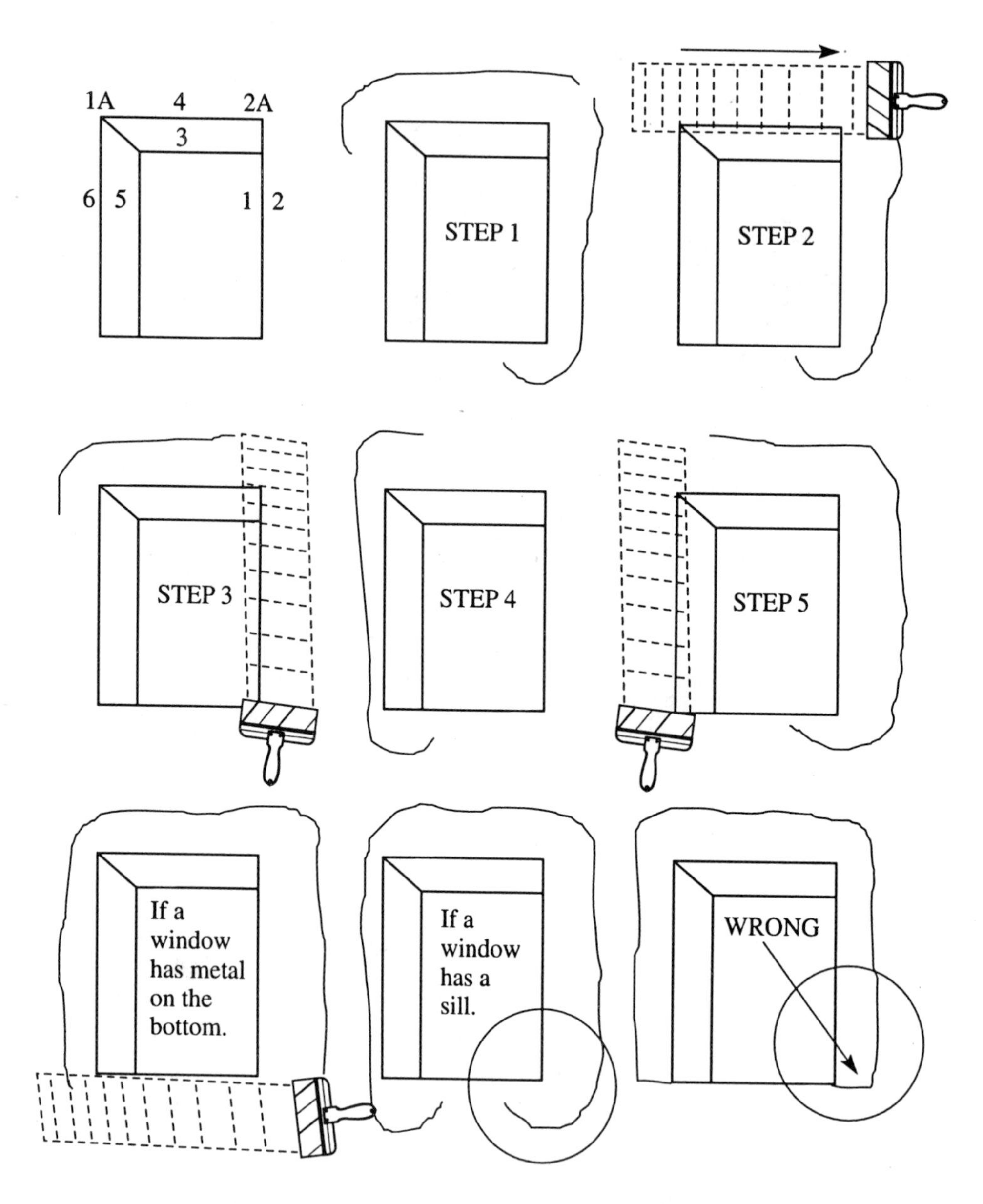

FIGURE 6–23 Detail of metal wrapped windows

Sometimes the metal is bowed between nails. If the metal isn't loose but still shows after being coated, try coating it more loosely. Fill with more joint compound, feather edge, and smooth very lightly. Lay the knife down and float over it.

If you are having difficulty learning to build, take a knife, put joint compound evenly across the blade, and lightly cover the bad spot. Use the edge of the metal to brace the knife so you don't dig into the fresh joint compound. This will look rough, but it's more important to get this area covered. You can sand off the roughness later, before you apply the second coat. If the metal is loose, it will have to be taped and then covered.

FUR DOWNS IN KITCHENS AND BATHROOMS

It is very hard to build fur down corners straight and square. These corners will test your hand control. Fill all three sides and about two feet along the side of the end of the fur down with joint compound (see Figure 6–24). Feather edge all outside edges first. Now, beginning with side 2, start at the wall to get the feel of the proper knife angle. Pull the knife from the wall and float it past the corner. Keep the knife

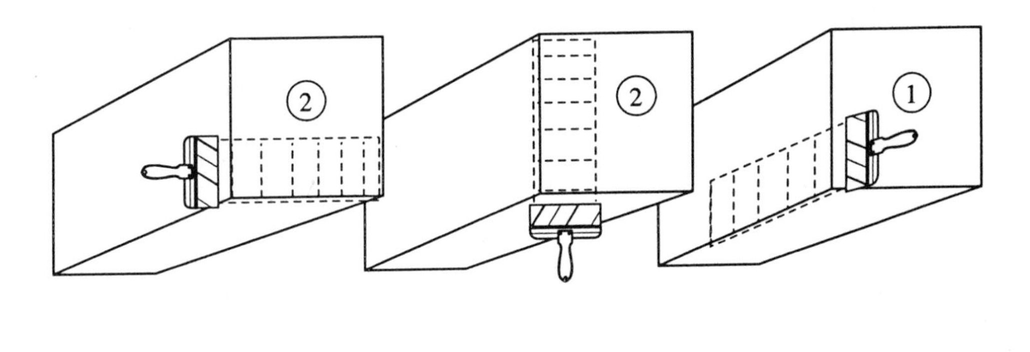

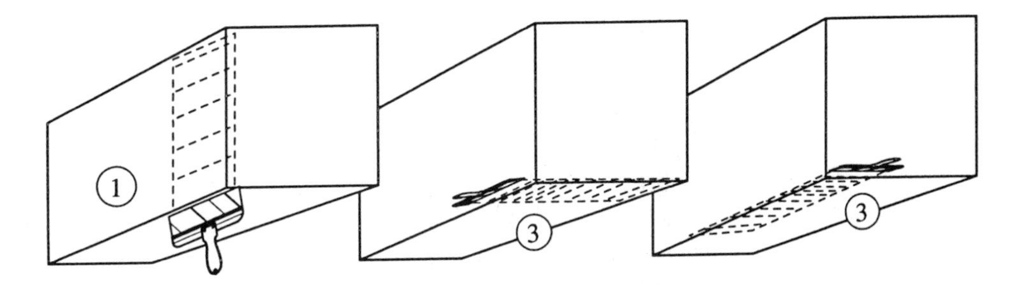

FIGURE 6–24 Floating and hand control procedure for kitchen or bathroom fur downs

resting on the metal, and avoid cutting into the joint compound at the corner. Now come down across the same corner, holding the knife against the metal to steady it. Float the knife over the metal. Fill the corner, making it square. Now start on side 1. Pull the knife along the bottom toward the corner. Holding pressure against the metal, pull the knife past the corner, floating on top of the joint compound at the corner. Then float from the top across the corner in the same way as you did side 2. Now do side 3 in the same manner.

FIRST COATING FLAT JOINTS

Flats are the easiest joints to finish. Two coats on a flat joint will make only a small line down the middle—is the worst. (You get this only when you coat over the tape wet.)

Use the recess to make a flat wall. Coat right across the recess. A good flat joint, taped correctly, should need a joint no more than six inches across to be perfectly flat. None of the joints will be perfect, though, so use a ten-inch knife to coat them. Spread the joint compound over the joint about three feet or as far as a knife-full of joint compound will go. Feather edge each side, and then lay the knife down and smooth it down. You shouldn't be leaving any joint compound anywhere but in the recess. The knife should be touching the board on each side of the recess. By the time you're done, you should see only six or seven inches of solid joint compound.

Spread joint compound as far as you can along the flat joint. (See Figure 6–25.) Clean both sides of the knife. Feather edge the top side going in one direction. When coming back, feather edge the bottom side. You'll have joint compound on the other side of the knife, so flip it over to the clean side and lay it down to smooth the center. If you always feather edge with one side of your knife and smooth with the other, your knife will develop a bow, which will make your work easier.

TWISTED JOINTS

In commercial work where the walls are framed with metal studs, you'll find a lot of bad flat joints (see Figure 6–26.), usually caused either by the hangers or by poor materials. Even though the joint is perfectly flat from recess to recess, the wall changes direction at the side of the recess. A yardstick placed across the joint will show that these joints need to be rounded out. It's impossible to make a flat joint where the wall comes to a point, so it needs to be camouflaged to look flat. This type of wall casts a shadow. If you can catch this type of joint while the job is being hung, check to see if the hangers are hanging from the right direction of the stud. Also check to see that the studs are up to specifications. Problems occur more often

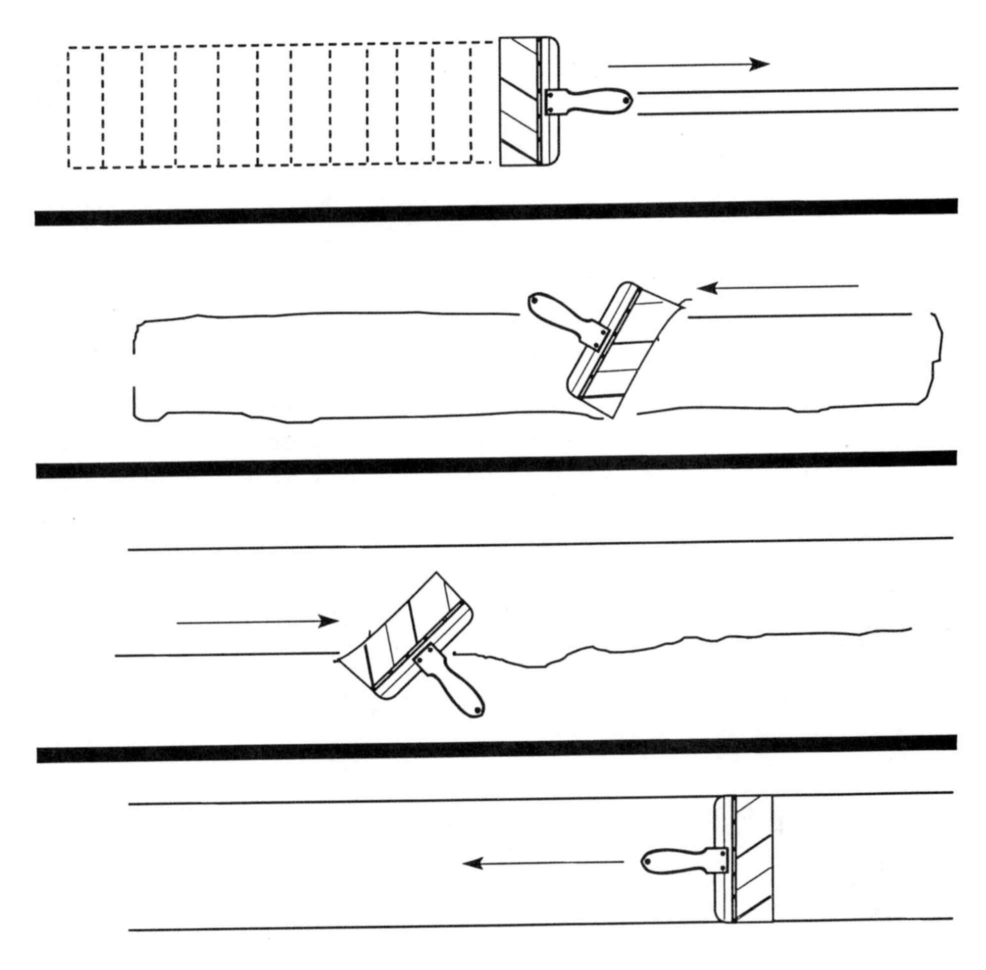

FIGURE 6–25 First coat on flat joints

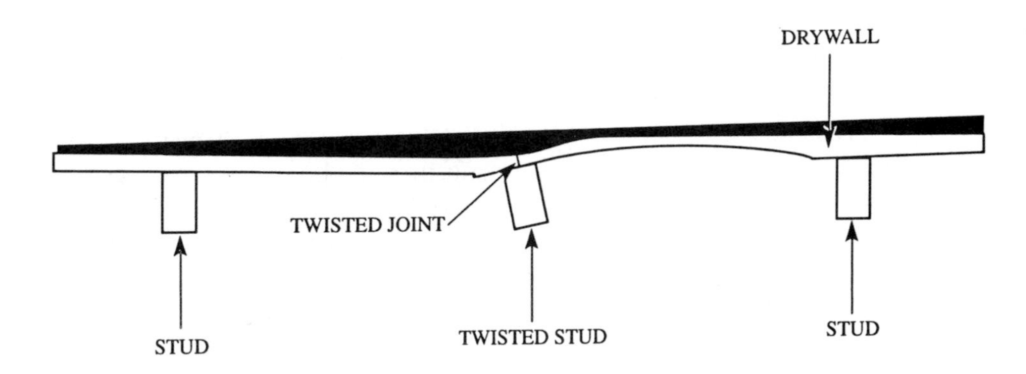

FIGURE 6–26 Twisted joint cross section

with metal studs. Metal studs twist easily if they are made of low-gauge materials. For a twisted metal stud, you need to coat around the high recessed edge.

If you can't avoid the problem at the hanging stage, the joint must be built out, just like a bad butt joint. Keep in mind that the low side gets built up to meet the high side. If these places are extremely uneven, build them out with building strips just like the butt joint. The high point will be one side of the recess (Figure 6–26).

COATING ACROSS WET BUTT JOINTS

Often, the joint compound on a butt joint will still be wet when you are ready to first coat the flats. If so, spread joint compound right across the wet butt joint, trying to spread evenly and not leave globs on the wet part. Feather edge, except across the wet joint compound. Skip that part. Lay your knife down and smooth the joint compound across the joint, putting pressure on the opposite side of the knife when crossing the butt joint. If you leave a small ridge but it is built right, leave it. You can take care of the ridge later, but you can't build later without wasting time and causing trouble.

COATING BASTARD ANGLES

At this point, bastard angles should have some sort of metal edge tape on them. Coat loosely and don't put pressure on the edge of the paper because it will skin up, leaving a rough edge. If you have taped the flex bead properly, it will be easy to coat. Watch this edge when sanding or scraping it after coating.

COATING INSIDE ANGLES ONE SIDE AT A TIME

Two different procedures are used for coating angles: coating one side at a time perfectly, so it needs only one coat, or coating both sides at once and coating them twice. Really good finishers can coat both sides at once with only one coat.

Most finishers coat one side at a time, usually with a six-inch knife. The goal of this method is to coat one side perfectly smooth, and then go back after that dries and coat the adjacent side. The angle has to be coated perfectly smooth, because it takes too much time to dry two coats (unless you're using quick set.)

Here's the procedure: First, spread joint compound on one side of the angle. Then feather edge down the outside. Lay the knife down, and very carefully pull it down the angle. When this side is the way you want it, clean the opposite side of any excess joint compound. When the first side (especially the center) is dry, lay the knife against the opposite side and pull joint compound down it. Take care not to scrape the first side. Then feather edge and smooth down, the same as the first side.

This procedure is by far the easiest way for a beginner to turn out a neat angle—but it is more time consuming than coating both sides at once.

COATING BOTH SIDES OF AN ANGLE AT ONCE

This procedure is most effective if you use thick joint compound and spread it thin. If you put on a heavy coat, you will create a line down the center of the angle, which will call for another coat. You don't need to cover the tape completely in the corner: if the tape has been put on correctly, it will look fine by the time it is painted. To ensure that your angles are square, use a four-inch knife, it allows the best control and accuracy.

Here's the procedure: First, spread joint compound on both sides of the angle. Feather edge both outside edges. Then hold your knife at a 90° angle from the wall and pull down the first side, resting the knife against the opposite side. This will smooth the first side and take off about ¼ inch of joint compound from the center of the second side, preventing build-up in the center and keeping the angle clean and neat. When you smooth the joint compound on the second side, hold the knife at a 45° angle (or less) and at an outward slant (point your guide finger into the center). This way, only one corner of the knife will be working the center. As you pull the knife down the angle, put pressure on the inside corner, forcing the joint compound to become smooth in the center and pushing the excess outward. (See Figure 6–27.)

Work to perfect your technique so you don't need any feather edging at all and you can produce excellent angles with only one coat. It pays to make a habit of skimming the right side first with the first coat, and the left side first with the second coat. This way, any center line is eliminated.

PROBLEM AREAS IN INSIDE ANGLES

It is common for two pieces of corner drywall not to fit tightly. Drywall is hung with a gap between boards to allow for house movement and settling. However, some cracks are larger than they should be. These should have been prefilled before taping, but if they still need work, they can be filled and taped a second time. If the crack is really wide, it can be flat taped. (If you're in a hurry, use quick set.)

Here's the procedure: Spread joint compound on both sides and feather edge each outside edge. Smooth the good side first, holding the knife out at a 90° angle from the wall. This way, the side of the knife is fairly straight and will keep the knife from cutting into the deep crack and pulling the joint compound out. When smoothing

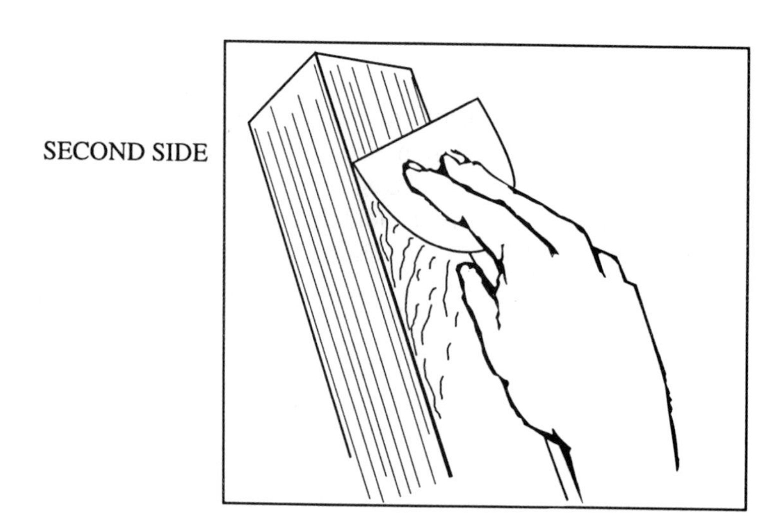

FIGURE 6–27 Knife positioning for inside angles

the second side (the deep crack), lay the knife down and use the corner of the knife to smooth it out. Take care not to dig into the center and pull out any joint compound—stay on the solid drywall. This side will probably have to be coated again when the joint compound shrinks.

FIRST COATING TOP ANGLES

A top angle is the corner that touches with the ceiling. In this angle, butts and angles run into one another. Coat each butt all the way to the center of the angle. When coating these angles, you can coat right across partially set joint compound. If you leave a knife mark across the joint, don't worry about it. If you use a four-inch knife on the first coat and a six-inch knife on the second coat, the knife will overlap this area, filling the low spot.

FIRST COATING 45° ANGLES

Coat one side of a 45° angle at a time unless it is a very good angle. If a weaving in it makes it crooked, build with your twelve-inch knife sideways. Build it right with this first coat. You will need to use the second coat for smoothing it out. If the angle is really crooked, you may need to put flex bead on it.

FIRST COATING ELECTRICAL OUTLETS (LIGHT BOXES)

Electrical outlet holes tend to be uneven, with a high and a low side. They need to be coated in two directions. Get into the habit of coating them in one direction for the first coat and then in the opposite direction for the second coat. For example, first coat horizontally, and second coat vertically.

Use a twelve-inch knife, spreading joint compound completely across the outlet. If wires are sticking out, roll them up and push them inside so your knife will float across it. Feather edge each side and smooth over, making it no thicker than necessary. The joint compound will fall out of the hole when it dries, so don't worry about covering it.

FIRST COATING PIPES

Use a five- or six-inch knife and spread joint compound around the pipe, feather edging and smoothing around it.

FIRST COATING AROUND BATHTUBS

Spread joint compound on with a four-, five-, or six-inch knife; feather edge and smooth by laying the knife down.

FIRST COATING NAILS

When the house was taped, all the nails should have been hammered and coated once. Torn paper should also have been coated. Paper stays in after being coated

FIGURE 6–28 Knife position for coating nails

with joint compound, so now you need to take a hammer through the house and tap in any paper that is torn or sticking out. Hammer in any nails that might have been overlooked. Don't hammer any deeper than is necessary to get below the surface of the board. Now coat the nails again, using one stroke across and one back. If you coat each set of nails separately you will be making six strokes. Save yourself some time! (For more details about this procedure, see also Figure 6–19.)

Preparation for the Second Coat

When you applied the first coat, you put on a thick layer of joint compound. That thick layer will shrink, crack, and harden, making the edges stick up and catch your knife when you are applying the second coat. This will create lines of joint compound that will have to be sanded out later. Avoid this problem by sanding off those edges before you begin applying the second coat. You are sanding not for smoothness but to get anything off that might catch your knife. You also want to remove the small hard pieces of leftover joint compound that will break off and cause streaks in later coats.

SANDING BUTTS

Just smooth off the top edges of butt joints. Then run over lightly to remove any pieces that are sticking up.

SANDING METAL

Metal needs more sanding than anything else. Be sure to clean off the corner edges of the metal; these pieces will fall off in the joint compound when second coating.

SANDING INSIDES OF WINDOWS

Push the sander against the insides of windows to break off any joint compound pieces that are sticking out. Also, clean the inside corners well: these areas really need to be square. Any joint compound left in these corners will cause ugly drag streaks. Look for ridges where the knife left off.

SANDING FLATS

Run the sander across flat joints, and sand down ridges where the knife leaves off.

SANDING ANGLES

It usually is not necessary to sand angles unless they have been coated with thick joint compound or if the inside has globs of joint compound. Angles of 45° need to be sanded very carefully. Don't sand the edge where flex bead was used. It's made of paper, and it will tear easily.

SANDING RECEPTACLE BOXES

Break loose all the joint compound that's inside the receptacle boxes. It usually sticks out where it settles. Sand these areas well.

SANDING PIPES

Press the side of the sander against the pipe to break off the edges and any globs of joint compound that are on the pipe.

SANDING NAILS

Sometimes the paper doesn't stay tucked in, so just tap such pieces with the end of the knife. In addition, if a ridge was made where the knife was caught by the paper, sand it.

SANDING AROUND BATHTUB AND SHOWER UNITS

Sand lightly around bathtub and shower units, making sure not to sand into the tape. Break off the joint compound around the edge of the shower unit. Obviously, you don't want to sand the bathtub or shower unit itself because it scratches easily.

THE SECOND COAT

For the second coat, the joint compound needs to be thinned down a little, so it spreads smoothly and leaves no air bubbles. The purpose of this coat is to smooth the surface. If the first coat was done correctly, you won't need to worry about building anything up. There are three different situations you might face with the second coat.

THE FIRST SITUATION

If the first coat was done with quick set and you are doing only two coats, you only need to smooth the surface and make it look good. Build only when absolutely necessary. This coat should be a loose skim coat.

THE SECOND SITUATION

If the first coat was done with joint compound and you are doing only two coats, the joint compound will probably have shrunk, and you will still have to build some. It's difficult to apply a lot of joint compound and still keep it smooth. You may have to work with it.

THE THIRD SITUATION

If the first coat was done with joint compound and you are doing three coats, you can build with the second coat and not worry about it looking perfect. The third coat will cover any scratches and problem spots. This is where you can save time: you don't need to play with the second at all.

SECOND COATING BUTT JOINTS

A twelve-inch knife is recommended. Cover the entire butt joint with joint compound, keeping in mind where you have built and where you still need to build. (See Figure 6–29.) Skim the entire joint, pulling joint compound off, but remember where the low areas are. Straddle them, leaving the joint compound there. If you are doing only two coats, you will have to be neat. Bad butt joints usually don't look good unless they have a third coat. If you have a really bad joint and are doing only two coats, you might mix some quick set so you can skim the surface again before you leave. Also, where the joint compound is thick, it will have some ripples, so a sideways coating will look better. A receptacle box in the middle of the joint should be coated sideways.

SECOND COATING GOOD BUTT JOINTS

For good butt joints, use a twelve-inch knife to spread joint compound, overlapping at least three or four inches each side. When pulling the joint compound off, you

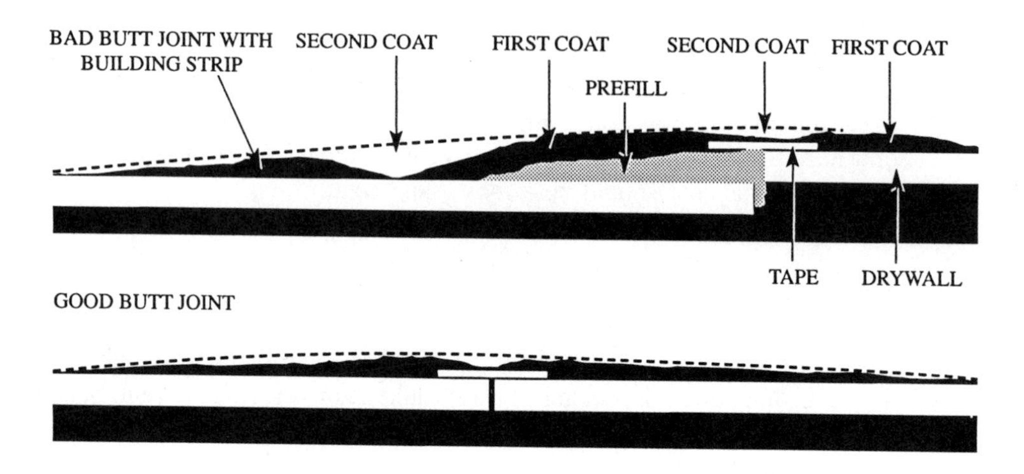

FIGURE 6–29 Second coating butt joints

need to straddle the middle and sides of the joint with the knife. This joint should be flat across the top with a gradual slope at each side. This coat should fill all the low spots and skim the high ones, leaving the surface flat and smooth.

SECOND COATING METAL

Metal should be skimmed very loosely with a twelve-inch knife. Joint compound should be thinned a little and mixed smooth to avoid air bubbles. Metal picks up small pieces of dried joint compound, making it difficult to keep out the streaks. When the joint compound picks up a lot of dried joint compound, you should dump it into an extra bucket and get some fresh joint compound. The problem of streaks in the joint compound can be minimized if you hold your knife down. This leaves the right amount of joint compound on the metal and also pushes the small pieces of dried joint compound down, burying them instead of dragging them along. Don't put too much pressure on the knife, or it can pull off too much joint compound. Most metal will still need some building to make it square.

SECOND COATING WINDOWS AND DOORWAYS

Windows and doorways are the most difficult areas to build. Spread joint compound in the same way as you did for the first coat. Corners that have been built up and have high spots should be coated to at least two to three inches past the first coat. Remember, when pulling joint compound off, hold the knife down loosely. Spread joint compound, feather edge, and smooth down loosely. If the corner of the window has not been built right or if it has a low spot, you can smooth it out and fill the low spot, as shown in Figure 6–30.

SECOND COATING INSIDE WINDOWS

A six-inch knife is recommended. Spread joint compound on and smooth it down, watching for scratch marks and air bubbles. Don't build any more than you have to and keep corners square and neat. Make sure the joint compound is filled all

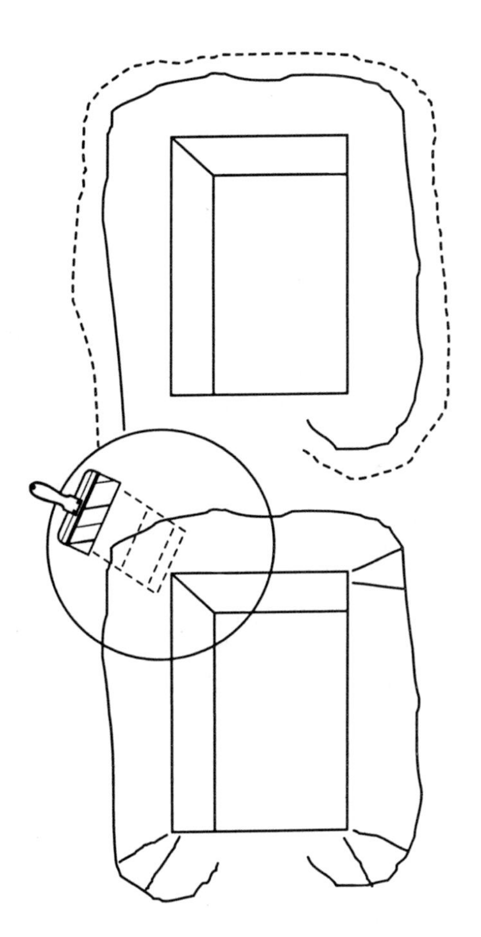

FIGURE 6–30 Second coating metal wrapped windows

the way to the bottom, if the area is getting a window seal. The inside of the window needs to look good, since it's always well lit. Almost all builders check inside the windows. If you are doing a second coat, and they need a third coat, it would be worth your while to skim it again. They dry fast and can be coated again easily.

SECOND COATING DOORWAYS

Skim the sides of doorways with a twelve-inch knife in the same way as you did the outside of the windows. The inside of the doorways and ends of walls have a lot of joint compound in the narrow center, and it normally needs to be filled quite a bit on the second coat. The insides of doors, like the insides of windows, catch light and usually need a third coat. Closet doorways aren't as important as the doorways between the kitchen and dining room, of course. While coating metal and butts that go to the floor, be sure to carry the joint compound to within an inch from the floor. Avoid leaving globs of joint compound at the bottom. This area needs to be kept neat, or it can interfere with the floor molding.

SECOND COATING FLAT JOINTS

Three different situations occur with flat joints:

Situation 1. Your first coat was done with an eight-inch knife, and you don't need a wide joint. In this situation, use a ten-inch knife for the second coat.

Situation 2. Your first coat was done with a ten-inch knife. In this situation, use a twelve-inch knife for easy covering.

Situation 3. Your first coat was done with a twelve-inch knife, and you need a wide joint. In this situation, overlap each side two inches.

No matter how the joint is coated, when you're skimming, it needs to be pulled off straight down the middle so your knife straddles the joint recess. Then pull the sides off with one stroke down one side and back on the other. By pulling joint compound off the center, you will be able to see all the high and low spots. If the area needs building on one side or the other, build accordingly. If the area will be getting only two coats, you will need to be careful and neat. If the area will be getting three coats, you can build it correctly now. (See Figure 6–31.)

SECOND COATING BOTH SIDES OF ANGLES

Two different situations occur when applying the second coat to both sides of angles:

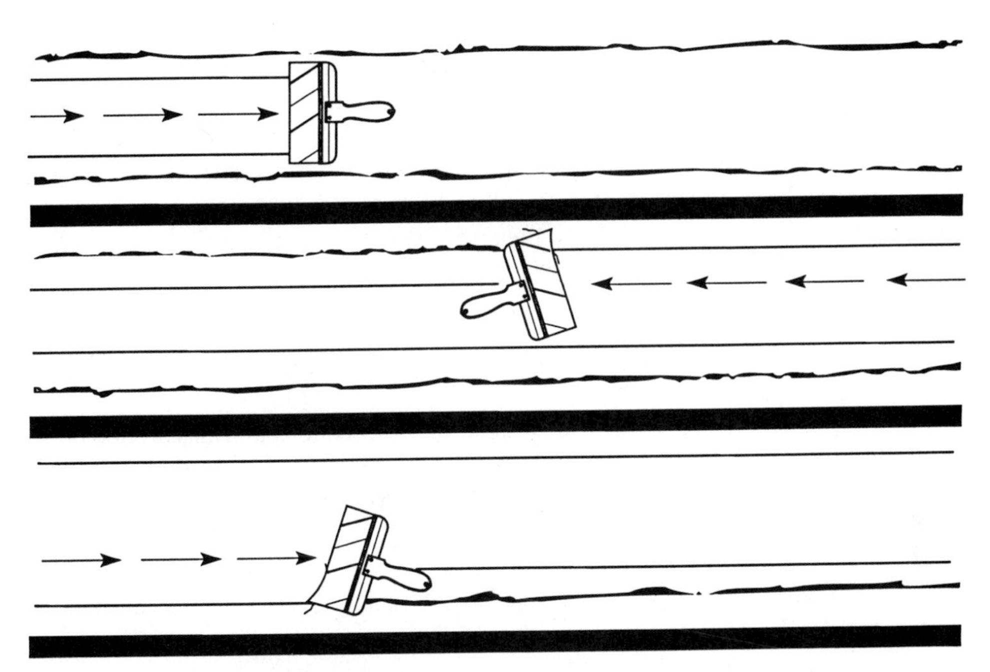

After putting the joint compound on the joint, pull the knife straight down the middle, going in one direction. Feather edge on top side; then, coming back, feather the other side. Turn knife over and smooth it down if needed.

FIGURE 6–31 Second coating flat joints

Situation 1. The first coat was done with joint compound. In this situation, make sure the center is dry. Otherwise, the joint compound will roll up in the center.

Situation 2. The first coat was done with quick set, so you don't have any drying problem. In this situation, the second coat will be a tight skim, done with a five- or six-inch knife. While skimming the joint compound off, hold your knife out with its side edge running along the center and braced against the other side. When you did your first coat, you skimmed off the same side first. On this second coat, reverse the procedure, skimming off the second side first. This way, if you have a crack to fill, you will be sure to fill both sides. If you used a soft joint compound on the first coat, you will have to be careful when holding your knife straight out. When you use the adjacent wall as a support, you can cut a groove into the soft joint compound. In this case, you might have to make yourself a knife with straight sides simply by taking an old knife and cutting its sides down straight.

SECOND COATING ANGLES, ONE SIDE AT A TIME

The second side is done exactly the same way as the first side. Hold the knife out and let the side edge ride against the other side for support. Be neat, as this method has only one coat. You will need to spend some time on it to get it exact. Any flaws can be sanded out. If the angle from the first coat isn't dry yet, don't bother coating the second side. It will only make a mess.

SECOND COATING NAILS

Use the same procedure as you did for the second coat. Nails around doors don't have to be coated this time unless they are fairly deep and you think they might show after the framing is in. Avoid having to come back just to coat a nail. You may have places where the rough edges have caught the knife and caused ripples. These areas need to be coated crossways.

Unless the hangers have dimpled the nails too deep, this should be your last coat, so be neat and overlap any edges.

SECOND COATING RECEPTACLE BOXES

If the first coat was done vertically, the second should be done horizontally. This way, you will be sure to fill any ridges and imperfections. Skim off tight across the middle first, as this always needs to be filled.

FUR DOWNS

Apply the second coat to the fur down with a twelve-inch knife in the same way you did the first coat. Overlap by a couple of inches and pull the joint compound off loose so it can build where it needs to. Refer to Figure 6–24 for review.

SECOND COATING PIPES AND BATHTUBS

The areas around pipes and bathtubs need to be skimmed tight.

PATCHES

Any patches where the tape had to be overlapped should be coated the opposite way from the first coat. All bad places need to be coated both ways.

Preparation for the Third Coat

If the walls will be painted with enamel, you will have to be very neat with the third coat. You will need a tight skim with no sanding. If you sand a joint, it will be smoother than the paper covering the drywall, and the joint will show up. Therefore, if you plan to use enamel paint, sand very well now so the joints can be skimmed tight and smooth without sanding.

BUTTS AND METAL

Sand butt joints and metal the same way you sanded them in preparation for the second coat. The wall should be smooth all the way to the bottom. Cut away the globs, or the trim won't be neat.

ANGLES

Angles won't need another coat unless you have problems. If you have coated one side at a time, you can now skim both sides if they need it.

NAILS

Nails won't need another coat unless they were very deep. You can tell if they need another coat by looking at a wall that has a window at one end of it. This wall will show every flaw.

BASTARD ANGLES AND JOINTS

Any joint that has flex bead used on it must be sanded very carefully. Take care not to sand the paper edge on the joint compound.

RECEPTACLE BOXES AND FLATS

Receptacle boxes and flats must be sanded lightly. Joint compound should be cleaned out of receptacle boxes.

THE THIRD COAT

PREPARING JOINT COMPOUND

The joint compound for the third coat needs to be fairly thin because you will be skimming everything off tight. The goal is to fill any shallow joints, scratches, or nicks left from other coats. Doing this will cut your final sanding time by about 70%.

A METHOD TO MAKE YOU FASTER

If you have an untrained helper, you can utilize this person's time in the following way. Have your helper roll the joint compound on the joints with a paint roller. Then, you follow and skim it off tight. Do not let the person rolling on the joint compound get too far ahead of the person skimming it off, because the edges dry quickly. The purpose of this technique is to produce a smooth job and to eliminate edges. If you do it right, you won't have to use sandpaper at all. You should have two buckets, one to roll the joint compound from and the other to empty your pan into. Before reusing the joint compound, you will have to mix it up again to eliminate globs and make it easier to skim off smoothly. This method enables your untrained help to be more productive.

THIRD COATING BUTT JOINTS

A twelve-inch knife is recommended, since almost all butt joints need to be coated crossways. This is to eliminate the ripples in the joint compound caused by an unsteady knife. All receptacle boxes, butt joints, flex bead joints, and bastard angles need to be coated crossways.

The butts are always the first thing to coat, since they require the most drying time. If a butt joint still needs to be built a little, it might dry in time for you to skim it crossways again before you leave.

Butts along the bottom of the wall have a common mistake: globs of joint compound on the bottom next to the floor. Eventually, you will have to clean this up, and it's better to do it now. Scrape off this joint compound and coat crossways if needed. The trim must fit flush against the wall.

THIRD COATING METAL

If you are rolling on the joint compound, the insides of the windows will be saved for last and done by hand. Skim all metal tight to make it smooth, filling in any mistakes. In the kitchen, a receptacle box is often close to the door, which is wrapped with metal corner bead. This is a problem area. See Figure 6–32 for tips on how to coat this. Use a twelve-inch knife and coat it sideways.

THIRD COATING 45° ANGLES

Outside corners where flex bead was used will need to be coated sideways for the third coat.

THIRD COATING FLATS

Spread joint compound to overlap previous joint compound slightly, and skim it off tight. Always pull the knife along the recess to make sure it is filled in. Then skim off each side with the same stroke of the knife. Skim one side while pulling the knife one way, and then turn your knife around and pull off the other side on the way back. Save strokes where you can.

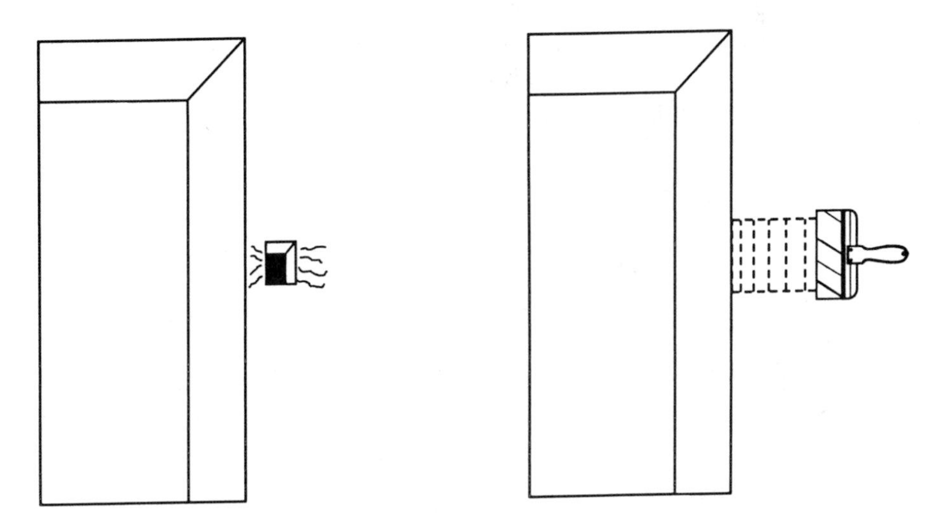

Switch box next to the metal corner bead-wrapped doorways usually are a problem area because the flat joint dead ends at the doorway, and the metal is filled vertically. So, this time, coat it cross-ways.

FIGURE 6–32 Switch box next to doorways

THIRD COATING ANGLES

The angles should be finished, unless you have a problem angle with a wide crack that needs to be filled. If anything, coat problem bastard angles crossways with a twelve-inch knife.

If you have coated one side at a time, you should have both sides coated now. If you have used quick set, you can follow the directions from the second coat for angles. Just hold the knife out from the wall so the angles will be square and the edge of the knife won't slide back into the recess. Hold the knife out straight from wall and skim.

THIRD COATING RECEPTACLE BOXES

If a third coat is necessary for the receptacle boxes, coat them in the direction most needed.

SANDING

Many people think that anyone can sand, but this is not true. Only a trained person should finish sand because this stage needs to be done right. This is your final product. See the next chapter or the chart in Figure 6–33 for the type of sandpaper you should use for each type of final coating. As you sand, keep an eye out for ridges, knife marks, and scratches. Also watch for problem spots such as the bottoms of butt joints, doorways, and end walls where the joint compound comes all the way down to the floor.

SANDING BUTT JOINTS

When sanding butt joints, be careful not to sand into the tape. If the butt joint is coated right, the tape will be close to the surface. If you do sand into the tape, coat it over with joint compound again so it won't stick up and show when painted.

Watch for ridges and scratches. Always check the bottoms next to the floor. Scrape off any globs of joint compound and coat crossways to fill any deep ripples.

SANDING METAL

When sanding metal, the edges of metal that are showing should be free of joint compound. When the metal is clean and shiny, it will look good, saving you a lot of trouble later.

Paint/Texture	# of Coats	Sanding	Fuzz	Sandpaper	Final Sand
SPRAY PAINT					
Enamel Paint	3	after second coat & skim	none	100 grit	no
Semi Gloss	3	yes	none	100 grit	yes
Flat Paint	3	yes	none	100 grit	yes
PAINT (*Roller*)					
Enamel Paint	3	after second coat & skim	OK	100 grit	no
Semi Gloss	3	yes	OK	100 grit	yes
Flat Paint	3	yes	OK	100 grit	yes
NAP TEXTURE (*Roller*)					
Enamel Paint	3, or 2 neat ones	yes	OK	80–100 grit	yes
Semi Gloss	2 neat ones	yes	OK	80–100 grit	yes
Flat Paint	2 neat ones	yes	OK	80–100 grit	yes
SPRAY TEXTURE (*Light*)					
Enamel Paint	2	lightly	OK	80–100 grit	yes
Semi Gloss	2	lightly	OK	80–100 grit	yes
Flat Paint	2	lightly	OK	80–100 grit	yes
SPRAY TEXTURE (*Heavy*)					
Enamel Paint	2	no	OK	n/a	n/a
Semi Gloss	2	no	OK	n/a	n/a
Flat Paint	2	no	OK	n/a	n/a

FIGURE 6–33 Finishing walls according to texture

SANDING INSIDE WINDOWS

Inside windows need to look neat. You should scrape off any joint compound against the metal window. As you do this, take care not to scratch the metal or the window.

SANDING BASTARD JOINTS AND 45° JOINTS

When sanding bastard joints and 45° joints, be careful not to sand into the paper edge of the metal edge tape.

SANDING FLATS

Flats are usually the easiest to sand. Watch for any knife marks and ridges where a piece of joint compound on the wall has caught the knife and caused a ridge.

SANDING ANGLES

When sanding corners, do not sand into the center. If you push the sander into the center, the side of the paper on the sander will cut into the adjacent corner. If something is in the center or small pieces of joint compound are left on it, the best thing to do is to fold up a piece of sandpaper and run it down the center. A second option is to keep a corner on your sander worn (if you are using a hand sander) and use only that corner—not the side. Don't try this with a pole sander because you don't have good control over it. A third option is to just carry a knife and run it down the center to knock off any pieces of joint compound.

SANDING NAILS

To sand nails, simply run the sander around the edges.

SANDING RECEPTACLE BOXES

Before sanding receptacle boxes, clean joint compound out of the inside; it will fall out with just a little help. Sand the area smooth, being careful not to sand into any tape, which should be close to the surface. It's a good idea to take a utility knife and cut out the boxes that were taped. Sometimes, an electrician might pull the tape up while trimming the box. You don't want to have to come back and fix it.

SANDING AROUND TUB AND SHOWER UNITS

In tub and shower units, the edges next to the joint compound should be cleaned off. Scraping with a knife or a sander will scratch into the fiberglass. The best way to clean the fiberglass is to wet it, let it sit a few minutes, and then lift it off with a knife.

CLEANING DOOR FRAMES

Plaster is easy to clean if you wet down the area that needs to be cleaned. After three or four minutes, the plaster softens and is easy to remove.

The Final Product

QUESTIONS TO CONSIDER

Before you sand, you need to know how the walls will be finished. In preparing this job for the painter (or for yourself, if you will be painting it), you will need answers to the following questions:

1. What kind of paint will be used?
2. What kind of texture, if any, will it have?
3. How will the job be done—with spray or with a roller?

IF YOU'RE USING A PROFESSIONAL PAINTER

Some painters need to see sand marks into the paper or they aren't happy. This is why you need to talk to the painter before you sand, if possible. Ask the three questions and discuss the kind of job the painter prefers. The painter can give you a lot of trouble, so it is in your own best interests to get along. If the painter isn't sold on your job, you will probably have to come back and fix it.

PAINTING METHODS

There are two painting methods for smooth walls: spray painting and roller painting. To prepare for spray painting, do not sand into the paper—stay on the joint compound. Any paper fuzz will catch the paint and hold it away from the wall. The result would be that at different angles, dark places would be visible underneath. If you fuzz up the paper by mistake, it can be fixed only by sponging the walls down with water, which can be time consuming. Sometimes, you will be asked to sponge the joints rather than sand them.

To prepare for roller painting, you won't have to worry about fuzz because the roller will press it down. Roller painting hides much more than spray. It can hide even better if you put a little joint compound into the paint and mix it up about half and half or whatever thickness you want. This is called a roller texture.

Smooth Walls, Spray Method, Enamel Paint

This is the most difficult method because this procedure shows everything. Walls done this way need three neat coats. Any imperfections will show, so never sand.

If joints are sanded, they will be smoother than the paper surface on the drywall. This difference will show. Preparation for this method starts after the second coat. Sand very well, skim the third coat on tight, and don't sand it again. Some finishers skim the entire wall, depending on what the builder wants.

Smooth Walls, Spray Method, Semi Gloss Paint

All smooth walls need three coats. For this method, sand very carefully, taking care not to sand into the paper. It's important to avoid getting fuzz on the surface. For any spray paint and smooth walls, use 100 grit sandpaper; 80 grit will leave scratches that may show.

Smooth Walls, Roller Method, Enamel Paint

This situation requires three coats and is best without sanding. The roller will help, but it will still be hard to hide the differences in the surface between the joint compound and the paper.

Smooth Walls, Roller Method, Semi Gloss and Flat Paint

Use 100 grit sandpaper. Sand well and don't worry about fuzz. This surface needs three coats or two neat coats.

Nap Texture, Roller Method, Enamel Paint

This situation requires three coats or two neat ones. Sand with 80 grit or 100 grit sandpaper because this texture is very light.

Nap Texture, Roller Method, Semi Gloss and Flat Paint

For this situation, use two neat coats. Sand with 80 grit or 100 grit sandpaper.

Light Spray Texture, Spray Method, Enamel Paint

This situation requires two very neat coats. Sand lightly with 80 grit or 100 grit sandpaper. This texture will hide small imperfections, but it will show bad joints.

Light Spray Texture, Spray Method, Semi Gloss or Flat Paint

This situation requires two neat coats. Sand lightly with 80 grit or 100 grit sandpaper. This texture will hide short scratches and bubbles, but it won't hide shallow metal or bad joints.

Medium to Heavy Spray Texture, Spray Method, Any Paint

For any kind of paint, use two coats and no sanding. This texture will hide most bad joints, shallow metal, scratches, and so on.

Questions

THE FOUR BASIC JOINTS

1. What are the four basic joints?
a. Angles, beveled, factory edge, and butt
b. Beveled, butt, corner bead, and bastard
c. Flats, butt, bastard, and angles
d. Beveled, bastard, butt, and angles

2. Which joint has a recess?
a. Bad butt
b. Bastard
c. Flat
d. Angle

PREPARING FOR TAPING

3. What is meant by the term "punch out"?
a. Popped nail
b. A process for cutting out windows
c. Things you need to fix after a job is completed
d. What hangers call the hole made for receptacle boxes

4. When the drywall is broken underneath but on the surface the paper isn't broken, what should the finisher do?
a. Cover it with joint compound
b. Tape it
c. Dig out the broken piece and patch it
d. Paint it

5. When the finisher is trying to prefill a hole in the wall and the joint compound falls behind the wall, what should he or she do?
a. Go around and tape it on the back side
b. Cut out a bigger piece and put drywall in it
c. Put some tape across the hole, prefill, and tape again
d. Hang a picture over it

6. What is flex bead used for?
   a. 45° outside corners
   b. 45° inside corners
   c. Rounded soffits
   d. All of the above

TAPING

7. For a beginner, which knife is best for wiping down a flat joint?
   a. 5 inch
   b. 6 inch
   c. 4 inch
   d. 7 inch

8. When spreading joint compound at an angle, what must you watch for when spreading the second side?
   a. That it doesn't get air bubbles
   b. That the knife doesn't cut into the first side
   c. That your joint compound isn't lumpy
   d. That the angle is square

9. When taping, why is the area where an angle touches the ceiling a critical place?
   a. It is hard to coat that corner.
   b. If you don't tape the complete center, the joint compound will fall out and leave a hole.
   c. Earthquakes shake that corner more than anywhere else.
   d. If that corner isn't taped completely, it puts stress on the butt joints.

10. When taping a residence, what type of joint should you tape first?
    a. Receptacle boxes
    b. Flats or horizontal joints
    c. Vertical joints
    d. Butts and headers

11. When taping by hand, how should you mix the joint compound?
    a. As thick as possible
    b. As thin as possible
    c. Half water, half joint compound
    d. One quart of water per gallon of compound

12. What happens if a spot under the tape has no joint compound?
    a. Nothing happens; it won't fall off because it's attached at each end.
    b. It shrinks and pulls the tape crooked.
    c. It forms a blister and needs to be cut out.
    d. The tape splits because it won't stretch.

13. When wiping down tape on a butt joint or header, you will
    a. use a lot of pressure so you can get joint compound off the low side.
    b. use the high side to set the pressure, so you don't take too much off the high side.
    c. wipe it down crossways as it is an uneven surface.
    d. wipe down one side at a time if necessary.

14. When wiping down tape on a butt joint, how do you hold your knife? Why?
    a. At a 90° angle for better control
    b. Upside down so it's easier to wipe the tape from the bottom up
    c. Laid down so it doesn't take too much joint compound off
    d. Held down so it's easy to get joint compound off.

15. What kind of tape should you use on an outside 45° corner?
    a. Fiberglass tape
    b. Perfa tape
    c. Flex bead
    d. Regular corner bead

16. What is a hot patch made of?
    a. Paper tape
    b. Fiberglass
    c. Drywall
    d. Joint compound

17. When plugging a hole, how do you keep the plug from falling through the wall?
    a. Put in a receptacle box.
    b. Fill it up with newspapers.
    c. Put a piece of tape across the hole and push the plug into it.
    d. Fill the hole with quick set.

18. Should you tape the inside angle in a window or doorway?
    a. No, since it usually gets a lot of joint compound
    b. Only if it has a big crack
    c. Yes, to guard against the effects of house settling movements
    d. Only if the metal is loose

19. When should you tape around pipes that will be hidden in cabinets?
a. When someone requests it
b. Always
c. Only if the hole is one inch or bigger
d. Only if in an earthquake area

20. When should you tape around a bathtub or shower unit?
a. Never, as it will be caulked
b. Only if it has a crack too big for caulking
c. Never, as a trim seal fits around it
d. Always

21. If a crack is in the drywall but the surface paper isn't broken, what should you do?
a. Coat it thick with joint compound.
b. Always tape it.
c. Tape it only if it has movement.
d. Tape it only if the paper is twisted.

22. In an area where paper is torn or pulled out, why should you coat it first and hammer it in later?
a. It saves time.
b. Joint compound help the paper stay in when hammered.
c. You should always hammer the first coat after you put it on.
d. Finishers should never hammer anything.

FIRST COAT

23. What is feather edge?
a. A procedure done while sanding and dusting off
b. A procedure used on inside corners of windows
c. A procedure used while coating joint compound and blending the edges into the drywall
d. A procedure used to build up butt joints

24. Why is a building strip used?
a. To trim 45° angles
b. To trim 90° angles
c. To build out a bad joint
d. To sand out a bad joint

25. What causes ripples?
a. Settling of the building
b. Sanding unevenly
c. Spreading large amounts of thick joint compound
d. Spreading thin joint compound

26. When coating a butt joint that runs into a flat joint, how do you first coat it?
a. Coat up to and across the flat joint.
b. Stop at the flat joint.
c. Wait until the flat joint dries.
d. Wait until the angle dries.

27. How should the joint compound be prepared for first coat?
a. Thinned down to allow for shrinkage
b. Thinned down so it has fewer air bubbles
c. As thick as possible for less shrinkage
d. Thinned down for faster coating

28. Where flat joints meet angles, how should you first coat?
a. Wait for the flat joint to dry.
b. Wait for the angle to dry.
c. Be sure to fill the flat joint into the center of the angle.
d. Coat the angle with a ten-inch knife.

29. Where flat joints cross butt joints, how should you first coat?
a. Stop at each side of the butt joint.
b. Wait for the butt joints to dry.
c. Coat right across.
d. Wait for the angle to dry.

30. With what type of joint is the building strip used most often?
a. Flat joints that are ten feet long
b. Bad butt joints
c. Good butt joints
d. Where angles and butt joints join

31. How is a header coated?
a. In the same way that an angle is coated
b. In the same way that metal is coated
c. In the same way that a flat joint is coated
d. In the same way that a butt joint is coated

32. When starting the first coat, which joints should be done first?
a. Flats
b. Angles
c. Metal
d. Butts

33. When coating metal, how do you scrape off the edges?
a. Toward the right
b. Toward the left
c. By sliding the blade of the knife along the edge
d. By using the side of the knife

34. What can you do to make a butt joint into a flat surface?
a. Sand it down to the tape.
b. Use a twelve-inch knife on it.
c. You can't; it merely can be camouflaged.
d. Spread it out at least 24 inches.

35. If you are a do-it-yourselfer and just learning to finish, you will want to
a. coat metal with a six-inch knife.
b. coat flats one at a time.
c. coat butt joints from right to left.
d. coat inside angles one side at a time.

36. If you are working to be a professional finisher, you should
a. coat the insides of metal wrapped windows with an eight-inch knife.
b. keep track of how much joint compound you are using.
c. take the time to learn how to coat angles two sides at the same time.
d. coat butt joints last.

PREPARATION FOR THE SECOND COAT

1. How do you prepare for a second coat?
a. Dust the walls.
b. Sand the walls until smooth.
c. Wet the walls down with a sponge.
d. Sand lightly.

THE SECOND COAT

2. Since all butt joints are different, what procedure should you follow for second coating?
a. Coat the right side first.
b. Coat the left side first.
c. Drag the second coat off sideways.
d. Straddle the low areas.

3. When second coating metal, it should be
a. skimmed tight for a smooth look.
b. coated loose because it will still need some building.
c. as thick as you can spread it.
d. very thin joint compound so it won't have streaks.

4. When second coating, you should
a. thin the joint compound to avoid streaks.
b. skip butt joints as they are always wet.
c. flatten out the angles.
d. overlap the first coat by a few inches.

5. When second coating a joint that goes to the floor, you should
a. sweep the area so you can coat all the way to the floor.
b. make sure you don't leave globs of joint compound at the bottom.
c. coat to within an inch from the floor.
d. hold the knife at a 45° angle.

6. It is important to guard against globs of joint compound along the bottom of the joint because
a. they would make it difficult to paint.
b. this is a waste of joint compound.
c. they would interfere with the trim.
d. wallpaper won't stick.

7. When second coating flat joints, you should spread them with joint compound. Then, when dragging the joint compound off, you should first
a. feather edge both sides.
b. pull the knife down the center of the joint.
c. pull the knife across the joint.
d. pull a six-inch knife along each side.

8. If you are second coating a receptacle box and the first coat was coated vertically, you should coat it
a. horizontally.
b. parallel to the floor.
c. parallel to the angle.
d. vertically.

PREPARATION FOR THE THIRD COAT

9. If you are smoothing a wall for enamel paint, how should you do your third coat?
a. Put a lot of joint compound on because it is the last coat.
b. The same as any other coat.
c. Sand before the third coat because it can't be sanded after.
d. Put some texture in the joint compound.

10. If you are sanding a bastard angle with flex bead on it, what is the most important thing to remember?
a. Press hard on the sander to get the ripples out.
b. Don't sand the paper edge because it will tear.
c. Don't sand too deep or the metal will show.
d. Be sure to sand the bottom next to the floor.

THE THIRD COAT

11. How can you effectively utilize an untrained person during the third coat stage?
a. Have the person use an electric sander.
b. Let the person sweep floors.
c. Let the person use a bigger knife for coating.
d. Have the person roll on the joint compound with a paint roller.

12. When you are third coating butt joints, you should
a. coat sideways whenever possible.
b. sand as deeply as you can.
c. be sure not to cross the flat areas.
d. be careful where the butt joins the angle areas.

SANDING

13. When sanding inside windows, you should
a. coat sideways because of ripples.
b. sand very carefully, as every one sees this area up close.
c. use an electric sander. It's much faster.
d. use the clincher.

14. When sanding angles you should
a. be careful not to let the side of the sander cut into the other side of the angle.
b. use heavy sandpaper to get out the big chunks.
c. use an electric sander.
d. sand the top a lot because everyone can see it.

15. When sanding around the tub or shower unit you should
a. sand fast so someone can take a shower.
b. use an electric sander.
c. be careful with the fiberglass unit because it scratches easily.
d. be careful with the surrounding wall because it may be wet.

16. When cleaning excess joint compound off doorways, you should
a. freeze it with liquid Freon and then chip it off.
b. use a hammer and chisel.
c. wet it and let it set a few minutes. Then lift it off with a knife.
d. use a hair dryer on it, and it will fall off.

THE FINAL PRODUCT

17. If the paper has been sanded, making the wall fuzzy, what is the best painting method to use?
a. Spray paint
b. Brush
c. Texture
d. Roller

18. Which painting method requires the most difficult of preparations?
a. Semi gloss, spray method
b. Enamel paint, textured
c. Enamel paint, spray method
d. Enamel paint, roller method

19. For which painting method do you need to sand?
a. Heavy spray texture, enamel paint, spray method
b. Heavy spray texture, semi gloss paint, roller method
c. Heavy spray texture, flat paint, spray method
d. Light spray texture, enamel paint, spray method

Chapter 7
Texturing

Textures add a great deal of interest to walls. The most important thing to remember about texturing is to be willing to experiment: there are many interesting and exciting ways to produce beautiful and unique textures for your walls.

NAP TEXTURE

Nap texture, which is done with a paint roller, is perhaps the easiest kind of texturing. Certainly, it requires the least amount of tools. Different types of rollers, of course, make different textures. A leather roller, for example, creates a unique look. Texture thickness varies, depending on nap thickness of the roller and paint thickness. Paint can be thickened by adding joint compound to it.

The illustrations show different nap textures. The big pattern in Figure 7–1 was made with a thick roller and thick joint compound. The patterns in Figure 7–2 were made with a fine nap roller and thin and medium joint compounds. The differences in texture are considerable.

ROLL-ON TEXTURE

Rolling on the joint compound creates a foundation for a series of textures. The important thing is to roll the joint compound on evenly. Joint compound on

FIGURE 7–1 Thick nap texture

FIGURE 7–2 Thin and medium nap textures

ceiling or wall joints absorbs moisture more quickly than drywall paper does. Therefore, this texture must be rolled on thick enough to prevent the drywall from showing through, and fast enough that it doesn't start to dry in particularly absorbent areas. Beginners should apply a coat of white primer to the ceiling before starting these textures. It requires some skill to put these textures on properly without primer.

Make the joint compound thin enough that you can roll it on the ceiling, but not so thin that it falls off the roller. Pick an area about six feet by six feet at one end of the room as a starting place. Roll on the joint compound, no thicker than is absolutely needed. The thinner it is, the more attractive the texture will be. Roll in one direction, (say, north to south). Start at one end and then, with a second roller, full of joint compound, start at the opposite end. This way, you will distribute the thick areas from both ends. Do about six rows, and then start smoothing the joint compound across in the opposite direction (say, east to west). Don't apply any more joint compound! Just smooth it across the opposite direction so it has a uniform thickness. (See Figure 7-3.)

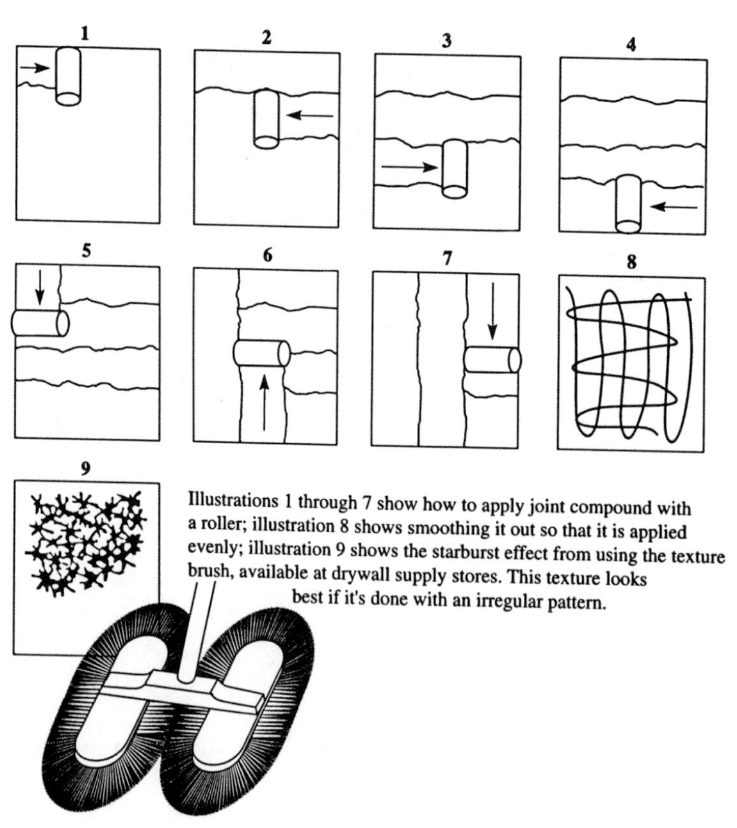

FIGURE 7-3 The roll-on texture technique

When rolling the six-foot-area square, overlap the first area so the texture can be cut in without showing. Be careful not to daub on a half-dry area because that would change the texture, and the difference would be noticeable. Be careful to get the joint compound the same thickness all over the ceiling because different thicknesses change the texture. See Figure 7–3 for roll-on technique. If an area is partially dry by the time you start daubing there, simply roll over it again to moisten it.

BRUSH PATTERNS

After rolling on the joint compound, you can make interesting patterns with a brush. (See Figure 7–4.) If you want rows, make them straight for a pleasing appearance. It's better to stagger the brush marks, making an irregular pattern, which, incidentally, is easier to repair than a regular pattern. This texture will get a lot of joint compound on the walls, which can be remedied by a process called glazing. The process is simple: just cover the lower part of the top angle with joint compound and drag it off tight. This joint compound can also be lifted off with a knife, but this method will leave edges and will have to be sanded. Choose the method you find easier.

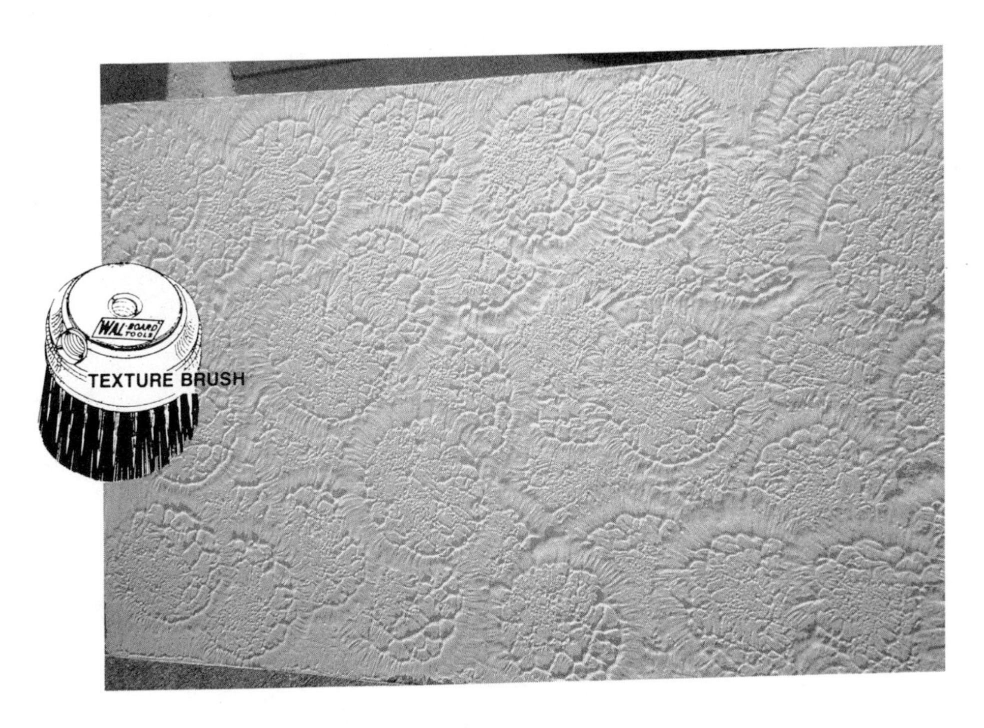

FIGURE 7–4 Brush patterns

SWIRLS

After rolling the joint compound, you can make swirls with a brush. Swirls are made best with the roll-on method. Instead of daubing the brush on the drywall, just place the brush and twist. Remember, when doing swirls, they must be lined up in straight lines. Use a chalk line to guide you. You can also twist the joint compound and pull it out in tips. For bigger tips, use thinner joint compound and put it on thicker. Different textures can be made with a small whisk broom, a brush, or even a lid. Try using different objects on a scrap piece of drywall.

A small kitchen scrub brush was used for the swirls here in Figure 7–5. Keep the swirls in the first row all about the same size, and make the row straight. Use the first row as a guide to keep the other ones straight. Check each row against the first row, not the one you just did, because you will begin to swerve. Overlap each row by the same amount to assure continuity and a regular pattern.

USING HOUSEHOLD OBJECTS TO MAKE PATTERNS

The textures in Figure 7–6 was made after rolling on the joint compound smoothly. Notice the household objects in the illustration. The small scrub brush

FIGURE 7–5 Swirls

FIGURE 7–6 Using household objects for patterns

was used to make the swirls. The lid was used in two ways: The flat side of the lid was pushed into the joint compound and pulled out, causing it to suck up some joint compound. The flower design in that texture was made with the underside of the lid. The glass was used to make design on the left. Other effects can be achieved by pressing heavy woven materials against joint compound and taking it off, leaving an imprint. All kinds of objects can be used: sponges, paper, spatulas, screens, and so on. Use your imagination, and create your own designs.

FIGURE 7–7 (*Courtesy U.S. Gypsum Co.*)

SPRAY TEXTURE ACOUSTIC

Acoustic-type textures can be rolled on with prepared mixes. These textures look better with a coat of primer underneath. You will need an air compressor and hopper. For spray textures shown in Figure 7–8 you will also need a roll of plastic to cover

General Applications

Gypsum Wallboard. Surfaces, including joint-treated areas, must be smooth, clean and dry. When texturing is the finished surface, first apply a coat of good quality, white alkyd flat oil paint or primer/sealer. Mask appropriate areas before spraying, and promptly remove overspray from unprotected surfaces afterward. Follow the instructions of the spray equipment manufacturer for adjusting controls and cleaning. If a second coat is desired, allow the first coat to dry completely.

Concrete. Allow concrete to cure for at least 28 days. Clip protruding wire ends and spot with rust-inhibitive primer. Remove all forms of oil, grease and dirt, or any loose or water-soluable material. Grind down any form ridges and level any remaining unevenness with Gold Bond Joint Compound. Apply a coat of alkali-resistant, white alkyd oil paint or primer over the entire surface to be textured.

NOTE: *These are general instructions. Complete, easy-to-follow application guides are printed on all bags of Gold Bond Textures. Close adherence to instructions for surface preparation and priming will avoid the problems of color variation, bleeding or sagging, and will permit the texture to achieve its full potential.*

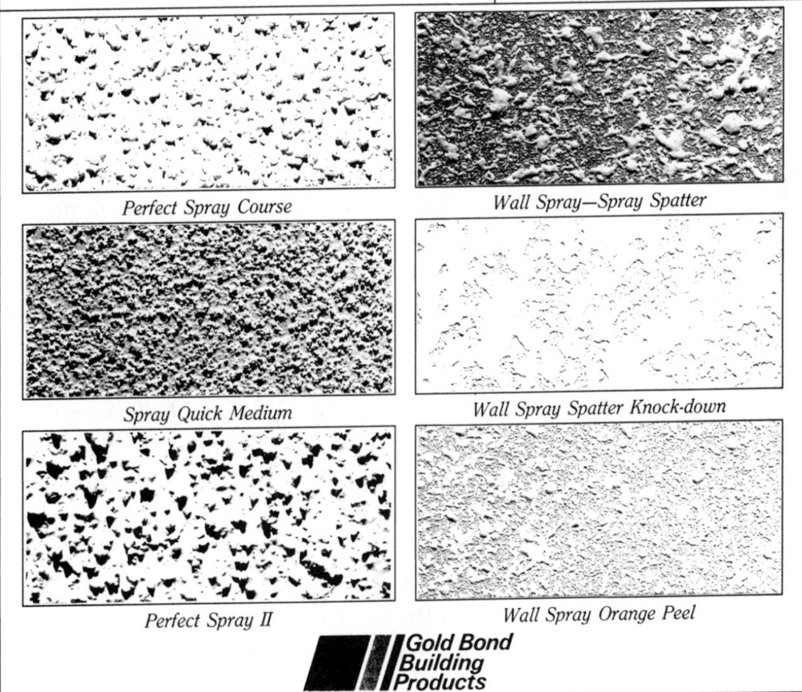

FIGURE 7–8 *(Courtesy Gold Bond and Wal-Board Tool Co.)*

all your windows and doors. Cover any furniture or carpets because this texture sprays all over. A drywall knife will be needed to scrape the walls after the texture has been sprayed. A ten- or twelve-inch knife is best for this task. After you prepare the mix, fill the hopper about halfway and spray the ceiling. You must cover all the drywall. You can make the mixture as thick as you want. However, don't let it collect in globs that drip or run. Spray evenly and lightly, going back to make it thicker so it doesn't run. Spray this texture in the same way that you would paint an area with spray paint. Don't stay on one spot or even hesitate, or the texture will run. Experiment on a scrap piece of drywall for practice. If the texture is too thick, scrape it off with a knife and start over. After you complete one area, a helper can scrape the walls off. The texture comes off very easily.

SPARKLE

Sparkle can be used on any texture. Put it on while the joint compound is still wet, and it will stick easily. You can buy a tool at the drywall supply to throw the sparkle evenly. It's just like a seed thrower. You can throw the sparkle by hand, but it probably won't be even. If the surface will need paint, put the sparkle on while the paint is wet, and it will stick well.

THE STOMP TEXTURE

The stomp is an interesting texture. To create it, you will need a special tool. This tool I call the dobber can be made with scrap materials such as a round piece of wood, an old frying pan lid or anything round and about ten inches in diameter. In addition, you will need a one-by-one piece of wood about three feet long, or an old broom handle. You will also need a piece of insulation, carpet padding, or thin foam rubber to pad the dauber. Finally, you will need a plastic garbage bag and a piece of two- or three- inch tape about two feet long. Nail the pole onto the round piece of wood, and cover it with your padding material. Cover that with plastic, pulling it down around the handle and taping it. This tool should fit into the bucket of joint compound you are using. (See Figure 7–9.)

You will also need to trowel the texture down smooth. To do this you can use a cement trowel or a ten- or twelve-inch knife. If you use a knife, bend each corner up a little so it won't cut into the joint compound.

There are tools you can buy to make the same texture, but they aren't as effective.

This texture can also be blown on with an air compressor and hopper, then troweled down flat, like the spray texture described (Figure 7–8 Wall Spray Spatter Knock-down).

1. Daubing leaves little piles of joint compound on the ceiling.

2. Troweling with a 12-inch knife, start at the corner and pull the knife back about ten inches, which will put a pattern of joint compound on the knife.

3. Then put knife back to the edge and press the pattern of mud in the corner while pulling the knife further into the daubed wall.

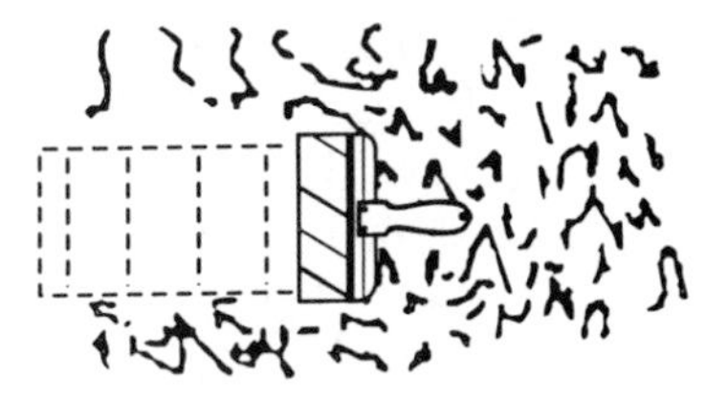

4. Now repeat the same thing on the other side of the corner and all around the edges.

5. The little piles of compound will flatten out into different shaped patterns.

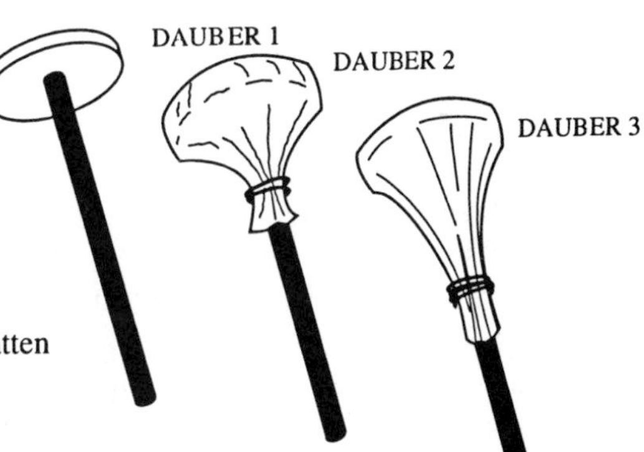

FIGURE 7–9 Steps 1–5 show how to trowl the stomp texture. Dauber 1 shows the round wood handle. Dauber 2 shows carpet over the round wood for padding. Dauber 3 shows plastic garbage bag pulled tight and taped at the bottom.

Stomp texture is good for accent walls. Paint a wall in an accent color and then texture over it, allowing the color to show through the pattern. Textured joint compound can be colored to give a two-tone color. This type wall must be sealed with clear lacquer so it can be washed. Sparkle can be added while the paint is wet.

For a fine pattern, use the joint compound straight out of the bucket; just mix it so it comes out more evenly. For bigger patterns, add some water to thin the joint compound. The thicker the pattern, the thinner the joint compound should be. Thinner compound goes on in bigger globs and spreads out more when it is troweled. The stiffer the joint compound, the finer the texture. Put the dauber into the joint compound and apply it to the wall. The joint compound should cover the dauber in globs.

If you want to, hit the wall in circles. Overlap them so you can't see definite circles. Hit the joint compound once and the wall three times for the best results. Don't try making circles out of a texture unless you mark off the ceiling and get all the lines straight. Continue to refer back to the starting line to keep the pattern the same. It's easy for the pattern to change a bit as you move around the room. After you have daubed an area for about ten minutes, you will need to check where you started, to see if it is ready to start troweling down. If one person starts daubing a room, that person needs to finish that room. A different person will daub a different pattern.

TROWELING THE STOMP

When the edges start looking white where they are drying, you need to stop daubing and trowel down. If you start troweling and the joint compound flattens out to the drywall, it is too wet. The trowel should float over the joint compound and knock down the high areas, spreading them into a pattern. If you trowel it wetter, it will spread out more and be a bigger pattern. For a smaller pattern, let it dry more so it will be more set up. The texture should be about $\frac{1}{32}$ inch thick after it is troweled down. This is ideal for painting, cleaning, and a neat appearance.

Start troweling from the edge of the area and move to the middle. This way, you won't leave trowel marks in the joint compound. Around edges next to walls and corners, press some joint compound into the corner. The reason for this is that the dauber can't get closer than two or three inches from the corner.

The wall shown in Figure 7–10 was painted brown and then daubed; it was not troweled down. The joint compound was Gold Bond joint compound, used straight out of the box. Taping joint compound was used because of its hardness. This texture needs to be sealed with clear lacquer so it can be washed. Otherwise, because the joint compound is water soluble, it would melt away and smear all over the wall when washed.

The background shown in Figure 7–11 was painted a dark color. The illustration shows the results of using two slightly different techniques. The left side was done by daubing the joint compound once and the wall five or six times. The right side

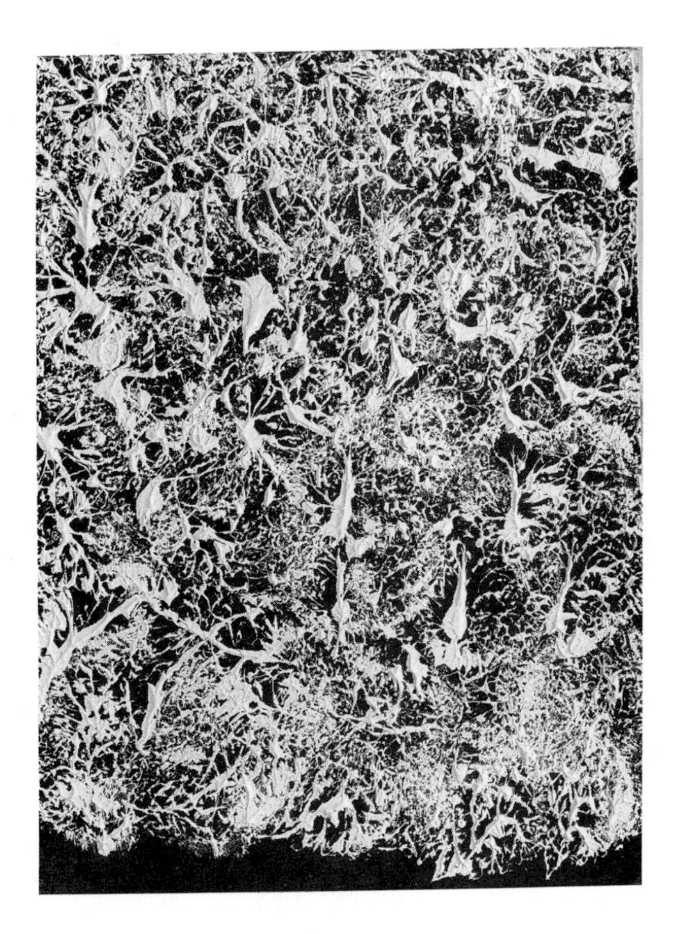

FIGURE 7–10

was done by daubing the joint compound once and the wall three to four times, spreading it out a little more.

The wall shown in Figure 7–12 was painted a dark color, then stomp-textured with Gold Bond taping joint compound straight from the box. The wall has to be sealed with clear lacquer to make it washable.

COVERING OLD TEXTURES

The wall shown in Figure 7–13 was painted green; then the same paint was mixed into the joint compound. When the wall was textured, is came out a two-toned green.

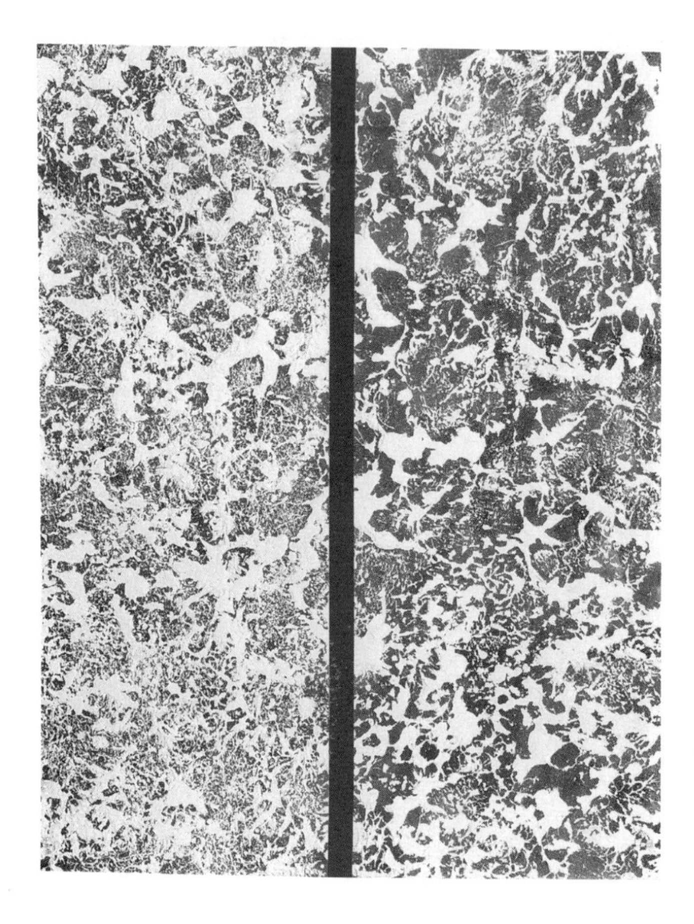

FIGURE 7–11

The green textured surface was textured over with a regular white joint compound. The result was a three-toned wall. This texture was done to show how effective this texture could be in covering over another ugly texture or a wall damaged in some way, like a wall that has had glued panelling or something. A rough surface can be camouflaged very well.

The wall shown in Figure 7–14 is dramatic and unusual. First, it was painted gold, and then black paint was mixed into the joint compound. The combination creates a dark charcoal color. This wall must be sealed with lacquer. When you get tired of a wall like this, you can always paint it white; the texture will still make it an interesting wall. If you are in the remodeling business or are trying to sell your home, a wall like this can make a good impression.

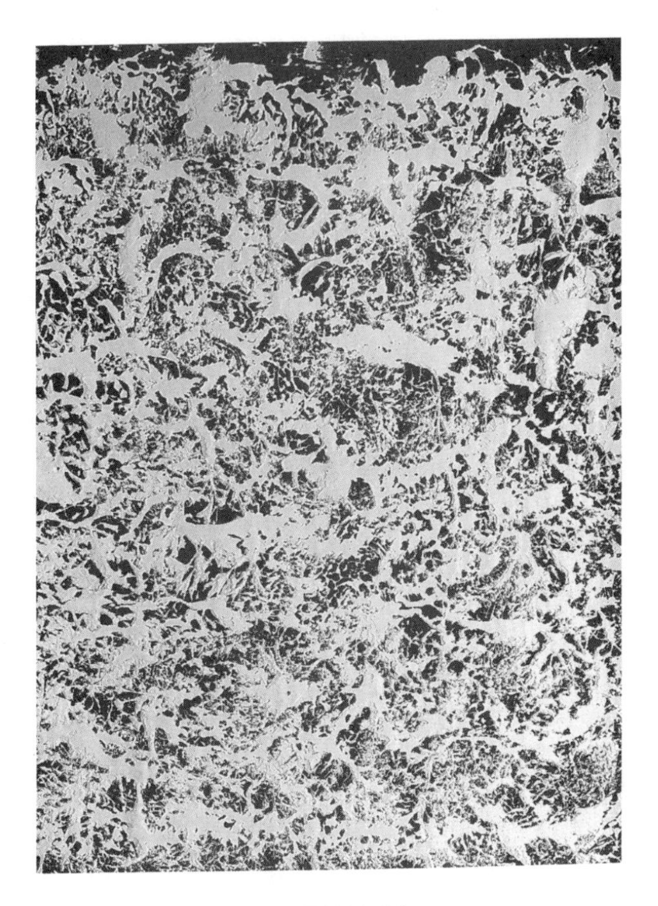

FIGURE 7–12

Questions

TEXTURING

1. What is nap texture?
   a. Texture made with a paint roller
   b. Texture made by using a nap rag to wipe it down
   c. Texture made by using a napsack
   d. Texture that makes you sleepy

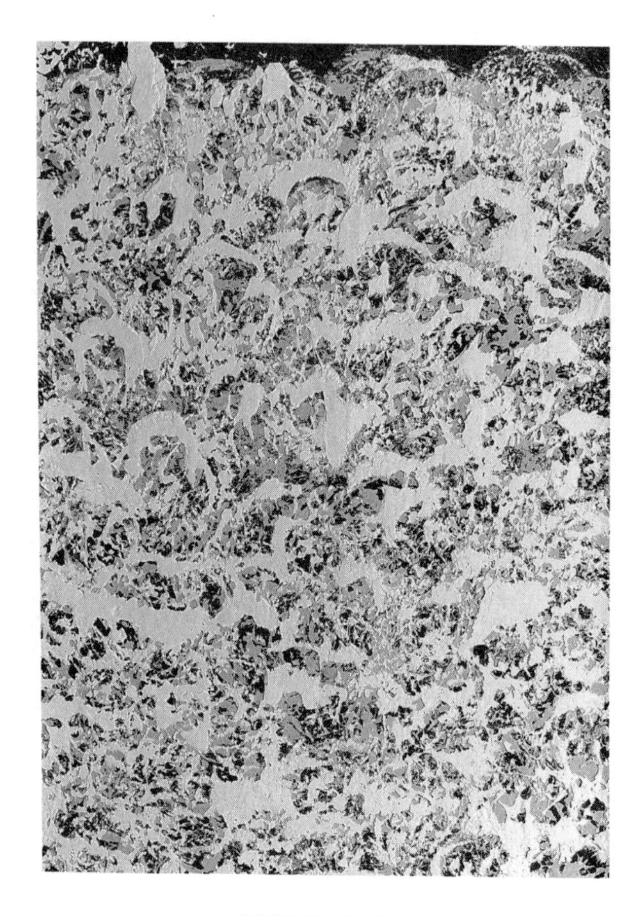

FIGURE 7–13

2. What two elements control the design of nap texture?
   a. The speed of the roller and the width of the nap
   b. The size of the brush and the thickness of the joint compound
   c. The thickness of joint compound and the speed of the roller
   d. The density of the nap on the roller and the thickness of the joint compound

3. What is roll-on texture?
   a. Texture made by first daubing with a brush
   b. Texture made by first rolling on joint compound
   c. Texture made by spraying on joint compound
   d. Texture made by the nap

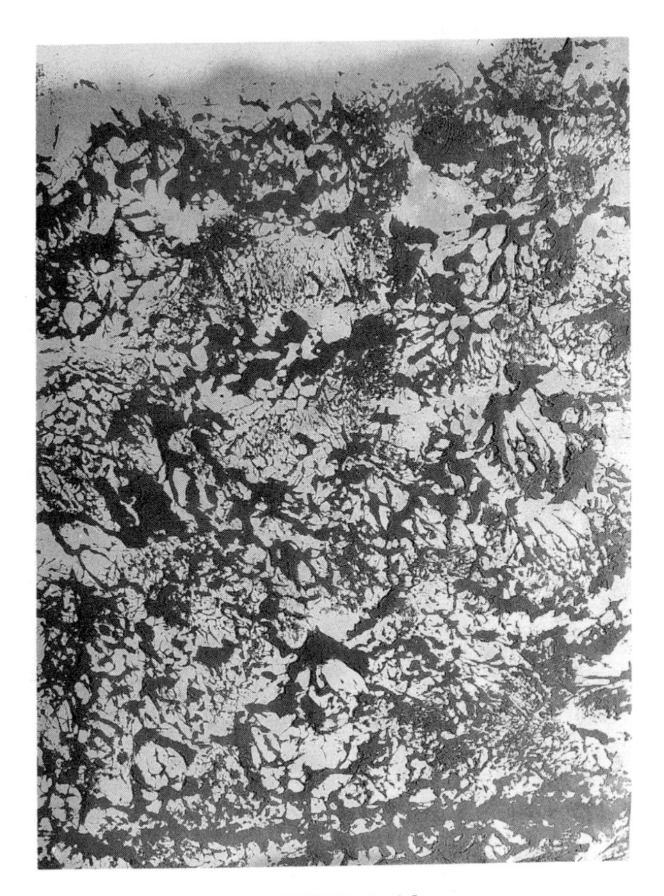

FIGURE 7–14

4. Swirl texture is made with the
  a. daub-on method.
  b. stomp method.
  c. roll-on method.
  d. toss-on method.

5. What kind of materials are used for a spray texture acoustic finish?
  a. Joint compound and prepared texture materials
  b. Prepared texture materials only
  c. Texture mixtures and gravel
  d. Joint compound

6. The stomp texture is made by
   a. spraying or daubing joint compound and then troweling down.
   b. daubing or stomping with special shoes.
   c. spraying or daubing joint compound and then sanding down.
   d. daubing and troweling it down.

7. If you do a stomp texture for an accent wall, paint it, then texture over it, you must
   a. put sparkle on it.
   b. color the plaster.
   c. seal it with clear lacquer.
   d. paint over it later.

8. If you want texture with a very fine or small pattern, you can
   a. use thick joint compound and daub many times in the same area.
   b. use thin joint compound and daub many times in the same area.
   c. use thick joint compound and daub fewer times, more spread out.
   d. use thin joint compound and daub fewer times, more spread out.

9. If you want a big pattern but thin to the wall, you should
   a. use thick joint compound and let it dry a few minutes before troweling it down.
   b. use thin joint compound and let it dry a few minutes before you trowel it.
   c. use thin joint compound and trowel it wet.
   d. use thick joint compound and trowel it wet.

10. If you are using the stomp texture to go over an old texture, you should
   a. use thick joint compound. Let it dry five minutes before troweling.
   b. use thin joint compound. Let it dry five minutes before troweling.
   c. use thick joint compound. Use pressure when troweling.
   d. use thin joint compound. Use no pressure when troweling.

Chapter 8
For the Professional

Things to Keep in Mind

1. Remember that time is money, especially if you would like to make hanging and finishing your trade.

2. Don't play around with joints too much. Of course, each coat needs to be built well, but don't worry about a little scratch in the first coat: the second coat will take care of it.

3. Every stroke of the knife takes time and builds habits. When something is okay, leave it. If it's not necessary, don't do it.

4. When you're spreading joint compound, always practice to spread it farther. Do nails in two strokes, angles in eight strokes, and so on. When you're feather edging a joint, use your back stroke to smooth it down. Don't waste strokes, and you will be working much more efficiently.

5. Use shortcuts in procedure but never cheat on quality. Your finished product should always make you proud.

The Professional Finisher

Here are some helpful tips for the professional finisher who wants to be as efficient and productive as possible.

UTILIZING HELP

Utilizing help efficiently and productively is important. This will oftentimes make the difference between making money and losing it. Always think of speed and production. Suppose you are working a crew of eight, and you have three journeymen who finish fast and well; three apprentices who can tape, sand, coat nails, and run tools; and two helpers who can sand between coats but can't finish sand.

How should you keep these workers busy?

HELPERS

The two helpers must keep the three journeymen spreading joint compound. That is their primary concern. They should keep joint compound ready, move it for the journeymen, fetch tools, and so on.

The three journeymen should never have to stop spreading joint compound to get a knife or anything. Also, helpers can clean plaster off door frames, mix joint compound, keep materials together, sand between coats, hammer nails or screws, tape around pipes, and so on.

APPRENTICES

The three apprentices' priority also is to keep the journeymen spreading joint compound. Other duties include sanding, taping, coating screws or nails, keeping the helpers working, and running tools.

JOURNEYMEN

The three journeymen keep spreading joint compound at all times. Always think ahead: look for things that might be in the way to stop them or slow them down. Get an apprentice or a helper to take care of the problem before the journeymen get to the problem area.

While you are supervising your help and assigning jobs, always have lower-waged people doing the grunt work, if possible. Keep your higher-paid people doing what they do best.

If you have a large area to float out and you're working with just one untrained person, you might want to try rolling out the joints with a paint roller. This way, you can utilize your untrained person. Have him or her roll on the joint compound while you come behind and float it out. This will make you twice as fast. Of course, this system wouldn't be a good idea for the first coat, but for the second and third coats, it works fine.

CONTRACT HELP: HOW TO HIRE

When you hire someone, start him or her as contract help. Offer so much money to do a certain job. After observation, you can figure out a fair hourly salary. If you hire hourly help right off, you take a chance on losing money. Some people don't put out any work; they can look busy all day but never accomplish anything. Where a contractor license is required, however, you can't hire this way.

CONTRACT HELP: WHOM TO HIRE

When interviewing a potential employee, ask questions that will help you to know the person's worth. For instance, ask "Would you rather be paid hourly, or so much per foot?" The prospective employee might answer in any one of a variety of ways. Each response tells much about the person.

A slow person is likely to say, "I work only hourly." That's because the person can't make any money working at a certain rate per foot. Remember if the worker can't make money working by the foot, you won't make any money either.

If the person replies, "It doesn't matter. Hourly or footage is fine," he or she can make average pay and will do the same for you.

The person might respond, "I would rather work footage, but I will work hourly." Chances are that this person can make you better than average money. He or she is likely to be both fast and good, because a contract employee simply doesn't get paid if the job is not right. Be aware that many finishers are quite independent and might resent being told what to do.

HOW TO SUBCONTRACT

Most drywall work is paid for on a subcontract basis. The rate of pay varies from one area to another. Most of the northern states pay 8 to 15 cents per square foot; in the southern states, the pay varies from 4 to 7 cents per square foot. I've worked for as little as 2.5 cents before.

If you are working on an hourly basis, you are not a subcontractor. The builder is required to withhold your taxes, F.I.C.A., and unemployment insurance. If he or she doesn't, you are losing your benefits and the builder is liable for a fine from the U.S. Government. Don't let this happen to you. If you are working as a subcontractor, you are responsible for your own taxes, and you are required to obtain a business identification number from the I.R.S. Just call the local I.R.S. office, and a clerk will send you an application form.

If you are doing work for anyone other than a drywall contractor, you should protect yourself with a contract. If you decide to contract your own work, ask yourself a few questions.

1. Can you keep track of the details of a business?
2. Does the quality of the finished job mean anything to you?
3. Can you work toward a goal, inch by inch?
4. Can you get along with people working for you as well as people you are working for?
5. Do you place much value on your word?

The success of a business depends on a good reputation. Repeat business grows from doing a good job and keeping promises. Word, good or bad, travels fast. You had better do a good job because often you won't get a second chance to change a bad reputation.

You are better off contracting in an area where a license is required and where the license law is enforced. If the law is not enforced, it's no help. If you are contracting in an area that doesn't require a license, anyone can contract. In such areas, nobody has any protection: not the property owner, not the builder, not the worker, and not the licensed contractor.

What happened in Houston is a good example of what can happen when no contracting license is required and jobs are underbid. Prices in Houston went from 10 cents to 4 cents per foot in a two-year period. That's cutting wages by more than half. Some people were working for 2 cents a foot, while others were working the same job for 8 cents a foot. If a builder can get the work done for 2 cents, why should he or she pay 8 cents? Chances are, wages in Houston will never come back. If people had been educated about contracting, workers in Houston would still be getting paid 10 cents a foot. Where there is no license, there is no protection for the worker or the contractor.

In a state where a license is required, you know that you are bidding against other people who are educated about business and law. Their employees are protected. Their employment and withholding taxes are paid. You can compete because all bidders have the same overhead to pay and the same laws to follow. These laws protect your professional future. The person holding a contractor's license has worked hard for it, and so will you. Take it seriously, or you won't make it in the business world.

After you have gone through the pains of getting a license, send a letter to all the builders and ask to be put on their bid lists. Send some references—builders don't accept just anybody. They will send you notice when they need bids on a building, telling you where and when. You might want to consider hiring a professional bidder, as a wrong bid can put you out of business before you begin.

FIGURING FOOTAGE

Here are some formulas that will help you to estimate footage for a job:

- An apartment, small and cut up: floor space times 4
- An average home: floor space times 3.8
- A large, spacious home: floor space times 3.5

An accurate way to figure footage is from the blueprints or by measuring the floor space (this gives you the ceiling drywall footage unless the building has cathedral ceilings, which would need to be figured separately). After you have the ceiling square footage, then measure the wall linear footage. Remember, the interior walls need to be counted twice, exterior walls once. Multiply the linear footage by the height of the ceiling. Add this number to the ceiling square footage, and you have the total footage. Remember, when measuring the linear footage, measure right across the windows and doorways. The extra board is used to wrap the windows, doorways, and soffits. The same footage measurements are used for the hangers, finishers, and painters.

Many things must be considered when bidding on a job: Is the job going to be ready? Can the hangers hang it all in one trip, or do they need to make two? When working apartments or a housing project where your work is lined up, it's no problem to come back two or three times. If you have to travel across town, however, you will lose your profit. Remember, time is money.

RESIDENTIAL PROBLEMS TO CONSIDER

Hangers:

1. Do the hangers put on the corner bead?
2. Where is the job located?
3. How big is the job? Is there a full day's work?
4. Does the builder want glue?
5. Is the thickness of the drywall ⅝ or ½ inch?
6. Does the builder want wood trim or metal wrapped and finished windows?
7. Are there any skylights?
8. Are there any difficult angles or other time-consuming items?

9. Do we stock the sheetrock?
10. If we do, how far do we need to carry it?

Finishers:
1. Does the finisher put on the corner bead?
2. Does the builder want wood trim or wrapped and finished windows?
3. What is the location of the job? (Normally, a finisher has to make two trips, maybe three, depending on how the job is finished out.)
4. What's the size of the job?
5. Are there any skylights, 45° angles, or soffits?
6. What's the size of the receptacle boxes?
7. How high is the baseboard trim?
8. What type of paint or texture will be used?
9. How is the painting to be done—roller or spray?
10. Does the finisher include texture, or does the painter do so? (Remember, a spacious home with wood trim can be bid for a lot less money.)

COMMERCIAL BIDDING PROBLEMS TO CONSIDER

Hangers:
All of the residential problems listed above, plus the following:
1. Are there many soffits and items like recessed lighting, round walls, skylights, 45° angles, and atrium buildings where scaffolding might be needed?
2. Is raco or some kind of metal trim to be used along the bottoms and tops of the walls, doorways, and windows?
3. Are there many expensive materials?
4. Who puts up the doors?
5. Are there any flimsy metal studs?
6. Are there any fire walls? What kinds of pipes are there? How high are they?

Finishers:
All of the residential problems and the commercial hangers' problems listed above, plus the following:

1. Will the hangers put up raco? If not, how many interior walls need L-bead along the top board? (This is a time-consuming task.)
2. Does the bottom have baseboard? How wide is it?
3. Are there fire walls? How high? What materials or specifications did the architect list? A few special requests can eat into your profit if you don't include them into the bid. Be aware that flimsy metal studs can be a big problem.

Never agree to finish out one side of a wall before the other side of the wall has been hung, or you will have to take responsibility for a bad finish job that wasn't your fault. Metal studs have a lot of movement. It's better for the hanging contractor to spend a little extra money for a higher quality metal stud than it is for you to spend all your profit on extra joint compound to fix the hanger's problem. Sometimes code materials aren't good enough to be problem free. Check out the hanging job carefully. If you start a job that already has serious problems, you won't win.

Insist on a contract that specifies the job you are doing and the amount you will be paid. Be sure you make provision for any extra costs and extra tasks you may have.

Many of the other trades' mistakes usually electrical and plumbing, will affect you. For example, if a plumber has to go back and change something after the drywall is up, he or she will need to cut a hole in your drywall, and you will have to repair it.

Keep track of these miscellaneous repairs. If the job goes smoothly and members of all the trades work cooperatively, the extras can be thrown in free of charge. But suppose the electrician is unwilling to cooperate and goes ahead and puts in the receptacles too soon. Such an action causes extra work and time for the hanger or the finisher. In such an instance, feel free to make up a bill, charging for extra time.

Sometimes, the architect makes a mistake. Maybe a soffit is to be made to cover the error. The extra soffit should be paid for separately from the original bid. Drywall is a catch-all: it serves to make everything else look good. There are often extras: keep track of them. They can eat up your profit easily if you're not charging for them. Be reasonable, though; give a person a break where you can. Remember that what goes around comes around.

Glossary

Angle—The point at which two walls intersect; a corner.

Banjo—A tool that applies joint compound directly to tape as it is laid out onto a joint; it makes taping a much easier job.

Baseboard—Wood or vinyl trim applied around the bottom of a wall.

Bastard angle—Any angle (corner) that is not 90°.

Bench—A device similar to a carpenter's sawhorse but made so that a hanger can stand on it with his or her head just touching the ceiling.

Beveled edge—The long edge of a sheet of drywall; it forms a recess when two sheets are hung side by side. (See also *Flat joint.*)

Building strip—A strip of joint compound the width of a knife and feather edged on each side; it is used to build out and camouflage particularly bad joints.

Bullnose—A type of metal corner bead that has rounded corners.

Butt joint—The shorter, unbeveled edge of a sheet of drywall.

Center line—A line drawn down the center of drywall used as a nailing guide.

Circle cutter—A tool, similar to a drafting compass, used to cut holes in drywall.

Clincher—A tool used to crimp on the 90° metal corner bead (Figure 1–7).

Corner bead—V-shaped sticks of metal that are applied to outside corners to provide straight hard edges and extra support as the house settles. (See also *Flex bead.*)

Dauber—A tool used for textures.

Drywall—Paper-wrapped gypsum board that forms the walls and ceilings of most buildings.

Drywall cutout—See *Router.*
Drywall door—In drywall, an area cut on three sides in the drywall that will lift up as if hinged.
Drywall lift—A tool used to lift drywall to the ceiling and hold it in place until it is nailed off (Figure 1–7).

Electrical outlets—Also known as receptacle boxes, light receptacles, electrical boxes, light boxes; these are holes in the wall through which electrical wires are threaded. See also *Receptacle boxes.*

Factory edge—See *Beveled edge.*
Feather edge—The act of spreading joint compound on a joint, applying more pressure to the outside edge of the knife, leaving the joint compound flush to the drywall.
Fire-rated drywall—Treated drywall that takes a much longer time to burn through; it is used on all fire walls.
Fire wall—Any wall separating two units, such as apartments.
Flat joint—The intersection of two beveled (factory) edges of drywall.
Flex bead—Flexible corner bead used for bastard angles or acute angles.
to Float—Is a term used for the process of finishing, as floating the knife on top of the joint compound to create the desired thickness and effect.
Fur down—A drop-down unit nailed to the ceiling under which the cabinets are put. (See also *Soffit.*)
Furring channel—Is used to adjust the wall surface by applying furring strips, then drywall being fastened to the strips. In this way the drywall is fastened to concrete without coming in contact directly to the concrete. Furring is also very often used to create a sound barrier, holding one layer of drywall away from another layer creating an air pocket.

Gypsum—*Hydrous Calcium Sulfate*; a mineral used in the formulation of drywall.
Glue—An adhesive sometimes used in drywall construction instead of nails.

Hatchet—A tool used to drive nails into drywall.
Headers—A system of hanging drywall that includes using a butt joint over the top of a door or window. (See also *Picture framing.*)
Hot patch—A method for filling a large hole in drywall by which a cutout piece of drywall is inserted into the hole.

Joint compound—A ready-mixed gypsum-based compound used to cover the joints in drywall; also called *mud.*
Joists—Boards that make up the framework of a house.

Mud—See *Joint compound.*
Mudder—Another word for *finisher.*

Nap texture—A texture produced by thickening paint with joint compound and applying it to a wall with a paint roller; also known as *roll-on texture.*

Pans—Metal or plastic trays for holding joint compound as one works.
Picture framing—A system of hanging drywall in which the drywall is hung over a window, covering it. The drywall is then sawed out of the window area. This system is the best because it leaves no joints above the window. (See also *Headers.*)

Quick set—A fast-hardening joint compound for use in jobs that need to be finished quickly.

Raco—A snap-on metal trim for walls (used in commercial buildings).
Rasp—Is a tool with a file-like edge and is used to smooth the edge of the freshly cut drywall so it will fit in place better.
Ream Machine.—See *Router.*
Receptacle box—A box in the wall that houses electrical wires. See also *Electrical outlets.*
Rocker—An attachment for a screw gun that feeds screws, allowing drywall to be screwed in place quickly.
Roll-on texture—Texture for a finished wall, made with thickened or thinned joint compound and paint applied with a paint roller; it is used as a base for other covering textures and designs.
Router—A tool used to cut drywall around receptacle boxes, windows, and doors, or to trim drywall (Figure 1–7).

Screw gun—A tool used to drive screws into drywall (Figure 1–7).
Set of nails—Two nails driven into the drywall one to two inches apart. The ceiling area is nailed with three sets, and the walls are nailed two sets.
Sheetrock—Another word used to describe drywall. (See *Drywall.*)
Soffit—A fur down in a kitchen or bathroom, nailed to the ceiling for the cabinets to sit under. (See also *Fur down.*)
Stomp—A type of texture.
Stress point—See *Weak point.*
Stud—The point at which you can nail a piece of drywall, usually a two-by-four.

Tape—A paper tape used to cover drywall joints.
Top plate—A horizontal board laid on a wall to receive the framework.

Toe jack—A tool used for hanging wallboard; it is used to lift the bottom board up to the top board.
Trap door—A procedure for cutting drywall around pipes that eliminates the need to patch large holes (Figure 2–25).
T-square—A tool used to aid in the cutting of the drywall.
Trowel—A procedure to flatten the daubed joint compound forming a texture pattern.
Wallboard—Another word for drywall. (See also *Drywall.*)
Water resistant drywall—A type of drywall used in wet areas, such as showers.
Weak point—A hanger's term for the area above a door or window that is the weakest point of a wall; it is also known as a stress point.

Index

Answers to Test Questions

CHAPTER 1

DRYWALL INSTALLATION TOOLS AND MATERIALS

1. b
2. d
3. d
4. b & d
5. d
6. c
7. d
8. d
9. d
10. c
11. c
12. c
13. c
14. a
15. d
16. a
17. c

CHAPTER 2

HANGING CEILINGS

1. c
2. c
3. c
4. a
5. b
6. c
7. c
8. c
9. b
10. b
11. c
12. a
13. b
14. c

HANGING WALLS

15. b
16. a
17. d
18. b
19. c
20. d
21. b
22. a

HANGING WALLS AND OPENINGS

1. b
2. c
3. b
4. c
5. b

HANGING KITCHEN WALLS

6. c
7. c
8. a

HANGING STAIRWELLS AND CATHEDRAL WALLS

9. b
10. c
11. d
12. c
13. c

HANGING ROUND WALLS

14. b
15. d
16. c

CHAPTER 3

METAL TRIM AND CORNER BEAD

1. b
2. b
3. c
4. d
5. b

CHAPTER 4

DRYWALL REPAIR AND SHORTCUTS

1. d
2. b
3. c
4. a
5. c
6. c
7. c

CHAPTER 5

DRYWALL FINISHING MATERIALS AND TOOLS

1. d
2. b
3. c
4. b
5. a
6. c
7. b
8. c

CHAPTER 6

FOUR BASIC JOINTS

1. c
2. c

PREPARING FOR TAPING

3. c
4. c
5. c
6. d

TAPING

7. c
8. b
9. b
10. d
11. a
12. c
13. b
14. c
15. c
16. c
17. c
18. c
19. b
20. b
21. b
22. b

FIRST COAT

23. c
24. c
25. c
26. a
27. c
28. c
29. c
30. b
31. d
32. d
33. d
34. c
35. d
36. c

PREPARATION FOR THE SECOND COAT

1. d

THE SECOND COAT

2. d
3. b
4. d
5. b
6. c
7. b
8. a

PREPARATION FOR THIRD COAT

9. c
10. b

THE THIRD COAT

11. d
12. a

SANDING

13. b
14. a
15. c
16. c

THE FINAL PRODUCT

17. d
18. c
19. d

CHAPTER 7

TEXTURING

1. a
2. d
3. b
4. c
5. a
6. d
7. c
8. a
9. c
10. a